CM

Russian Dance

Also by Andrée Aelion Brooks

Children of Fast-Track Parents: Raising Self-Sufficient and Confident Children in an Achievement-Oriented World

Out of Spain: An Educational Program for Children Covering the History and Culture of Sephardic Jewry

The Woman Who Defied Kings: The Life and Times of Doña Gracia Nasi— A Jewish Leader during the Renaissance

Russian Dance

A TRUE STORY
OF INTRIGUE AND PASSION
IN STALINIST MOSCOW

Andrée Aelion Brooks

WILEY

John Wiley & Sons, Inc.

Published by John Wiley & Sons, Inc., Hoboken, New Jersey
Published simultaneously in Canada

Source for the pictures on pp. 5, 6, 12, 23, 35, 36, 37, 71, 192, 263:
Private family collection, courtesy Clifford Forster

For general information about our other products and services, please contact our Customer Care Department within the United States at (800) 762-2974, outside the United States at (317) 572-3993 or fax (317) 572-4002.

Wiley also publishes its books in a variety of electronic formats. Some content that appears in print may not be available in electronic books. For more information about Wiley products, visit our web site at www.wiley.com.

Library of Congress Cataloging-in-Publication Data:

Brooks, Andrée Aelion.
    Russian dance : a true story of intrigue and passion in Stalinist Moscow / Andrée Aelion Brooks.
        p.   cm.
    Includes bibliographical references and index.
    ISBN 0-471-64866-3 (alk. paper)
    1. Cheftel, Marc Solomonovitch, b. 1884. 2. Rabinoff, Bluet, d. 1976.
3. Rabinoff, Max. 4. Soviet Union—Biography. 5. Soviet Union—History—
1925–1953. 6. New York (N.Y.)—Biography. 7. Americans—Soviet Union—
Biography. I. Title.

CT1218.C36B76   2004
947.084'2'0922—dc22
                                                                    2003020624

Printed in the United States of America

10 9 8 7 6 5 4 3 2 1

*Dedicated to the secondary heroes of history
who also labor to build a more compassionate world.
Unlike those of world leaders,
their contributions are too often lost to posterity.
Yet the dreamers deserve recognition too—
even when their dreams turn to nightmares.*

*But you know, it is sometimes curious that the Russian fatalistic
attitude to life is similar to the Chinese or Asiatic. He says,
"I know I am going to die. But I will go just the same."*

From testimony by Dr. David Dubrowsky,
head of the Russian Red Cross in New York,
before a special congressional committee on
communist activities convened in 1939

Contents

Preface   xi

PART ONE   Manhattan, 1928–1930   I

PART TWO   Marc's Story: Un Mèdico Benèvolo   89

PART THREE   21 Bolshoi Lubianka   169

Epilogue   271

Author's Note   275

Bibliographical Note   277

Index   279

Preface

The Bolshevik revolution in Russia in 1917 gave rise to heroes as well as to villains. It was many things to many people. Intellectuals and the poor embraced it as the magnificent dawn of a brave new society. Ruling families and the landed wealthy in neighboring countries looked on aghast, terrified that the proletarian spirit of Bolshevism might spread like a virus, consuming them all. Pragmatic Western business entrepreneurs recognized a rare opportunity to reap profits from the untapped resources of the vast Russian interior. Overnight, political dreamers and exiled revolutionaries were placed in positions of power. Many in the West wondered if these earth shakers were indeed the wave of the future or simply misguided idealists with dangerous dreams. In time, the visionaries and the idealists would be crushed—not by outside foes but by Russia's innate longing for dictatorial rule. But for a while, reformers the world over were counting on these early revolutionaries to spearhead the kind of compassionate society they hoped would emerge.

I have re-created the true tale of one of those visionaries—Marc Cheftel—and the woman, Bluet Rabinoff, whom he loved. I had already known Bluet for many years when she finally shared this story with me. For more than forty years she had lived with a fearful guilt—convinced that through her actions, she had condemned her lover to an untimely death and had destroyed a brilliant leader. We all pay a price for our passions. But the price in this instance was exceptional.

This story needed telling for an even more important reason. Through its recounting unfolds the panorama of those Russian Jews who chose to alleviate the suffering of their own people, and indeed all Russians under czarist oppression, by remaining to reshape their own society, rather than fleeing to other lands. Because the revolution rapidly deteriorated into a regime equally as brutal as czarist rule, and communism became such an abhorrent doctrine, the contributions of these early Jewish revolutionaries are rarely discussed in mainstream Jewish circles. It remains one of those episodes, like so many others in Jewish history, that are too often dismissed in favor of a few choice topics and epochs. Yet their idealism sprang from the loftiest of motives, and in the process they had hoped to emancipate the very Jewish people who today still find it disturbing to talk about them.

Because of its passionate nature, the story had to be rebuilt and written in a novelistic style. However, I made tremendous efforts to remain meticulous in my reporting. Real names have been used. And I re-created the scenes and the incidents exactly as they were reported to me by either Bluet herself, her close friends, or members of Marc's family. Nothing has been added or embellished. The letters in Part Three that Bluet sent to her daughter clearly needed editing to make them more easily understood by the reader and to incorporate contextual material that helped further the story. Some are a compilation of several letters. But most stay close to the originals (I still have the entire cache tucked away in a safe deposit box, along with the worn red passport that became key to Bluet's survival, and the guidebook she took to Moscow). I also took care to retain the cadence of Bluet's voice.

Obviously, the dialogue had to be reconstituted. But even this was based upon countless interviews with my various sources. Added to these were audiotapes of my long talks with Bluet and others close to the events, plus the books and documents I culled from archives and agencies that are listed at the end—written material that helped corroborate and expand upon the oral accounts. Where government hearings are quoted, the testimony has been taken verbatim from the public record. The official letters and the diplomatic correspondence used in the story are all based upon archival sources available to any reader or scholar.

It has frequently been said that a Russian story is the story of an undoing of a life. This, then, is indeed a Russian story.

Part One

Manhattan, 1928–1930

One

IT WAS THE SEVENTEENTH DAY of the ninth month of the year 1930. It had not been a normal year for anyone. The party atmosphere of the 1920s and the explosion of ideas—in arts, literature, science, lifestyles, and politics—had abated with the stock market crash. Hopes were being dashed along with fortunes. Yet people still clung to dying dreams. Nobody wanted to wake up.

Sinclair Lewis, attacking the selfish complacency of middle-class America, had just won a Nobel Prize for literature. In Russia, ushering in a new somber mood under Stalin, Maksim Litvinov had recently been appointed Soviet foreign minister. In the wake of the Big Red Scare, the works of Leon Trotsky were being banned by the city fathers of Boston. The death had been announced of Arthur Balfour, British statesman and author of the Balfour Declaration (championing the establishment of a Jewish homeland in Palestine). An elated Nazi Party had gained its first major victory in Germany. People were singing "I Got Rhythm," "Body and Soul," and "Something to Remember You By." They flocked to Broadway hits like *Strike Up the Band* and *Girl Crazy*. Reflecting a new isolationist mood, *All Quiet on the Western Front* won the Academy Award for Best Picture of the Year. Amy Johnson's dramatic solo flight from London to Australia signaled a last hurrah for the daredevils of the 1920s. And everyone from beggar to billionaire was laughing over the comic-strip antics of *Blondie.*

It had rained lightly earlier that day in the city of New York. A mild thunderstorm at dawn had cleansed the summer dust from the parched streets of Manhattan, so that now a mist was slowly rising from curbside and stoop. At the pier of the White Star Line, along Manhattan's West Side, the luxury liner *Majestic*—so much a symbol of the glitter and the pomp of the 1920s—stood bedecked in multicolored bunting, waiting patiently at her berth as eager passengers and well-wishers crowded aboard. Everybody was anxious for a good time. Perhaps there would not be many more, so any opportunity for a champagne farewell party was not to be missed.

On the main deck, in one of the ship's luxury suites, Helene Rabinoff—known to everyone as Bluet, for the cornflower blue of her eyes—knelt down to open her trunk. Outside, the unseasonably hot summer wind was drying up more than just dreams. Life was going to be far different for her from now on. Usually, the noise and the bustle of a departure would thrill her with the anticipation of yet another journey with her husband, Max, to her beloved France and the excitement of dashing from one European capital to another, ferreting out new talent for his productions.

Highly volatile, the famous American millionaire opera impresario Max Rabinoff had devoted all his energies and his life to such a quest. Bluet had been his diplomat, the only one with sufficient tact, social flair, and understanding to knit all the explosive elements together.

Today she was alone. Only a few weeks earlier she had divorced Max after sixteen years of marriage. She had persuaded him with some difficulty to give her one year's alimony in advance so she could make the trip abroad. That had come to $3,000, a sum far in excess of anything she had personally ever held in her possession before. Max always kept a tight rein on the family purse strings. Though he allowed his wife to shop with abandon, he never permitted her to have her own money. Cautiously, she checked once again to make sure it was still there—a bundle of travelers' checks carefully folded inside the black calf handbag that lay on the satin bedspread.

Glancing around at the gleaming wood of her first-class cabin, she smiled briefly as she remembered the unexpected gaiety and warmth of the farewell party her friends had just given her. They had been in high spirits. This was even true of Dr. David Dubrowsky, who ran the Russian Red Cross in New York and who was the only one who really knew where she was going. She had told the others she needed some months alone to travel and think things out. It troubled her to have to lie.

Then there were the flowers. She had received so many lavish bouquets, she had not realized until now how many of her friends genuinely wished her well, even though she and Max were no longer together. Tied with red, yellow, and pink taffeta ribbons, they sat on a tall dresser in elegant crystal vases with tiny white cardboard message cards tucked neatly into the blossoms. Full-bodied chrysanthemums, tall gladioli, delicate roses, Bluet loved them all. The scent reminded her of her childhood in the Auvergne in central France. In the springtime and throughout the long, hot, torpid summer, the hilltops and the meadows would be ablaze with the colorful brilliance of wildflowers.

Helene (Bluet) Rabinoff, c. 1911

She picked up a half-empty champagne glass from the collection that stood on the low coffee table. Even though her guests had all left, she could still sense the buzz of their voices.

One final toast—to Marc. To their future. Together.

Trite, she chided herself, but true. Marc Cheftel, the magnetic but enigmatic Russian physician for whom she had abandoned Max, would have composed a far more original and pithy toast, probably a quip about the pious wags who would be set astir by the thought of such a respectable pillar of society as herself stealing halfway across the globe on a lover's tryst. She adored the boyish delight he found in setting the cat among the pigeons and watching the pompous elite wriggle uncomfortably in any situation that mocked their stuffy self-righteousness. For despite his quiet mien, his urbane appearance, and his impeccable manners, he was the most irreverent anti-establishment figure she had ever met.

Marc Cheftel as a young man

Though the end of the 1920s was at hand, all sorts of people were still chasing madcap dreams. It was the thing to do. The swirling and dizzying magic of the decade had not totally dissipated. Marc had been caught up in this atmosphere as much as she had.

Putting down her glass, she left the cabin to wander onto the deck to watch the familiar chaos of a departure. Deckhands, loosening fat ropes from their moorings, worked feverishly as dockside crowds waved and gawked and shouted their farewells at departing friends and relatives. Then, with the grace of a seabird, the liner gently, almost silently, slipped into the open channel of the murky Hudson. Glancing up at the cloudy, windswept sky, she worried about the unsettled weather—all the ingredients for a storm. She shuddered. She hated stormy seas.

She looked around. The three-funnel, 56,000-ton *Majestic*, the flagship of the White Star Line, was one of the most luxurious passenger liners of the day. Built in Germany in the early 1920s, it sported all the finery and the trappings of that era: superb restaurants overstocked with lavish and exotic foods, deck tennis, movies, plush nightclubs, cocktail bars decorated with outrageous motifs, expansive lounges with tall picture windows. There was just about everything for its passengers' pleasure, from caviar to calisthenics. The *New York World* assigned a reporter aboard each journey merely to report on the gossip. And just one year earlier, amid feverish publicity, a ship-to-shore telephone had been installed.

Yet this time she was somehow unimpressed with all the finery. There was no escaping the guilt she felt about leaving Anna, her sixteen-year-old daughter, even temporarily. She was equally uneasy about turning her back on her comfortable and familiar world of servants, opulence, and a glittering social life, to embark on a romantic adventure that hardly befitted an elegant matron of thirty-eight. She was, after all, no longer a starry-eyed youngster. With difficulty, she choked back a sudden and unexpected flood of tears.

She was sacrificing a way of life. Yet without Marc, it had lost its flavor. She had become so overwhelmed by a consuming passion for the man that there was no possibility of making any other decision. The thought of saying good-bye to Marc was impossible to face. Their affair had become too special. With time her enemy, she feared it might never be recaptured. So she opted for the path her emotions dictated. And in doing so, she was equally willing to blind herself to the stark realities of the life that she might have to face in Moscow.

BLUET RABINOFF was a petite French woman standing only five feet tall, with hair the color of ripened wheat, an hourglass figure, and such finely drawn features that her picture had appeared in *Beauty* magazine only a few years earlier. She was considered a vivacious coquette, exquisitely chic in clothes that were custom-made by her personal dressmaker in Paris. Even her shoes, an incredibly small size three, were hand-sewn for her in France. Since she traveled to Paris with Max at least once a year, she scorned American ready-to-wear as assembly line and commonplace.

Though she and Max had drifted apart in recent years, mainly due to his neglect, constant bullying, and the vulgar flaunting of one new sexual conquest after another (usually a singer he would seduce with the cliché of a promised role in an upcoming production), their lives radiated glamour and excitement.

Since Max not only possessed a fluent knowledge of Russian, but also claimed extensive familiarity with Russian business affairs, in addition to his cultural activities, he had been appointed an adviser on Russian matters to the U.S. government in 1917, immediately after the Bolshevik revolution. He attended the Versailles Peace Conference and the equally important Genoa Conference of 1922, serving as a liaison between the Russians and Americans. He acted as the official representative of the newly organized Estonian and Azerbaijan governments. Though not avidly political by nature, Max employed his diplomatic credentials more as an opportunity for a wily entrepreneur like himself to edge his way into the lucrative markets he was confident would blossom between the United States and Russia—a country recognized for its enormous untapped natural resources, as well as for one hundred million potential consumers. Max tended to gravitate toward those portions of the business and the diplomatic worlds that would provide him with the highest profits, the most grandiose headlines, and the jauntiest publicity.

Thus, to their wide circle of performers was added an increasing number of diplomats and politicians. Parties at their triplex apartment adjacent to Central Park at West Sixty-seventh Street, and occasionally at the permanent suite Max maintained at the Shoreham Hotel in Washington, were the envy and the talk of both the concert and the diplomatic world—a heady brew of glamorous names and powerful statesmen. Even this was not all. Max had recently introduced a third element: the crowd from the Amtorg Trading Corporation, those secretive Bolshevik Russian traders who were slipping in and out of the country on a wide variety of missions.

It was one of the most fascinating and cosmopolitan circles in the city of New York. Few could resist the excitement and the sophistication of an invitation to dine with the Rabinoffs. Max enticed everyone with his showman's charisma and the glamour that regularly surrounds a leading man of the theater.

Bluet attracted them with the quality of the evenings. For, undoubtedly, she was the one who reigned supreme over the glittering setting. Even Max recognized her as a jewel in this respect. She was charming and a scintillating conversationalist, and she possessed a delicate grace that enchanted everyone she met. It was she who set the tone of evenings that were inevitably full of fun, laughter, and refinement.

All of which was in total contrast to Bluet's own lowly beginnings among the hill folk of the Auvergne, a rustic region where the weathered timbers are blacker, the grass grows taller, and the scent of pine and fruit-filled orchards leaves indelible impressions of nature at its most bounteous. Her early childhood had been spent in the care of a foster mother she called "maman," an illiterate peasant woman with enough maternal warmth for the needs of a dozen children. In the Augerolles, a group of medieval granite and cobblestone hamlets where they lived, everybody had been accepted for what they were, with never any pretense; for their weaknesses, as well as for their strengths; for their learning or even for their unschooled peasant wisdom. Poor or rich, it did not matter. There was enough kinship to go around.

But they were a passionate lot, those people of the mountains. Like the torrential rivers of the spring, the violence of the thunderstorms in summer, and the whistling winds of winter, their characters were in harmony with their surroundings: stronger impulses, stronger characters, stronger voices. They loved more deeply, cried more bitterly, and laughed more heartily than those from less dramatic settings. Indeed, had it not been so, she might have been better able to resist the current temptation.

It was at her Manhattan home, at one of those magnificent dinner parties, that she had first met Marc almost three years earlier. Max always made a point of welcoming newcomers from Moscow and introducing them into his circle of highly placed Americans in politics, banking, industry, and the arts. This would continue throughout the years between the Russian revolution of 1917 and the official American recognition of the not-so-new Soviet regime in 1933.

Marc had just arrived in the United States to head the Russian Red Cross mission in New York—an outpost seeking to raise funds and purchase modern medical supplies for a people recently ravaged by famine and civil war. The mission was spearheading a humanitarian effort on behalf of all Russian people. Max had a special admiration for such vital work, volunteering his services to gather a distinguished array of artists for benefit performances.

That particular night the Rabinoffs were giving a formal dinner party for fourteen guests at the long refectory table in the huge downstairs living room where they did all their entertaining. To step into that room, friends would tell Bluet, was like stepping across the Atlantic into Paris. She had decorated it with period pieces she had carefully selected in France and had shipped to New York. The floor was polished parquet and scattered with oriental rugs that were rolled aside for dancing after dinner. Paintings hung in ornate gold frames over crimson damask wallpaper—an eclectic mixture of Serge Soudeikine's theatrical interpretations (this particular Russian émi-gré painted much of the scenery for Max's productions), pastoral French landscapes, nudes, portraits—anything and everything that came their way. But if there was an underlying theme to the art, it was one of strength and passion. "Nothing safe . . . nothing proper," as Bluet would express it.

Yet concerning the etiquette of her dinner parties, Bluet was very proper indeed. She was much taken with manners, courtesies, and grace, believing they reflected the care that one individual took toward the sensibilities of another.

On this occasion the table had been set with one of the hand-embroidered tablecloths that the commercial attachés at Amtorg had been trying to peddle in America for desperately needed dollars—cloths that had been painstak-ingly patterned by Russian peasant women into intricate designs of foliage and native birds, representing the natural beauty of each province. The blend-ing of colors in those linen-and-lace tablecloths was a visual delight.

The china was blue and white from Bluet's own native Sèvres, and the tableware was pure British sterling. Even the crystal wine and champagne glasses were the finest the Bavarians, superior in glass blowing, were produc-ing. As a finishing touch, tall twisted candles had been placed at each end of the table, name cards sat at each place setting, and a spray of fresh orchids served as the centerpiece. To ensure the smooth flow of the meal, a button bell was hidden under the rug at Bluet's regular spot at the end of the table, so that servants could be summoned at exactly the most propitious moment. But all this effort was not entirely her own idea.

As other first-time guests, including important bankers, had been invited on this occasion, Max had insisted upon everything being just so. Bluet therefore gave orders to the French couple who ran their household that there should be no skimping on the groceries, ordered by telephone as usual from Park & Tilford, the "corner grocery store" preferred by the city's elite. For the main course she had chosen rack of lamb with tiny new potatoes in butter and parsley sauce. Each guest would also be offered a side plate of fresh asparagus, as it was early in the spring and asparagus was in season.

Briefly that morning she had taken a few minutes to see her thirteen-year-old daughter, Anna, off to the Lincoln School, considered one of the more progressive private schools in Manhattan and one heavily patronized by the avant-garde. Anna was a conscientious student with a natural inclination toward the theater, a field she had already shown a desire to enter. Bluet was tremendously attached to her daughter. One of her obsessions, friends would say, was being a doting and devoted mother. There is no doubt that Bluet lavished so much affection and time on her only child because her own mother had abandoned her as a baby to the care of a foster parent, being too wrapped up in her life in Paris to be bothered with the care of an infant.

After seeing Anna off, Bluet took a leisurely bath and dressed. She pored over the morning mail and attended to housekeeping matters—including the evening's schedule—with the servants. At that time she employed a household of five: a French couple, an austere but devoted governess from Paris they called Mademoiselle, a maid, and a chauffeur.

That evening Bluet chose to wear a black chiffon sleeveless dress that clung close to the body. It was cut provocatively low in a steep V at the front and had a layered, pleated skirt starting at the hip, with a hemline finishing a shade below the knee. The opera crowd was known for its formality of dress, and Bluet preferred to keep it that way.

Max also took infinite pains dressing for these occasions. His reputation for flamboyant attire had led a reporter to mockingly describe him as "Tamerlane or Genghis Khan without the turban." Gold rings adorned his fingers. He favored raspberry-colored shirts with a matching cravat, a diamond stick pin, and studded cuff links. Around his neck he regularly wore a twisted rope of gold. A fob watch dangled from a breast pocket on a gold chain. When outdoors, his fedora, worn at a rakish angle, was not only his personal trademark, it was part of the legend of Max Rabinoff, dandy-about-town—"the impresario who looked like an impresario." It would trigger imitations of a Max-like character that would embellish the theater and entertainment world for decades to come. Here was the original, the man who initiated the legend—a caricaturist's dream.

Max's obsession was his bushy mustache. He regularly had it curled and set with hot wax by one of his young office girls. Since his office was in his house, it was a convenient arrangement. Max was the sort who could never keep his hands to himself, and he inevitably managed to run them all over the young assistant. It was an exercise that obviously gave Max pleasure, but it sorely irritated his wife, since he did not even have the good taste to refrain when she happened to pass by. It did not matter if the assistant was a niece or a cousin, as was often the case, provided she was female and attractive.

Although Max lavished jewelry worth at least $30,000—a small fortune in 1928—upon Bluet over the years, she felt uncomfortable decked out in too many jewels. She considered it inelegant and ostentatious. That night she

Max Rabinoff

chose a pair of plain gold circle earrings, a small round brooch of twisted gold, and a gold bangle bracelet.

Had it been one of the theater parties that she and Max often gave, she would have added her favorite white silk shawl with the long tassels and a silver filigree evening purse. These were the other kind of parties the Rabinoffs had become popular for giving, the kind where invitations would be sent out to guests in advance, with tickets clipped to a card on the inside of the envelope. Everyone would be requested to gather in a reserved section of the theater, usually upstairs, and enjoy an opera or a ballet performance by one of the newest companies that Max had imported from Europe or Russia. Later they would return to the house for a buffet supper, dancing, and much animated conversation.

But on this particular night the guests had been invited by telephone and would be arriving at eight. As they filtered in, they gathered for cocktails around a magnificent grand piano that took up an entire section of the Rabinoffs' large living room. They were a talented group, and it was not uncommon for someone to extemporaneously start up a tune, most often something by Irving Berlin or George and Ira Gershwin—also friends of Max.

Since they were a crowd that loved to keep up with the latest books, not to say the latest fads, Bluet knew her guests also secretly hoped to rub shoulders with John Galsworthy or Sinclair Lewis, two Nobel Prize–winning novelists equally well-known to Max. They gossiped excitedly about the latest daredevil flights across the North Pole and high-profile rescues from mountaintops and underground caves. They were especially taken by the fact that religion was losing its grip and churchgoing was being tolerated only so long as the preacher finished in time for a Sunday drive in the newest and most popular acquisition of all: an automobile. They were equally full of chatter about the most recent innovations in radio, something still experimental called television, and the latest electric gadgetry for the home. Talk was fast-moving, exhilarating, and chock full of new ideas.

Such was the scene when Marc entered Bluet's home for the very first time.

Two

HE ARRIVED LATE THAT NIGHT, together with his wife—a shy and somewhat severe woman. Bluet slipped out to meet them personally in the large square foyer, before introducing the couple to the group. Offering only the briefest apology for their tardiness, Marc seemed quiet and a little withdrawn, yet exceedingly self-assured.

The eloquent bearing of the man appealed to her from the start. He greeted her graciously in a soft-spoken manner with a slight nod of the head, a broad smile, and a firm shake of the hand. Respectfully, he made sure his wife remained a step ahead of him. They were both tall, although he was decidedly the slimmer of the two. Observing him carefully with unconcealed curiosity while the maid took their coats, Bluet could not help but notice Marc's impeccable taste in clothes. His topcoat, conservatively cut, was made of the softest black mohair. His dinner suit was luxuriously hand-finished with fashionably wide lapels. His shirt was made of the finest silk. This was hardly the new type of revolutionary Russian she had been accustomed to meeting. More aristocrat than proletarian, she mused to herself. In accent, mannerisms, and clothes, he did not even appear Russian. He reminded her instead of an Italian nobleman. This intrigued her, as Max had insisted that Marc Cheftel was a physician from Moscow.

There was not even a trace of the waistline paunch most men develop at midlife. Glancing up, she could see that he still had almost a full head of hair, which was only just beginning to recede and turn silvery gray. Above all, his facial features were unbelievably handsome in a dark, Mediterranean sort of way. And his eyes—she had a weakness for eyes—were the deepest brown and the most penetrating she had ever seen. When he chose to focus them directly upon someone, his magical gaze could make that person believe that the two of them were discussing the most important matter in the world.

That night, however, she chose not to let him linger in her thoughts. She was constantly meeting attractive and distinguished men and making dozens of new acquaintances. Moreover, she preferred to concentrate on her role as hostess, a job she undertook with professional care. So, after the usual pleasantries, the evening settled into its usual conviviality.

Except for Max. His voice boomed even louder than usual, and it irritated her. He was also flirting outrageously, this time with a dancer, fawning over the girl with his typical roving eye and hands. It was more out of place than usual, considering the formal circumstances. Bluet's close friends were well aware of how Max's public displays humiliated her. That night was especially discomfiting because of all the new guests. Bluet detected a note of sympathy and embarrassment in the wry smile that crossed the face of the handsome Russian physician, as he maintained a certain distance from the clatter of the party.

Afterward, she would look back and remember one particular feature about Marc that passed almost unnoticed at the time—the way the rest of the Russian guests paused in their chattering as soon as he entered the room, somehow holding him in awe all evening long. It was not something you could put your finger on, but she sensed a hush, a lowering of the volume the moment he walked in. As long as he remained, the members of the Russian crowd continually glanced over their shoulders as they talked, casting a wary eye on him. From that very first moment she had been conscious of his almost indefinable power.

Marc dazzled the company that night with his dinner-table conversation. He was clearly a classical scholar—his quick and pungent retort, his ability to convert any topic into an amusing and fascinating anecdote, intrigued and captivated them all. Marc could quote the philosophers with facility and change languages with the same ease that the musicians among them could transpose keys. German, French, Italian, and Russian all rolled effortlessly off his tongue. Only English seemed to bother him, and he hesitated and appeared decidedly uneasy when trying to say anything in the local vernacular.

Still, he managed to eclipse even the omnipresent Max. For once, Max's substantial achievements in organizing the Chicago Grand Opera Company and the Chicago Philharmonic and his period of ownership of the Boston Opera Company paled against the eloquence of the good doctor. It had, after all, been Max who combined the Boston Opera Company with the Pavlova Ballet Russe in 1915 for one of the most glittering seasons the company ever had. Max had first introduced Pavlova to America. Moreover, his underlying philosophy of exposing all this culture to the masses through open-air concerts and budget-priced tickets—considered a radical departure in those early years of the twentieth century—was entirely in harmony with the social aims of the new Soviet Russian society, whose goals were being beautifully expounded that evening by this most urbane of philosopher-physicians. Gradually, Bluet sensed that even Max viewed the newcomer with a combination of jealousy and awe.

She had always been attracted to learned and scholarly people, lamenting that her own formal education had ended when she was taken out of her convent school at only fifteen—a convent being the place her parents decided it would be proper for her to attend following those early years in the country. A top student in her class, she was the one Mother Superior always chose to call upon when visitors were present. But fifteen was late enough for a girl to attend school in those days, her parents insisted. Somewhat of a bookworm, she remained a voracious reader nonetheless, so that now she was regarded as knowledgeable and well informed. That night she also listened to Marc with avid interest.

Marc spoke with energy and enthusiasm about the developing Soviet society he had just left, appearing to take exceptional pride in his own health department, which had organized the world's first national health service. He talked about Lenin and what Lenin had been trying to accomplish before dying after a long illness nearly four years earlier. Those middle years of the 1920s have often been described as the Golden Age of Bolshevism—a brief interlude when the Russian people, recovering from war and revolution, disease and hunger, managed to muster the energy and the spirit to launch new publications; enthusiastically attack widespread illiteracy and ignorance; take part in an explosive rebirth of the theater, music, and visual and architectural arts; and even permit political debate. Lenin's retrenchment in allowing a small measure of private enterprise in those interim years, called the New Economic Policy or NEP, had even made it appear that compromise and consensus would rule and a less implacable ideology would develop.

In fact, the Moscow that Marc had just left proudly proclaimed the previous year as the most prosperous since the revolution. Shops were again packed with merchandise. Commerce had returned to normal. People were out dancing and drinking at nightclubs and cafés. Even the food shortages had eased. Socialists the world over were expecting great things to come, as nearly every major nation now officially recognized the new Bolshevik regime. All, that is, except the United States. So, despite having a long road to travel, the Soviet experience seemed bursting with promise—the first truly proletarian state where a laboring person would no longer be exploited for someone else's financial gain.

"From each according to his abilities . . . to each according to his needs," finally seemed like more than just a revolutionary slogan. The Bolsheviks were ridding Russia once and for all of the dreaded *bourgeois* element—the term these revolutionaries regularly used to describe anyone belonging to the capitalist class, whose pampered lifestyle had been won through the sweat of laborers toiling in unspeakable conditions.

But this mysterious Russian physician was not all serious that evening. Marc made them laugh with his Chaplinesque tale of an idealistic young American doctor named Armand Hammer. A sort of Don Quixote of the steppes, Dr. Hammer had gone to Russia to alleviate some of the disease and the suffering. Churning his ambulance through the muddy roads of Russia shortly after the revolution, he heard tell of Lenin's great campaign against illiteracy. Pondering, as he drove along, that the peasants were therefore going to need a hell of a lot of pencils, Dr. Hammer persuaded the government to grant him the pencil concession for the entire country. Almost overnight, it catapulted this impecunious young American physician into a millionaire. Capitalism could hardly better that!

Marc, she would later learn, could always sense something amusing, even whimsical, in the twist of events in any political or human situation. But he often had a gravely serious intent. That night he was determined to demonstrate that many a capitalist profit could be turned from a Bolshevik need, if only Americans would cease fearing the "Bolshevik beast." Responding to a question from one cynical banker about the subversive activities of the dreaded Comintern, the international wing of the Communist Party dedicated to spreading communism throughout the world, Marc patiently explained that the whole emphasis—since the recent expulsion of Trotsky and his elaborate aims for world revolution—had changed. The energies of the party leadership had now turned inward, toward building socialism at home. Was this perhaps only one of many calumnies being brandished about in the United States regarding Soviet intent? Was it another Red Scare fable? Surely, a man as worldly and perspicacious as the banker could not genuinely believe such fairy tales emerging from a nation that could barely feed itself.

Because of the nature of this particular crowd, people also began chattering about the Russian theater and cultural developments in Moscow. All were anxious for news of the remarkable new staging and acting concepts of

Stanislavsky, Meyerhold, and the world-renowned Moscow Art Theater. As Marc filled them in, it seemed as if the new Moscow represented the jewel of a Renaissance society blossoming in an otherwise decadent world.

But Marc was artful enough not to appear dogmatic in his views, retaining the philosopher's ability to gently win over his opponents through irrefutable logic. He left the dogma to his wife, Katya—a dark-haired, matronly type, rather too correctly dressed. She was seated next to Bluet at the far end of the table.

Bluet quickly observed—mischievously, perhaps—that Katya gave the impression of a soap box orator every time she spoke about Soviet Russia. She did not say much, yet when she did, her manner was deadly earnest. It lacked the humor, panache, and good fun that sparkled through her husband's conversation. She was so political that Bluet soon concluded that Katya must be a professional propagandist. It therefore came as a surprise for Bluet to learn that Katya was also a physician—in fact, a specialist in the treatment of tuberculosis.

"What a perfect team!" Bluet commented to Katya, halfway through the meal. "You have so much in common."

"Many people tell us that."

"You must be proud of such a husband."

"I am. I do love him. Very much," she added, looking up and glancing over at Marc. It had come out so unexpectedly and with such deep feeling that Katya's words would haunt Bluet many times in the future.

"And your children?" Bluet inquired politely. "How are they settling in?"

"We have no children. Just the two of us," Katya explained.

Then Bluet asked the question that had been uppermost on her mind all evening. "Your husband . . . he sounds so much more Italian than Russian. Was he born in Italy?"

Katya shook her head. "No. You see, we both lived out of the country, in Italy, for many years. Marc moved there while he was still a student, so I suppose he appears more Italian than I do. We only returned to Moscow a few years ago."

Tactfully, Bluet did not press the matter further because she suspected he had probably been a political exile. Many Bolsheviks they knew in New York had originally sought political refuge abroad during the latter years of the czarist regime and then filtered back soon after the revolution. Changing the subject, she declared, "And now I'm sure you're going to enjoy New York!"

"We do want to see some of those famous Broadway shows," Katya admitted.

"And that's not all. Just about everything's going on here at the moment," Bluet continued, becoming increasingly animated as she spoke. "New fads every week. One year everybody's doing crosswords. The next they're getting a Model T. Last year we had that famous Lindbergh flight to Paris—you must have heard about it—and a few crazy people made quite a sensation filling their swimming pools with champagne! Now I'm told the thing to do is to read that new book from England called *Lady Chatterley's Lover.* Its frank language is supposed to shock us all."

Katya did not look as though she could be either shocked or readily amused. It made Bluet feel as if her own frivolity, her own exuberance, might be striking a discordant note. So once again Bluet quickly changed the topic, discovering that the couple had arrived only two weeks earlier aboard the *Paris.* And that Marc and Katya had experienced such a choppy, gale-swept crossing that Katya had remained confined to their cabin for the entire voyage. Marc, a far better sailor, thoroughly enjoyed the trip, despite his wife's indisposition. Katya also explained that Marc had set his heart on crossing on the famous new ship the *Ile de France,* but mechanical difficulties had temporarily withdrawn it from service.

After dinner they all crowded around the piano again, this time for some Russian songs, in deference to the many Russians among the guests. Mostly, they sang old folk songs with new Soviet words—marching songs from the revolution. Afterward, they broke into melodies from *Show Boat,* the biggest current hit. There was never a Russian, Max would say, who did not love to sing.

When it came time to leave, Marc brought Katya over to thank them warmly for such a magnificent party. "It's been one of the most delightful evenings we've spent since we arrived," he said. "You've made us both feel very welcome." Then, as he graciously lifted her hand to kiss it, Bluet noticed a disarming twinkle in his eyes.

Max stood next to her, as he usually did to bid his guests good-bye. He beamed so broadly and was so flushed with pride that it almost melted the wax in his mustache. If anyone had been attracted to this intriguing Russian physician that first night, it was Max. Marc obviously knew many of the founders of the Soviet Republic, and Max was clearly anxious to cement their relationship. It offered an opportunity not to be dismissed lightly.

Max kept on talking about Marc and Katya for days afterward, even suggesting that they invite the Cheftels up to their country home, a colonial-style fieldstone-and-clapboard house on thirty-six acres at Stony Point on the upper reaches of the Hudson River. Max was especially proud of this property. With the peculiar respect for American history that is so strong among the non-native born, he was impressed that it had originally been part of a historic battleground. It was here, on July 16, 1779, that General Anthony Wayne, under the direction of George Washington, overran the garrison and captured the British stronghold during the Battle of Stony Point. Nestled in a wooded setting at the end of a winding dirt lane, their holdings now consisted of a group of small farmhouses and some agricultural land that Max had purchased in 1923 and combined into one estate.

As a site for a wholly American operatic school, another of Max's dreams, it was especially meaningful, as one of the houses on the estate had been the "cottage" where "Mad" Anthony maintained his headquarters. It was also conveniently situated near the Haverstraw railroad station, only an hour or so from Manhattan. Even by car, it took no more than two hours to cover the distance.

Lately, Max had grown more preoccupied than ever with this school, ambitiously named the American Institute of Opera and Allied Art. The cornerstone had been laid six years earlier by Senator William King of Utah. Among its backers had been such notables as Vincent Astor, Condé Nast, Adolph Ochs, and the Rabinoffs' good friend, the millionaire banker Otto Kahn. President Coolidge had dispatched a personal envoy to the impressive ceremonies attended by a crowd of more than 5,000 well-wishers and high-lighted by a thundering thirteen-gun salute fired by an artillery detachment commandeered from the United States military academy at nearby West Point. Ever since, it had become a gathering spot for performers. This meant that they continually mingled in such rarified circles as those of Anna Pavlova, Mordkin, Racine, Fokine, Soudeikine, Galli-Curci, Rachmaninoff, Isadora Duncan, Ravel, Nijinsky, and Chaliapin—many of whom had first been introduced to America by Max. A zealous and active promoter of the new Bolshevik Russia as well, Max considered the regime such a marked improvement over the loathsome czarist rule of his boyhood days that he wanted to do all he could to help.

As a consequence, the house teemed with guests during the warmer months, especially people connected with Max's various endeavors. The Cheftels visited many times following the dinner party, especially over long holiday weekends. Max and Marc soon formed a close relationship, both eager for different reasons to feed on each other's goodwill and contacts. Business aside, Marc thoroughly enjoyed Max's musical friends. Bluet learned from Katya that Marc had been an ardent opera, ballet, and concert buff during the many years the couple had lived and worked as physicians in Italy. Now, through these visits to Stony Point and the parties at their New York apartment, Marc finally had an opportunity to meet many of these performers in person. In return, Max avidly studied Marc's political know-how and tried, albeit clumsily, to ape the intellectual prowess of his newfound acquaintance.

Often Bluet discovered them sitting for hours in the rustic living room or relaxing on the wide porch in Adirondack chairs, sipping Russian tea in the traditional way, out of a tall glass into which they dropped a spoonful of jam or honey. Chatting and laughing, they sometimes stayed there far into the night.

At other times the two couples took leisurely strolls through the grounds of the college while Max strutted around, pointing with pride at his accomplishments. Such a venture had been the dream of a lifetime, into which he had already invested $750,000 of his personal fortune. His aim had been to develop an arts center where American-born talent could be professionally trained in the United States, instead of undergoing lengthy and expensive periods with the maestros of Italy, Germany, or France. To avoid excluding those who could not afford such training, he structured the entire project to be self-supporting. Students would receive free food, lodging, training, and living expenses in return for a thirty-city tour at the end of each scholastic year. Box-office receipts from such a tour were designed to defray costs. The sole entrance requirement was a rigorous audition that tended to weed out all but the most promising.

Max was especially proud of his scenic studio, a huge concrete-and-steel structure the size of a giant aircraft hangar. It contained the original sets from some of his best productions. The top floor had been designed as a workshop for the use of his Russian émigré friends who specialized in theatrical sets, like Serge Soudeikine and Boris Anisfeld. It was tailored to their special horizontal way of working canvases (stretched out on the floor) that they had brought with them from Russia. American sets were still being built on the spot and worked upon vertically within the theater by handymen, rather than by artists. By contrast, these loose horizontal canvases could be folded into bundles for easy shipping. Using this method, even a touring company could employ a top-name designer to prepare a backdrop.

The downstairs had been designed to house a costume archive and a record collection, including a library of folk music gathered from all corners of the world. The Persian and the Japanese collections, considered the most rare, were already being made available to American composers. Max boasted that there was no shortage of wealthy backers anxious to associate their names with his institute. However, he was careful to conceal the fact that the entire project was still financially shaky.

He also made a point of showing his guests the huge red barn on another part of the grounds, which served as a rehearsal hall. It was a temporary arrangement while a fully equipped theater was being completed, along with a complex of dormitories, dining rooms, kitchens, and recreation rooms that would meet the residential needs of over one hundred students. Meanwhile, seven acres of fertile hillside were being plowed and spread with topsoil for a vegetable garden and a fruit orchard that would supply fresh produce to students and teachers.

One of his favorite stories—so indicative of the establishment attitude of the 1920s—was how the dormitories had originally been planned for coed use. But since he had received irate letters from the Daughters of the American Revolution and the General Federation of Women's Clubs, he had rearranged the facilities. As he put it, "They wanted me to appoint seven women supervisors to maintain the problematic purity of the project."

Max delighted in recounting in great detail the color, the splash, the organization, and the pomp of the original dedication ceremony—the one with the thirteen-gun salute. He had arranged the entire production (it could be called no less) to coincide with that same day in July when Mad Anthony had waged the Battle of Stony Point 145 years earlier.

Not content to let his guests find their own way to the estate that day, Max had chartered the Hudson River steamer *Observation* for the occasion, ferrying hundreds of people up from New York City in the carnival atmosphere and the cool breeze of a river ride. Those who did not care for boat travel were invited to board a special car attached to the noon train on the West Shore Railroad that ran up to Stony Point. The guest list read like an establishment handbook: representatives from the White House and Capitol Hill, the Grand Army of the Republic, the Sons of the Revolution, the Daughters of the American Revolution, the Boy Scouts of America, the American Legion, the National Federation of Women's Clubs, the National Federation of Music Clubs, and the American Federation of Musicians. Max had cornered the market on Americana for a day.

At Stony Point in the summer of 1924: Bluet (third from left) holding Anna, and Max (far right).

But Max could never admit the most upsetting part of what really happened. How, in full view of the 5,000 assembled guests and dignitaries and just as the guns were being fired for the climax of the proceedings, one of the gunners—a West Point cadet named Rose—caught his hand in a breech block, and the entire exercise stumbled to an embarrassed halt while a frantic call was sent out for a physician to attend to the injured cadet.

His house parties at the estate were different. They touched a warm and informal note in the lives of all their friends—musicians, bankers, and politicians alike. Invariably, Bluet made a discreet effort in advance to discover the personal taste of the visitors, whether for a particular food, a desire to sleep late, or even a wish to bring along a friend or a lover. She arranged matters so that each guest left marveling at the talents of such a warm hostess. However, problems still arose, such as the time, late one night, when one ardent gentleman tried to reach the object of his passion by climbing a tree outside the window of the woman's room. Mistaking the man for a prowler, the family's German shepherd awakened the entire household and cornered the would-be Romeo in a most embarrassing situation.

It was a place to relax, to walk among the pungent-scented pine trees or hike across the open meadows, alive with the sounds and the smells of summer.

Some guests preferred to sit outside and enjoy the cool breezes that floated across the wide flagstone terrace. Relaxing in wicker chairs, made comfortable with soft blue-and-white calico cushions, they were left in peace to read or chat. Alternatively, if the weather were bad, they all gathered around the great stone fireplace in the living room for more substantial conversation or an opportunity to listen to a recording of a new musical talent. They were not an athletic crowd, the only exception being horseback-riding. Max and their daughter, Anna, were both keen riders, stabling their horses at a farm nearby.

Conversation at Stony Point was the highlight of the weekend. It drifted from music to politics to world affairs in a fashion that could humble all but the most intellectually sophisticated. Though she was far too discreet to admit it to anyone, Bluet loved the politics most of all.

The evening meal provided the only real ritual of a weekend. Guests returned to their rooms at about five o'clock to change into something more formal before coming back down again to gather for cocktails in the large living room. Vodka was the favorite, and newcomers were initiated into the rites of this most traditional of Russian drinks, taken straight in a small glass and swallowed in one quick gulp. The choking and the tearful gasps of the first-timers never failed to evoke a laugh. The meal was the exclusive province of the loquacious Russian woman who ran their country kitchen. It also tended to be Russian, with a blend of French dishes. As a respite, desserts were as American as Boston cream pie.

What was apparent to all during these weekends was Bluet's own position as the confidante of the crowd—a factor even Marc soon commented upon. She had earned this role over a long period of time because of a gentle, sympathetic ear and her unfailing ability to keep a confidence. She even acted as matchmaker once between Soudeikine and the diva Jean Palmer. The couple had met at Stony Point while Serge was working in the scenic studio. Jean had been rehearsing with a chorus of students. Eventually, they married, although Max had opposed the match. He preferred to foster Jean's career, while Serge was reluctant to have a wife singing professionally. Bluet had scorned Max's opposition as self-serving. She considered a happy marriage and personal relationships far more important. Max raged, but Bluet promoted the match nonetheless.

Marc even spoke to her once about the way people confided in her. He wanted to know her secret. But she turned the conversation around, commenting instead upon his own passion for privacy. "I'd get nowhere with you," she teased. "You'd guard your age like a state secret."

"Not at all. I'm forty-three. And that's the truth," he conceded.

Bluet had made the first dent in the doctor's shield.

They spent a great deal of time together over the following weeks, though there was never a hint of a blossoming romance. The Cheftels merely slipped into that broader orbit of warm friends who meet each other regularly but never become too deeply involved in each other's lives.

Marc, however, found a special place in Bluet's affections from early on because of the attention he paid to Anna. Often he appeared in the afternoon while in New York to talk business with Max. Anna was frequently around, having just returned from school. And sometimes Marc accidentally met her as she walked through the apartment carrying piles of homework. It was then that Marc thoughtfully stopped to talk about her studies and laugh with her. Often they discussed Anna's perpetual agonies over violin lessons. Marc had learned the violin as a child and offered to assist Anna; he followed her achievements and setbacks with seemingly genuine concern.

Obviously, Marc had a great deal of patience and related well to youngsters, far better than did Max, who often seemed oblivious to the fact that he even had a daughter. Indeed, Max could not tolerate children. And he had refused point blank to have any more.

These midweek meetings between Max and Marc developed into regular events. Max had unquestionably become a valuable contact for Marc, due to Max's close working relationships with many of America's wealthiest families. He knew that they were all engaged in a philanthropic rat race to outdo one another as patrons of the arts and the charities. They were particularly intent on fostering their image as humanitarians. And it seemed clear to Marc that these families could be persuaded to contribute their talents and money to improving the lives of starving Russians, were it possible to divorce their actions from political involvement. In 1921 the American government even donated $20 million for famine relief, despite its avowed political antagonism toward the Bolshevik revolutionaries and the expansionist policies of their Communist International (Comintern). The private charitable donations that subsequently poured in from a concerned American public boosted this amount to a gigantic $60 million.

One particular need Marc constantly discussed with Max was for money to help train medical personnel and develop modern hygiene in the outlying villages. To this end, Max persuaded a personal friend and philanthropist, Francis Drury of Cleveland, to donate $6,000. The plan was to send two Russian physicians to train at the famous Cleveland medical laboratories so that they might return and educate their own people. Drury even offered to equip a similar laboratory inside Soviet Russia. Marc and Max were left to work out the details, with the actual cash being entrusted personally to Marc.

The Rabinoffs were often invited to the three-room apartment that the Cheftels had rented on upper Riverside Drive. It was very correct, very 1920s modern—total simplicity of line and a somewhat insipid choice of colors. Comfortable, yet without character. But it was neat and pleasant, and evenings there were fun.

Then it happened. One evening, totally unexpectedly, Marc drew Bluet aside. Would she care to have lunch with him the following Wednesday?

Bluet was flattered. If anybody occupied the most important place in the hierarchy of their Russian friends, it was definitely Marc Cheftel.

"That would be lovely," she said. "I will look forward to it."

They agreed upon an Italian restaurant he recommended in the East Sixties and settled on one o'clock. For some reason Bluet chose not to tell Max. At first she convinced herself, in all modesty, that Marc simply wanted to discuss a problem he might have encountered with Max. Many friends approached her when further dealings with Max became futile. His abrasiveness often antagonized them at a pivotal moment. Usually, she managed to smooth things over. She considered it part of her job.

Nevertheless, she took extra care that Wednesday morning as she dressed, put on makeup, and arranged her hair.

Three

BLUET WAS, BY NATURE, a fastidious person. She lavished a great deal of care, thought, and time on her appearance. Her long, thick, wheat-colored hair had been arranged that morning in her favorite way—pulled back into a chignon with a few loose curls brushing the corners of her cheeks. From her ample wardrobe she chose one of her favorite outfits: a gray wool flannel suit, simply but expertly cut to fit her waif-like waist. Over a pure silk white blouse she slipped on a tapestry vest—her fashion hallmark. She then selected a brilliant crimson cravat to set it all off. No jewelry whatsoever, aside from a plain wedding band. Completing the ensemble was a gray felt cloche hat, her one concession to the fashion fad of the day. Bag, shoes, and gloves were of plain black suede leather. She stayed with the simplest designs, no matter what changing fashions dictated.

She left the apartment in plenty of time to call a cab and arrive at the restaurant by one o'clock sharp. Even so, Marc was already there, pacing up and down and smiling eagerly. She climbed out of the taxi just as a nearby church clock chimed the hour. Opening the car door with a flourish, he insisted on paying the cabbie.

"I thought Russians were habitually late," she teased.

"Not all of us. And not when we're meeting such an elegant lady. You look magnificent today," he observed, sounding genuinely impressed by her appearance.

"Do I?" His compliment surprised her. Max hardly ever noticed what she wore anymore.

"You're too modest," he added. "You don't think enough of yourself." He took her by the arm and gently led her inside.

As they reached the dining room, she realized he had taken the trouble of reserving a table in advance, tucked away in a corner. He seemed so utterly at home with the Italian surroundings and the Italian language that their waiter even paused to inquire what part of Italy he was from. "Rome," Marc answered simply, his eyes lighting up.

After ordering drinks and discussing the menu—on which he gave quite positive opinions as to which dishes to choose—they settled back to relax and talk. Immediately, there flowed such an ease of communication, a delight of shared thoughts and observations, mainly on people and places they knew in common—which by this time were manifold—that she hardly realized how quickly the time was passing. When she glanced at her watch, she was aghast at the lateness of the hour.

In a panic, she spluttered, "I promised to take Anna shopping after school today. I'll be late."

"I'd better not keep you any longer then," he apologized and motioned to the waiter to bring them the bill.

"You know," she observed, as she stood up to leave the table, "You must learn to speak better English now that you're here. It sounds so . . . ," she halted mid-sentence, not wanting to offend. "It doesn't suit you at all."

"You're absolutely right," he said. "It's been a difficult problem right from the beginning. So I was hoping," he added more slowly, looking directly at her with his magnetic gaze, "that you might help me. A few more lunches like this, speaking only English, of course, and correcting me as we go along. . . ."

She laughed, agreeing at once, even though they both knew it was only an excuse.

"We'll choose a French restaurant next time just for you," he promised her on the way out.

And then he hailed her a cab.

It was only on the way home that she realized he had never come around to speaking about Max or any problem that might have prompted the lunch. It intrigued her, but she certainly wasn't going to ask. All she cared about, anyhow, was that she had thoroughly enjoyed her afternoon with this strange yet captivating man.

THEY SAW EACH OTHER for lunch often after that. It became a regular part of both their lives, although he constantly changed restaurants, times, and even the day of the week. He seemed anxious that nobody should gossip about these meetings, even mentioning on occasion, "Let's just keep it to ourselves."

Most of all, she loved to listen to his stories. Spending time with him became an entertainment and an education all rolled into one. He told her of the years he had spent as a doctor in Italy, a country he clearly missed a great deal. He seemed to have a tremendous affection for Italian warmth, gentleness, and love of life. He marveled at cities like Rome, Venice, and Florence and the spectacular beauty of Italy. He found America bland by comparison, lacking the depth, history, and traditions that made European life so colorful. American women, he confided, disappointed him, too. They had little of the chic and the sensuality of European women. Still, he adored the gaiety, the sparkle, and the holiday atmosphere of New York. He had taken Katya to see Gershwin's *Funny Face,* laughed at *Animal Crackers* with the Marx Brothers, been to the famous Ziegfeld Theater, and was surprised at the popularity of Chekhov's work on Broadway.

"We were born in the same town, Chekhov and I," he mused one day, adding playfully, "giving it a double claim to fame!" Marc also loved to quote Spinoza, his favorite philosopher. He talked, too, about the genius of Freud and how much research was being conducted in the new Soviet Russia in psychology.

Bluet had never thought much of Freud's theories, observing, "If people can't be honest with themselves, then how can they possibly be with an analyst?" He refused to agree.

He loved to laugh and make others laugh. His Chaplinesque view of life, which she had noticed from that very first night, invariably left her chuckling. She picked it up instantly, and their eyes met in laughter with an intimacy easily as intense as any physical contact. He had a zest for living that was positively infectious, as though life itself was a madcap adventure to be lived and enjoyed at all costs. But she was also well aware from the many formal dinners he attended at her house that he could be as serious as any corporate executive when the occasion warranted.

He often discussed the friends they both knew. He regularly steered the conversation toward these people, especially the Russian artists, émigrés, and Amtorg couples they knew in common. She often shook her head in amazement because he invariably understood more about them than she did herself.

This led her to observe that she found him so very different from most communists, who typically came from very humble circumstances. And that led to his acknowledgment that he had, in fact, come from a wealthy family in Southern Russia. By contrast, Max's background, she told him, had been far more plebeian: a simple boyhood in the village of Moghilev, interrupted when he was forced to leave school at fifteen after an ugly brush with the Russian authorities. Afterward, Max's parents decided it would be wiser for him to leave the country, dispatching him to relatives in Chicago. From then on, Max's story became a classic Horatio Alger tale of the American entertainment world. First he had a job as an upholsterer's apprentice, then as a tobacco stripper, finally landing a salesman's spot with the Kimball Piano Company, where he did so well that he was allowed to open a branch of his own in a poorer, immigrant section of Chicago.

Convincing the management that he could sell pianos to these people equally as well as bread, he intuitively understood that they hankered after more than material well-being. Max began by obtaining permission for outdoor Sunday concerts for indigent workers. This grew in time to a founding role in organizing the Chicago Philharmonic, after which came opera (in conjunction with Oscar Hammerstein of New York) and ballet (in conjunction with Pavlova and the Ballet Russe), until Max's magic for developing and producing entertainment for the masses spread halfway across the world. He became a self-made success in the truest American tradition.

Marc was the opposite. His ambitions for himself and aspirations for his fellow human beings seemed to stem far more from a social position. Perhaps it was this element in his background that occasionally gave him the disturbing mien of a dilettante. There was no doubt that the thrill of the game appealed to Marc equally as much as the substance.

As his own boyhood may have been even more upper-crust than he cared to admit, especially as a Soviet representative, Bluet found it curious that he was comfortable among the other leaders of this workers' revolution. The only way she could explain it was to recall how a handful of the original Bolshevik leaders she had met at trade conferences with Max in Europe were equally eloquent and erudite: Old Bolsheviks, as they would eventually be called. She concluded that Marc must be one of them.

Whatever their background or label, all these early communists were eager to argue at length about their distrust of the greedy, buccaneer-style capitalism they saw all around them in those early years of the twentieth century, with its callous attitude toward the fate and the well-being of the ordinary working family. Marc was especially in agreement with their hatred of modern warfare, especially the conduct of the leaders in the recent World War, later known as World War I. Millions of ordinary people had been used as cannon fodder by both sides, he insisted, so that munitions suppliers could reap huge profits. He had witnessed much suffering personally as a physician working in Italy. Had the masses been in control at the time, he insisted, both sides would have sought a way out, as the Bolsheviks did after taking over in Russia in 1917.

Marc appeared totally consumed by these injustices. He also had little respect for American-style democracy. He considered the right to vote merely an exercise in throwing a bone to the workers each election day, while the real power remained in the grip of the major industrialists, regardless of the outcome. He had been shocked, he said, by the discrepancy in America between enormous wealth and acute poverty, finding it even more striking than he had imagined—the "two nations" he had read so much about.

The concept of a vast new political order had obviously infected Marc—he was plainly an idealist—far more than it had Max, even though Max was always anxious to help people like Marc. Max remained squarely focused on the success of his many theatrical enterprises and on perpetuating the legend of Max Rabinoff.

In general, Bluet agreed with Marc's position. Eighteen years under Max's liberal influence, plus her own lowly childhood, made her comfortable with the aims of the extreme left. Besides, it was the most fashionable philosophy of the day, despite Washington's anticommunist stance. Left-wing politics had dozens of respected followers, from Max Eastman to Jack London, Upton Sinclair, Theodore Dreiser, George Orwell, W. H. Auden, Bertolt Brecht, Stephen Spender, Arthur Ransome, Sylvia Pankhurst, and George Bernard Shaw. It would reach a crescendo in the upcoming days of the Depression—the era of the radical left.

But it was not in Bluet's nature to speak out on such matters. She was too modest, taking the view that she could better express herself through the men in her life than through personal endeavors.

With the guile of a tightrope walker, Marc repeatedly avoided such topics as his wife, his parents and siblings, and—most especially—his work in the United States. It struck Bluet as unusual. Most men she knew rambled on for hours about themselves and their accomplishments.

On one occasion, he did mention that the Rockefeller Foundation was helping to introduce him to the American medical establishment so that he could learn about new technical developments for hospitals. He also admitted that he had spent time with Katya at the Harvard School of Public Health, studying disease control and the aftereffects of industrial poisoning among factory workers. Ultimately, Bluet put his evasiveness about his own life down to his natural Russian preference for secrecy. The relentless

Red-baiting throughout the 1920s had taken its toll. Gradually, she stopped even trying to find out and enjoyed letting him remain a mystery man. The unparalleled deference his Russian associates afforded him created an indefinable aura of power. And that made him even more attractive.

Their conversations dwelled only on the personal, as when she told him about her own childhood and later years at the convent. Marc was curious to find out how she first met Max. Back in 1911, she explained, when she worked in the offices of a luxury hotel in Paris, Max had checked in while on a business tour of Europe. He needed bilingual help to trace a certain French composer. She was the only one with sufficient command of both languages to provide assistance. An extra year in a convent school in London, plus two more years as a governess with a British diplomatic family, had given her fluency in both tongues.

The week Max arrived, she had just finished reading Du Maurier's *Trilby*. And Max's dark face and green eyes—"like a tiger but shadowed with long soft lashes," as she put it—had fascinated her. "My Svengali," she joked. "Only much nicer."

Prudently, she left out certain details. How she had become infatuated with Max and his artistic way of life. How she had gone to America to live with him in an apartment over the Manhattan Opera House in New York, where he was organizing his upcoming season of opera. She had stayed on, even though he would not consider marriage. Life had been so exhilarating. Theaters or concerts every evening, parties, constant travel, living in luxury suites, and being lavished with exquisite clothes—not to mention meeting some of the most outstanding celebrities of the era. The lifestyle was irresistible. Eventually, she had become pregnant with Anna. They married only after the baby was born. By then, propriety and legitimacy demanded it.

The wedding took place before a justice of the peace, as she was Catholic and Max was Jewish. As a major concession to her faith, she promised to raise Anna according to the rites of the Catholic Church. Max, not at all a religious man, did not argue. Only later in life would he find it troubling.

The ceremony had hardly been the essence of romance. Max forgot to bring a ring, an oversight that stung her and looked absurd. Compounding the slight, he sent it to her the next day, delivered by his office boy. That typified Max's attitude to the marriage all along. He gave her the impression it was only one of household and sexual convenience. Nothing more. That cut deepest of all. Though addicted to sex, he had no place for love, not even at the beginning. Love was a commodity he exploited for the stage.

Tenderness and affection were not part of his world, except as a stratagem for seduction. He exhibited neither the patience nor the need for a spiritual bond.

They had not planned to tell anyone about the wedding. But the press picked up a rumor a week later, hounding them both for details, as Max was already considered a well-known personality. He did not even want to waste time on a honeymoon. After the ceremony, they simply went out for the evening—to the theater, of course. They saw a hilarious comedy called *Potash and Perlmutter,* about a pair of Jewish businessmen. Max laughed and laughed, but the hurt lingered with Bluet.

While Anna was still small, Bluet told Marc, she had gone every Thursday to the Garrick Theater, where Jacques Copeau, the innovative French producer and critic, was staging a superb season of French classical plays. "I put Anna on my knee," she told him, "and she fell asleep while I enjoyed the cadence of my own language, losing myself completely in the conflict of the drama. Then one afternoon Monsieur Copeau bolted out on the stage in the middle of the second act to tell us that the armistice had been signed. Of course, the play never finished. Instead, we all ran outside laughing and hugging each other in delight."

Afterward, she and Max attended the Versailles Peace Conference, where Max lobbied energetically for more realistic attitudes in dealing with the Bolsheviks. But the hysterical fear that a similar revolution might soon sweep the entire continent of Europe, fomented by the Bolsheviks, made such a quest impossible. Instead, the aging leaders of Western Europe vowed individually and collectively to isolate and eradicate this workers' virus before it spread any further. Marc peppered her with questions about these recollections.

Later, she told him, she and Max attended the Genoa Conference of 1922—the international trade conference where the Bolsheviks scored their initial breakthrough by signing a major treaty with certain European powers. Max had been invited to participate as a personal observer for President Harding, as well as the "official representative" of the All-Russia Cooperative Societies—sitting, as it were, on two sides of the diplomatic fence. Only someone as audacious as Max Rabinoff could have pulled this off, she giggled.

She particularly amused Marc with the story of their arrival back from the Genoa Conference on the liner *Olympic.* The customs officers in New York discovered a dozen bottles of champagne and Napoleon brandy that Max had carefully hidden by stuffing them into her precisely folded piles of underwear. He was worried that due to Prohibition, the bottles would be confiscated. When the officials threatened to take away the lot, Max pleaded that his sick wife needed them for medicinal purposes. Since he had gone abroad specifically in the service of the president, he would "take the matter up with President Harding himself." But with a wry look that suggested they had heard such tales once too often, the customs officials seized the entire booty.

Occasionally, she entertained Marc with her gossipy tales of the legendary performers of ballet and opera she had come to know personally while they were under contract to Max (who had recently granted an ambitious and eager young entrepreneur named Sol Hurok the candy and program concession for one of Max's seasons).

At the beginning, so much of the Rabinoff couple's lives had revolved around Anna Pavlova and her partner, Michael Mordkin, as Max plotted and schemed with Sergei Diaghilev, the Russian ballet producer, to bring them to the United States. These artists had not been as welcome as one would expect; Bluet told Marc that Max had difficulty persuading Giulio Gatti-Casazza, the excitable Italian who was running the Metropolitan Opera, to let the Russians dance at all during the season. Gatti feared it would mar the dignity of an operatic repertoire by including a lesser art. Even though the arrangements had been made, Gatti, a corpulent bearded man of Edwardian proportions and a terrifying temper, stubbornly refused to have the Ballet Russe on his schedule. Finally, he agreed to let them dance—but only on Tuesday nights when opera was not given. Max had to employ his utmost powers of persuasion to explain this humiliating turn of events to Pavlova and Mordkin, who were accustomed to dancing before royalty and the finest of European society.

Max also had to explain why, on other nights, they were scheduled to dance only after the conclusion of the opera—an additional late-night exposure he had squeezed out of the reluctant Gatti. But so many patrons of the opera turned up after ten o'clock just to see the ballet that Max could not contain his delight. He made the most of this personal victory against the artistically myopic Gatti, whose word was normally sacrosanct.

The Ballet Russe became an overwhelming success for more than just the brilliance of the dancers. As Max had long been an enthusiast of spectacular scenery and costuming, it also demonstrated the visual glory of combining the creativity of both dancer and scenic designer. To this end, Max spent considerable effort persuading Serge Soudeikine, Boris Anisfeld, and

A 1935 cartoon in honor of Max Rabinoff's twenty-fifth anniversary as an impresario of international repute underlines the breadth of his standing.

Leon Bakst, the best of the Russian set designers who had relocated to New York, to consider the American theater as an ongoing outlet for their work. This in itself was radical, as Americans were still not convinced that original art belonged on the stage. But, eventually, they embraced it. And the new "theater of illusion" led in time to that wholly American product: the Broadway musical spectacular.

Bakst created the decor for the first performance of the choreographer Mikhail Fokine's *Ballet Orientale*, later known as *Scheherazade*, since it had been set to Rimsky-Korsakov's famous score. The highlight of the evening had been the "Bacchanale," in which Pavlova and Mordkin danced together. From then on, the combined talents of Pavlova, Mordkin, and Bakst took the country by storm. Swept into the orbit of such success, Bluet and Max named their own daughter Anna Pavlova Rabinoff when she was born in April 1914, only hours after the finale of one of the most hectic seasons of the Ballet Russe.

Graciously, the dancer Anna Pavlova accepted their invitation to become the godmother to the child named in her honor. Bluet had grown to admire Pavlova more than most of the other performers she knew, finding Pavlova curiously modest.

Their brush with Feodor Ivanovitch Chaliapin, the incomparable bass of the 1920s, had been of interest to Marc, too. Perhaps it was Chaliapin's outspoken ways that were an embarrassment to the young Bolshevik regime. Rules, conventions, and social niceties meant nothing to this bombastic

Advertisement for the Boston Opera House, winter season 1915–16. Bringing Anna Pavlova and the Ballet Russe to the United States was a major coup for Max Rabinoff.

36

Bluet (backseat, left) riding in an open car with Anna Pavlova (at right), c. 1915.

Russian peasant. Given as he was to inexplicable fits of fury and erratic stage behavior, only his genius as an actor-singer—few could match his ability to combine the best of both—permitted him to get away with so much. Chaliapin was a formidable personality. Even Max could never bind him to a regular contract.

Still, at the pleading of a mutual friend, Max had arranged a special dinner for Chaliapin the very night of his arrival in New York in December 1921. Even back then, the new regime had been unable to keep him home, with so much of Europe and the United States clamoring for appearances. Bluet and Max invited twenty-one of their Russian friends to a surprise party in Chaliapin's honor at their Central Park triplex. This delighted him. He remained in excellent humor all evening, "keeping us roaring at dinner with spicy stories about Bolshevik intrigues," she said, "and singing for us after dinner far longer than he would have done at a professional concert."

Bluet also told Marc about the interpretive dancer Isadora Duncan, whom she first met in the early 1920s at Claridges in London at the height of Duncan's fame. Isadora, she explained, "looked down her nose at me," seemingly astonished that Max could have married such an insignificant woman.

"She greeted me with the pronouncement, 'I don't like women. Women *bore* me.' After that," Bluet continued, "Isadora monopolized the conversation for the entire evening without saying anything original or interesting." But, Bluet admitted, she had been entranced by Isadora. "She had such a unique face, the face of an innocent. Her silhouette was so magnificent, I would watch expectantly for her entrance into Claridges and the long walk she would take from the door right across the foyer. It was as beautiful a sight as I have ever seen." But Duncan never seemed to care what people said or thought about her. "If she had any philosophy," Bluet concluded, "it was the philosophy of Carmen. She loved, but knew she might cease to love tomorrow. She followed her passions no matter what. She was destined to come to a tragic end. It was inevitable."

By contrast, she mused, "Greta Garbo is the only one with the right idea. She instinctively knows that besides her exquisite and enigmatic acting, the most intelligent thing to do is to give nothing else to the public. Mystery completes the picture more powerfully than any press agent's tricks."

As Bluet and Marc became more comfortable with each other, she found herself drawn to share confidences with him, as though for the first time she had a friend who really understood her dilemma. One time she told Marc how Max, following his usual pattern, had started an affair with Oda Slobodskaya, a soprano from the Petrograd Opera. It had begun right after the season opened to rave reviews, and Oda was the center of it all. Their whole crowd knew what was going on. Max even bragged about his conquest. In the end, her only hope was that Max's ardor would quickly cool, as it always had before, and the woman would be dropped. It did. But he went on to seduce so many others that by now she had lost count.

It had reached a point where "he behaves as if he isn't even married. He hides nothing." And then she added quietly, "I'm beginning to feel more like a hired hostess than a wife."

"Why do you stay?" Marc gently inquired.

"Become a divorced woman!" Bluet screwed up her nose. Even among their carefree circle, a divorcée was still stigmatized. Divorce was not a step to be taken lightly. Besides, as Max's wife she enjoyed an enviable social status, as well as considerable wealth. "And there's our daughter," she continued, trying to justify her behavior to herself as well as to Marc.

As the weeks passed and they came to know each other more intimately, Marc seemed captivated as much by her exquisite appearance as by her delicacy and charm. "My Limoges miniature," he affectionately called her.

But it was not until late that fall that he made his first tentative advance. Unexpectedly, he placed his hand gently but firmly over her own as they were sitting at lunch. Startled, she flushed. It impelled him to remark, "You look so pretty when you blush."

Somewhat agitated, she ignored the comment. In truth, she felt angry at herself. She normally retained her composure no matter what. Such a gentle advance was really quite innocent. She was surprised and confused by her own reaction.

Later, as he helped her on with her coat, she felt the extra pressure of his hands against her shoulders as she fastened the clasps, lifted the thick fur collar up to her chin, and slipped on her hand-stitched leather gloves to guard against the unseasonable chill. She had not hurried. He understood.

So it was not unexpected that at their next meeting, when he again helped her with her coat after the meal, she turned to discover him standing unusually close, smiling down at her. Almost in slow motion and with infinite care, he stooped to tilt her chin upward and brush her lips lightly with his own, right there in the corner of the restaurant. It was not a passionate kiss, yet he held her momentarily so very close that his message was undeniable. She savored every second of it, lingering to enjoy the intimacy as long as possible. It was not simply an encounter. It was a growing enchantment.

That afternoon, instead of their usual cab, he suggested a walk. The air was crisp and the sky a deep winter blue. Although the temperature had fallen close to freezing, it was ideal weather for a stroll. She immediately agreed. Their time alone had become a precious commodity. They chose to amble slowly down Madison Avenue toward Midtown—even then lined with some of the most interesting and unusual shops in the city—and occasionally paused to enjoy the window displays.

As he walked just a bit ahead of her on the curb side of the pavement, she was again aware of his elegant appearance. She envied Katya for having married a man who looked so distinguished, by anybody's reckoning—quite a contrast to the clownlike Max. "Did anyone tell you that you look far more like a diplomat than a doctor?" she observed.

"Do I?" he replied somewhat vaguely. "My life does seem to be going in that direction."

"How long is it since you practiced?"

"A number of years. Since I returned to Moscow."

"Why did you give it up?"

"There were other things to be done. Other priorities. I try to be of service."

"Do you miss it?"

He laughed. She had obviously hit close to the truth.

"Well," she declared, "I think you'd prefer to be a diplomat." She slowed down, then paused to watch as one of the shopkeepers worked on his window, dressing it for the coming Christmas season. The stock market crash some months earlier had not dampened the festiveness in this affluent section of town. Adorned with silver tinsel and winter green holly, red berries and cotton-ball snow, the displays had remained the same for years.

The shopkeeper placed small gift items on the blanket of white cotton and continued to arrange the merchandise around his decorations. As Bluet watched, she found herself drawn to an exquisite jewel box of inlaid black enamel and mother-of-pearl. It gleamed and subtly changed shades as the shopkeeper maneuvered it into place—a mosaic so delicate, it was just the sort of piece she adored. It would be ideal for her tiny earrings, which were continually being mislaid in her large jewel case. But she dared not step inside to ask the price. Not with Marc. She would return in a day or so to buy it on her own.

Marc looked at the box, too. Then back at her. Hurriedly, he grasped her arm, saying, "Wait here. I'll be right back."

He disappeared inside the shop before she could stop him. So she just stood outside while he talked to the shopkeeper. She could see the man reach over to remove the box from the window. She felt guilty. She had not intended for Marc to do this.

"For you," he said shyly, handing it to her as he came out of the door.

"But I didn't mean . . . ," she stammered. "You shouldn't have done it. It's not even a special occasion."

"I think it is," he declared, then added enigmatically, "don't you?"

This was the same day he asked for permission to take Anna to a concert that upcoming Saturday afternoon. There was a violin recital at Carnegie Hall, and he thought Anna might enjoy going to a matinée. "Perhaps we'll have something to eat at the Russian Tea Room next door afterward," he added.

Anna came back from the concert in a great state of girlish excitement and let her mother know that it had been magnificent—"and Dr. Cheftel was so charming and amusing," she blurted out. "He knew everything about the program. And he told such great stories on the way home. He says he'll take me again when he has time."

Bluet could not help comparing Anna's response to this outing with the many times Max had arranged to take her somewhere, usually horseback-riding in Central Park, and had canceled at the last moment for one reason or another.

Max was home that afternoon. And Marc stopped to speak to him, poking his head around the door of the cluttered, pocket-sized office located near the entrance to the apartment. Max sat chin-deep in papers, preparing for a ten-day trip to Washington. Marc seemed anxious to remind Max to discuss certain matters with various officials while there. They never involved Bluet in any of this, but she hovered around anyway until it was time for Marc to leave.

"Don't be too lonely while Max is away," he teased, gently squeezing her arm and giving her a paternal peck on the cheek as he passed her on the way to the front door.

"Oh, don't worry. I'll manage quite nicely," she assured him. She looked forward to those times when Max was not at home. The house calmed down to a point where she could have more hours to herself—an appealing inter-lude between the never-ending noise and bustle of Max's life. It was a time to catch up on reading, browse in the shops, spend more time with friends, and even take overnight trips to see those who lived outside the city. It was a welcome change from the incessant churn of theater and late-night parties, a time to renew her own inner resources.

Four

THERE ARE CERTAIN TRUTHS in life that are known between two people but that defy words or explanation. Once past, it is often difficult to remember exactly the nature of the unspoken communication, except that it was as strong and as real and tangible as anything with form or substance. It is an atmosphere of knowing, of understanding that once experienced can be more meaningful than almost everything else in the pattern of human relations. It is the thread with which some of the most precious memories are woven.

Such was the case at that moment between Bluet and Marc as 1929 drew to a close. She was positive he would not leave their relationship suspended in this way. But she was also well aware that he possessed a philosopher's patience, an ability to wait out others for exactly the ideal moment.

The waiting turned out to be not as prolonged as she had anticipated. That same week, while curled up on the living room couch reading quietly one evening, she was startled by a knock at the door. It was past ten o'clock, and the servants had gone to bed. Max was still in Washington. Anna was fast asleep and the governess, too. Bluet slipped into a floor-length satin robe in her favorite shade of cornflower blue.

Curious to see who could possibly be calling at such a late hour, she put down her book and walked to the front door. She stood on tiptoe to peer through the round peephole. Instinctively, she knew even before looking out that it would be Marc, his shadowy figure unmistakable as he paced anxiously up and down in the gloom of the hallway. She let him in. She led him back into the living room, closing the door silently behind her. Neither seemed anxious to speak. He scanned her face, seeming to search her mood, her soul, just one last time, for the answer he already had. She sensed a momentary hesitation, lest at this crucial juncture all his intricate strategy might collapse for want of a perceptive gesture, an appropriate word. She had been wanted many times by many men, but more as a prize. A trophy. For sport. The warmth of a very personal love had eluded her in childhood

42

and later as a woman. Now it was here—a little late perhaps, but finally here. She had convinced herself of that, even though she knew in the deepest recesses of her mind that she could be deluding herself.

The next move was up to her. She felt herself trembling. He held out his arms. There was a pause. She felt impelled to say something—anything—but the words stuck in her throat. Suddenly, it was as if someone else were running toward him, showering him with kisses. He began to caress her with a tenderness she had never encountered before. It had never been this way with Max. Max was the most insensitive of partners, never profiting from all his rapacious experience. As a lover, Max had no soul. His artistry was reserved strictly for the stage.

But Marc's timing and approach had been perfection. Intuitively, they became caught up in each other's passion and needs. It became a joy of giving equally, as much as receiving. Yet they each felt just a whisper of shyness, acutely aware that such a precarious mood could be lost at any moment by the smallest blunder. It was a culmination of more than just sexual passion. They were like two figures on magic spinning wheels who became irresistibly propelled toward one another.

Or so it seemed. It was not a moment to dwell on reality or upon the obvious futility of it all. Or even on where it might lead in the end. It was too precious.

By midnight, he had left the house. For days afterward, she was aware of little else than her own daydreams, recapturing the event. Sometimes she wondered if indeed it had even happened. Though she continued to see him among the regular ebb and flow of their customary visits between friends, he never alluded to the incident.

Until the day he drew her aside at one of the parties to remark, "I hear Max is going to Boston for the weekend. Katya has to travel up to Niagara Falls to clear up a problem with a friend . . . so . . .well . . . I was wondering if you were free to come over to the apartment. To stay over perhaps?"

He was an artful man. He knew perfectly well that the question was a rhetorical one. She would never have turned him down. His miraculous ability to influence people by weaving a magnetic spell had been especially effective with her.

"I'll be there," she nodded. "I'll arrange it."

Arrange it she did. She told the household she was going to stay overnight with some friends. This was nothing unusual, as she often did so when Max was away.

But it did not turn out quite as expected. In layout, furnishings, and character, she knew the apartment well by this time. But the reason for her being there that evening made it all appear so different. From the moment she walked through the door, she knew she had made a mistake. Katya may not have been physically present, but she was there in every other way. An extra toothbrush was still standing upright in a holder in the bathroom. Open jars of make-up stood ready on her dressing table. Her velvet slippers were under the bed, and her clothes gaped accusingly from a half-open closet door. Scribbled notes were intermingled with piles of reports that lay on a living room table (with no sign of Marc's papers)—envelopes and letters clearly addressed to Dr. Katya Cheftel. The kitchen was all Katya, from the well-thumbed recipe books on the shelf to the peculiar way in which she stacked the pots and pans next to the stove.

Bluet felt cheap, something she hated to concede in her own behavior. She disliked herself for having accepted the invitation. It reminded her of the way she had felt when Max brought another woman into her house. But her anticipation of the pure sexual joy of spending a night with Marc was too tempting. So she rationalized. After all, she was there. It would be pointless to walk out now. It might even hurt his feelings.

She stayed. But her discomfort must have made itself evident. Although she never said a word, never even hinted at what was on her mind that night, Marc was sensitive enough to absorb the message. He never asked her there again.

THEY SPENT A GREAT deal of time together after that, endeavoring to be at the same gatherings as often as possible, though their opportunities for meeting alone were few. Bluet included him (with his wife, of course) in invitations to her own house. Since they entertained as frequently as three times a week, it was easily arranged. At least they shared the pleasure of just being near each other, of finding moments during these evenings to spend time in each other's company, even within the confines of a crowd. Though scarcely a man to play his cards openly, Marc's growing attachment to her made itself manifest in small ways, such as the evening when she happened to be dancing with one of his colleagues at a party in her own home. Marc abruptly cut in, admonishing the man in feigned anger, "You're poaching on my territory!" As he took over, Marc winked at her. It was more meaningful than a score of platitudes.

One day Marc even approached her for some professional help. He had been trying to raise $600 for a small but vital shipment of drugs needed at that moment in Russia. He suggested that she use her influence with a mutual doctor friend. He thought that such a sum could be obtained through the generosity of the medical staff at the doctor's hospital. She arranged it easily.

It gave her pleasure to help him. One quality she found irresistible was his obvious appreciation of anything she did for him and his constant care and concern for her own well-being. She was never used to such consideration from Max, and this made Marc's attentions even more appealing. The very reality that they had so little time for each other made every phase of their relationship all the sweeter. The irritations that can corrode everyday togetherness were blissfully absent.

There was also the special way she found herself reacting to him, even in a crowd. She invariably became nervous, unusually animated, her face glowing with an inner radiance. In turn, he let those magnetic eyes, which were accustomed to zeroing in upon the individual at hand, wander with her around a room and seek her out visually, no matter where she might be. Even friends began to notice and tried to pry some news out of her. But she did not dare to confide in anyone. She was too afraid of Max's temper. Besides, she sensed that Marc would not like it at all.

But these friends did not need much imagination to determine that here were two people who were falling deeply for one another. Their love had grown so potent that it had become a totally consuming passion, powerful in its intensity and so euphoric for them both that tactful suggestions of caution were tossed completely to the wind.

Max was the only one who seemed curiously oblivious to it all. His wife had lately become so estranged from his consciousness that her moods and actions were something upon which he spared not a whit of attention. He took her too much for granted. She remained faithful, reliable, understanding, and a magnificent asset in all his endeavors. She took his sarcastic tongue, abrasiveness, and violent fits of temper—to say nothing of his flagrant pursuit of other women—like a trouper. Yet Max was so vindictive a personality that not even his closest friends dared whisper that the man he had lately been treating like a brother had recently seduced his wife.

Moreover, it had become a chronically difficult year for Max. As he perpetually balanced life on a financial seesaw, with one project going bankrupt while another rose from the ashes of the previous debacle, the Wall Street crash of the previous October had taken an exceptional toll. Overnight, Max had lost $350,000 in securities—the bulk of his capital assets. A few months later, a fire consumed the scenic studio at Stony Point—the storage deposit for thousands of dollars' worth of costumes, musical scores, and oil-painted canvases. A caretaker had been burning brush near an outside wall of the building. Knowing that the studio had been built of concrete and steel, the caretaker did not expect it to catch fire. What he did not realize was that the cross beams worked into the concrete and the steel could ignite and rapidly carry the flames throughout the entire structure.

It had not even been insured. Because the studio was outside the local fire protection zone, it would have been exceptionally costly to maintain a policy. Max had therefore taken what he considered a reasonable risk. But the studio was the linchpin of the college program, containing library materials impossible to replace. Stony Point would have to close. At that moment, not even his millionaire friends had any spare cash to bail him out. Besides, Stony Point had never been a financial success. As with so many of his projects, Max had never followed through on the development of the theatrical college with sufficient care, dissipating his energies on too many enterprises at one time. This was true of so many of his opera endeavors, true of his trade deals. Though Max was a brilliant innovator, he lacked sufficient patience to nurture any single plan or project to maturity. After the fire, the possibility of retaining any of the college programs in the early days of the Depression was out of the question.

Max was crushed. The college was to have been his personal legacy, something he intended to bequeath to aspiring young American performers of the future, particularly those with more talent than funds.

Still, Stony Point would flicker to life again a few years later. In 1933, at the height of the Depression, Max would go to Harry Hopkins, President Roosevelt's closest adviser—then acting as federal relief administrator—to suggest a vintage Rabinoff idea: bringing out-of-work musicians and performers together to present low-budget productions that would tour the country and revive the flagging spirits of the people. Hopkins loved it. Army issue officers' tents were speedily erected on the disused Stony Point grounds, after which the plan took off with a carnival of national publicity.

But that was still four years in the future. Understandably, with his business life in disarray, Max had no time or inclination to concern himself with what was occurring in his own household. But, as might be expected from someone under such financial strain, he lashed out at those closest to him, ultimately causing the tension at home to drive his wife—though she could not admit it to herself—further into the arms of her lover.

But the interlude was about to be rudely interrupted, albeit from a totally different quarter. When Bluet and Marc met one day around the middle of May for one of those lunches that had become a routine part of both their lives, there was a harassed look on Marc's face. Bluet could not recall having seen anything quite like it before. He arrived half an hour late, and she had begun to wonder if she had made a mistake about the time. Throughout these months, he had never once communicated with her by telephone, so she could never confirm anything. Nor would he put anything down on paper, even so much as a perfectly innocent note.

When he finally appeared, he rushed up to grab her by the arm and push her into the restaurant. "It's too warm in here," he grumbled. "Let's eat and leave quickly."

She pressed him for an explanation. It did not take long before he confessed. "You might as well hear it from me as from anybody else," he announced. "I'm going back to Moscow. Katya and I are leaving at the end of the month."

Her mouth dropped open. She controlled a gasp. "So soon?" she asked lamely. "I thought you were supposed to stay much longer." It would have helped, she thought, if he had displayed at least a small sign of regret about leaving her. She tried again. "Was it something you requested? Are you pleased about going back?" She searched his face for a glimmer of feeling.

He paused. Weighing his words very carefully, he replied, "Yes. Yes, I am very pleased. I do want to leave as soon as possible." His manner was cold and businesslike. A lump swelled in her throat. She felt tears in her eyes. Obviously, she had deluded herself. She had never meant anything to him. They did not say a word to each other for the remainder of the meal, picking aimlessly at the food while avoiding each other's eyes.

During the silence, she tried to pull herself together, wondering whether this abrupt departure, and even his seeming lack of concern for her, might have evolved because their affair had become something of a problem for him.

Nor could she dismiss the notion that his leaving might also be due to the latest Big Red Scare that had rocked the country. Periodically, the government descended upon the entire Russian operation in New York, accusing it of spreading propaganda, fomenting riots, and committing other types of mayhem. Whenever this happened, senior members would be reshuffled.

Generally, matters died down quickly. That spring the problem had become more serious because of a possible political backlash from the looming Depression. In March a particularly ugly demonstration had occurred in Union Square. It led to riots and bloodshed. Communist sympathies were spreading among the unemployed, and the authorities were becoming decidedly uneasy. She was also aware that a congressional committee, on its way to New York under Representative Hamilton Fish Jr., was about to investigate the entire Soviet trading organization. Marc and the Russian Red Cross just might be implicated in some way. Already that year he had personally been accused in the press of spreading communist propaganda, but the accusation had never stuck. This in itself was not particularly noteworthy, so far as Bluet was concerned. These types of charges were rarely proven. And by now they were considered puerile, scorned by the Rabinoff circle as mere harassment.

A few weeks earlier, concerned about the possible impact of a May Day demonstration, the New York police had issued allegedly "top secret" papers called the Whalen documents. Named for New York Police Commissioner Grover Whalen, these were supposedly stolen from the Manhattan offices of Amtorg. Marc's name had been included among those mentioned as spearheading the Comintern offensive in the United States. But even these had eventually been exposed as inept forgeries, derided by more serious commentators of the day as yet another ludicrous chapter in the hysterical Big Red Scare.

However, Bluet reasoned, the publicity may have been sufficiently damaging to make it a propitious time to move Marc around, too. Or had Katya been at work behind the scenes, anxious not to lose him?

Bluet broke the silence by suggesting, "Let's take a walk in the park." It was a glorious day in May—one of the prettiest months of the year in New York. He nodded his approval.

They left the restaurant, crossing the street and heading for Central Park, where a lively lunchtime crowd was celebrating the arrival of warmer weather. Sleeves were rolled up and coats were tossed casually aside. Arms and legs were stretched out horizontally across the grass so that pallid complexions could absorb the first strong rays of a sun revitalized after its customary winter anemia. Even the economic chaos could not dull the delights of the season.

Unlike the European spring they both knew so well, the American reawakening bursts forth later and faster, with lazy yellow forsythia, delicate

MANDATE

The executive committee of the Comintern and Profintern have accredited us to issue to you this mandate, according to which you are again dispatched to the United States in capacity as a general representative of operation administrative section of the above-named organization.

In your duties is the execution of all decisions accepted on the last joint meeting of the foreign sections of Comintern and Profintern, all the changes and all new orders will be forwarded to you through the diplomatic couriers of one of the European countries which have representation of the U. S. S. R.

All your work you have to coordinate with Comrade Bogdanov and consult him on questions having any relations to business.

Comrades Dubrovsky and Sheftel must turn over to you all files which have some relations to their work in our line and activities in the future must be limited by notarial functions under the flag of the Red Cross. Comrade Sheftel is being redispatched to Europe.

You must be in permanent contact with Comrade Kraievsky who in his political work of the territory of South America must be subordinated to you.

In connection with the last mad outbreak of the traitors your headquarters will be temporarily in Seattle, in the State of Washington, where you will be sent by Amtorg as a manager of their branch where you must move all the current files. The archives from illegal work must be sent to Moscow by freight boat.

Between the 15th and 25th of March, you will have to call in Seattle a reunion of all our general representatives which must receive instructions, literature for organization of the 1st of May outbreaks from you and sums of money from Comrade Sversky who continues to be in charge of the financial department.

Comrades which we are dispatching from the U. S. S. R. in your charge distribute in the regions according to attached list.

Use all efforts to finish the work at Seattle within six months when the organization work of a solid base with connections, apartments, warehouses and printing shops will be furnished return to New York.

On all important changes of the program inform us by cablegram. The date of legality of this mandate is closed December 31, 1931.

FEODOR,

Accredited Representative of the Executive Committee of Comintern.

Correct : ALEXIV.

(Inclosure mentioned.)

AMTORG TRADING CORPORATION,

New York, March 10, 1930.

Personal and very confidential.
Copy Komintern International, Comrade A. Fedorov,
I. POLIAKOV,
Amtorg, Moscow.

DEAR COMRADE: Herewith I am complying with your telegraphic requests about sending a list of party comrades which are hard to be replaced, of those sent to New York for work:

Belitzky, Berlin, Bogdanov, Garin, Delgass, Ziavkim, Kanevitz, Kassilov, Kilomoitzev, Konovalov, Kopelevitch, Koffman, Lavreatiev, Lindorff, Magidson, Mamaiev, Mr. and Mrs. Markov, Petrov, Poverman, Potrubotch, Ruttenberg, Rykoff, Mrs. Sverdlov, Fetvaiss, Zukerman, Tsurupa, Sharatov, Sheftal, Shulga.

The recall of any one of those might result in a very serious handicap in our work, but if the political situation will require we request to make the replacements gradually, informing us at least three months in advance. Unfortunately the full report about the removal of the base is not complete, but I am working hard on making it and hope to be able to send you in a few weeks copy of the present list and will also send to other interested organizations.

With comradely greetings,

G. GRAFPEN.

From the Whalen documents compromising Marc, issued by the New York Police Department, and published in full on Saturday, May 3, 1930, in the New York Times, among other newspapers.

bone-white dogwood, pink cherry blossoms, and rich-bodied rhododendrons erupting in swift succession in a mixed blaze of pastel shades and flaming hues. The park then becomes alive once again with people, as well as flowers; with puppies whose stubby legs cannot keep pace with the measured trot of their mothers; with children and teens anxious to try out shiny new bicycles, baseball skills, grown-up clothes, and proud new dates. The handles of baby carriages sprout multicolored balloons tugging at their restrictive strings in an attempt to soar free to the heavens. As if on cue, the peanut vendors and the organ grinders return as well.

As they ambled in silence on the cobbled pathways and under the humpback bridges while the cars and horse-drawn carriages rumbled along on their journeys, a lone tear slipped out of the corner of Bluet's eye. It rolled down her cheek, tracing the side of her face and over her mouth, finally falling from her chin to leave a dark wet spot on her white woolen dress. She could not hold back her tears any longer. She began to cry.

"Here . . . let me." He pulled a handkerchief from his vest pocket and wiped her tears.

Holding her arm, he steered her gently over to a long park bench. They sat in thoughtful silence for a while before he suddenly asked, "Would you come with me?"

She looked up in surprise. "I don't understand."

"Come to Moscow. Join me there."

"That's impossible. It's ridiculous. You know that."

"Is it? What if I told you," he continued, as he carefully wiped the last tear from her face, "that I intend to divorce Katya as soon as we get back—divorce is easy there right now. You could come over by the end of the summer. We could be married. Would you do it?"

She didn't know what to think. Many of their friends had affairs, but not one of them took matters to this extreme. It was tantalizing and yet so utterly impractical.

"And Anna?" She knew she would not abandon her daughter to the vagaries of a life alone with Max.

"She could join us as soon as we're settled. We get along well. The theater's flourishing, and there's nowhere better than Moscow right now to study the latest techniques. She only has a short time left in high school. She could come immediately after that, sooner if you would take her out early."

"You're being too hasty," she said, upset by the suddenness of it all. "It's not like you."

Aside from her temporarily leaving Anna, what was upsetting was that it was one thing to take a lover, but it was totally another to contemplate severing a secure relationship. Over a period of twenty years, she had built a life with Max. Despite its disappointments, she had developed habits, patterns, expectations, and ways that would be difficult to discard. Moreover, even within their artistic circle, steps such as marriage and divorce were still considered drastic.

Marc could be so unpredictable, she thought—exceptionally clever and cautious most of the time, yet, on a day like this, utterly capricious, throwing caution to the wind. He had to be making a highly emotional, rather than a considered, decision. She could not make up her own mind in such a hurry.

So she told him, "I'd like to walk home today—all the way across the park by myself. It will do me good. Anyway, I can't arrive back with my eyes like this. What will everybody say?"

He pressed her relentlessly for an answer after that day, mainly because there was so little time. He managed to postpone his departure an extra few weeks, but he was running out of time.

Mostly, her concerns had been about Anna, rather than about Max. Max would survive and even prosper, despite his present gloom. She was certain of that. He never remained down for too long. She had experienced it all before. But Anna was a different matter—her only child and a responsibility she took more seriously than any other in her life. She did not want to leave Anna behind even for a brief period, nor did she want to take her daughter out of school. But the possibility of sharing her life with somebody who genuinely loved her—actually becoming Marc's wife—was something she wanted more than anything else at that moment.

For days she went about her errands and engagements, tortured by the choices that faced her. Finally, she convinced herself that it would have to be up to Anna. If Anna did not mind her going to Moscow, she would go. But if Anna hesitated even a little about staying behind to finish her schooling, then Bluet would remain in New York with her daughter, taking her chances as to her future relationship with Marc.

Marc even offered to speak to Anna personally. Bluet's own willingness, even eagerness, to leave the job to him said much about her true sentiments at that juncture. She was fully aware of how persuasive and charming he could be when he really wanted something. An impressionable sixteen-year-old was something of a pushover for a man of his abilities.

So she arranged for Marc to come out to Stony Point for a weekend with several other Russian friends. The Rabinoffs still used the house as their regular summer and weekend retreat, despite the setbacks at the college.

Marc suggested taking Anna for a long walk alone through the adjacent woods on that Saturday afternoon. Bluet remained at the house, talking to her other guests. But her thoughts were constantly on the pair and their conversation. She found herself pacing up and down the flagstone patio, weaving a path in and out between the wicker chairs and tables, alert for the first sign of their return.

Her thoughts centered mainly on Anna's reaction. Her daughter had changed noticeably in the last two years, blossoming from a hesitant and lonely child into an appealing young woman. Anna had attracted a growing crowd of her own friends—something Bluet fostered, having worried over Anna's prior tendencies as a loner. Not as naturally outgoing as her parents, she had instead developed a religious streak that they attributed to the dominant influence of her governess, Mademoiselle, who was a rigid and devout Catholic. It was a factor that quietly pleased Bluet. But it irritated Max. The more Catholic Anna became, the more Max seethed. The more he seethed, the more Catholic she became.

But Anna adored Marc and the endless time and attention he devoted to her. She must have noticed how much more kindly Marc treated her mother than did Max.

As soon as Bluet spied them coming through the tall pines at the back of the house, she knew it had turned out as she hoped. They were smiling and laughing together.

"It's settled, then, isn't it, Anna?" Marc said, as Bluet ran over to them, searching Anna's expression for true signs of her daughter's reaction.

"I'm all for it, genuinely I am," Anna insisted, "because I know it will make you happy. We've even agreed about keeping it to ourselves. I do understand, truly I do."

Even so, Bluet still felt uneasy. She continued to hesitate. Marc must have sensed it because he even let her know some days later that he was in line for an ambassadorial post, probably in Japan. Their future could be exceptionally bright. Her life could even be as luxurious as it was right now.

It helped. It gave Bluet a practical reason why Marc might have been so eager to return to Russia. They were offering him a promotion. But it also became the first crack in the solid medical front he had persistently presented. Though Bluet let this remark pass without comment, she had been tempted to suggest that it was somewhat curious for a mere physician to be appointed an ambassador. Yet she liked the idea. Being an ambassador's wife would suit her just fine. Her mind was now made up.

Max, away on business in South America, still had no idea of the affair or of their secret plans for a future together.

THE WEEKS THAT FOLLOWED were frenetic. Before Marc left, Bluet urged him to buy as many warm clothes as possible for the frigid winter ahead. In a maternal way she worried about the cruel climate, as well as about the lack of modern heating. She was also well aware of how little was available to purchase in the Moscow stores, though Marc insisted there had been a gradual improvement since he had left. Nevertheless, at her insistence, he hurried to Saks for a brown-flecked Donegal tweed suit, some heavy sweaters, and a camel-hair topcoat.

Marc arranged for her to keep in contact through David Dubrowsky, their mutual friend at the Russian Red Cross. Marc also promised to make the necessary arrangements for her ongoing journey to Russia as soon as he arrived in Berlin. He gave her the name of the official in charge of the Berlin office of the Russian Red Cross, who would clear the visa arrangements. And he promised to personally meet her at the border.

He repeatedly cautioned her not to let Max know until the latest possible moment, and even then not to reveal the truth behind her request for a separation. They both feared the impact of Max's wrath.

Then, suddenly, it was time to see Marc off. Saying good-bye became easier than expected because Bluet was now so sure she had made the right decision. Momentary pangs of loss that welled up when she thought about the long weeks of separation were soon cast aside. Besides, flushed with the anticipation of an exceptional life ahead, she immediately became immersed in her own preparations.

It was not even difficult to initiate a legal separation from Max. For years, Max had threatened to start divorce proceedings on the most trifling of pretexts, knowing full well that she loved their life together, even if she no longer loved him. It was his way of maintaining control. He also gave her the distinct impression that if she had given in to his demand, this would have been okay with him, too. It was enough to make her want to scream.

Now Max seemed almost relieved. The initiative was actually coming from his wife, and that cleared his conscience and allowed him to take the high road among his peers. In somewhat indecent haste he made plans to travel down to Mexico for a clean, quick break. Not concerned about her own legal protection in the suit, Bluet left the details to Max's lawyers. She simply wanted to be free to marry again. She cared neither for Max's property nor for his alimony—at least, not at that moment.

She didn't even move out upon Max's return from Mexico with their finalized divorce in hand. She just explained that she had booked passage for a lengthy trip to Europe in September, immediately after Anna returned to school. He seemed oddly pleased to have her stay on at the house until that time. Sometimes, she thought, it is difficult to put a rational explanation on why people act the way they do. The fact that they remained together all summer long as husband and wife, living as they always had, even sharing the same bed, was something . . . well, it was just that way.

Max began telling everyone she would be away for only a few months, and then it would all blow over. In his clever way, Max was playing the hero. The divorce, he implied, had merely been something to humor the unfathomable moods of a woman. His ambivalent attitude had become as inexplicable as her own.

Time, however, crept up on her a little too swiftly.

She told Max she had decided to leave all her personal belongings behind, since she would be traveling constantly. In truth, she was worried about loss since she did not know where she and Marc might be living, or if they would be on the move for a while. She only wanted the assurance that her jewelry—except for those favorite pieces she chose to take along—would be placed in safekeeping, fearful that in the passion of the moment, Max might casually give pieces away to his girlfriends.

All that she planned to take along was one large black cabin trunk and a valise—enough for her clothes, a few books she was anxious to read, her favorite brand of soap, and a generous supply of those cosmetics, toiletries, and perfumes she knew were unobtainable in Russia. It was too far away to take anything more extensive. She also packed a small red guidebook, purchased in Berlin several years earlier—the only up-to-date travel book on the new Soviet Russia published in English. It might just come in handy.

Thus far, she had purchased a ticket only to Southampton, with ongoing train reservations to London. This had been Marc's suggestion, as Max would then conclude that she was merely planning a lengthy stay in England.

54

Max knew she had many friends in London, especially those she had kept in touch with from her convent days and her years as a governess. She also had friends in the British entertainment and political world—acquaintances of Max, especially those associated with the British Labour Party. But she dared not write to anyone in advance. Marc had been so insistent upon caution.

It was only on the night before her departure, as Bluet placed her final belongings into her trunk and her valise, that the full impact of her decision hit her. That evening Anna spent hours sprawled out on the winter-white carpet of her mother's bedroom, watching as, one by one, the clothes were carefully folded between tissue paper and neatly layered in the giant steamer trunk. The sight of lightweight summer outfits going in with winter clothes and a few basic household items—two favorite tablecloths, some cooking utensils, soap powder, and a bottle of Lysol cleanser—made Anna morose and even snappy. It looked so final.

"Mother," she complained. "Aren't you going too far? I mean . . . do you need all that?"

"There's nothing in the stores over there," Bluet reminded Anna. "And you know how I feel about dirt." Bluet shuddered, remembering some of the grimy hotels she had encountered on her many visits to Russia with Max. Only a year earlier, as the leaders of a special American trade delegation, she and Max had traveled the country extensively.

"And while we're on the subject of what I need, don't forget to send the *New York Times* at least twice a week, and my monthly magazines. The subscriptions should be good until the middle of next year. I'll never be able to get them there. Send them care of the Red Cross address. That will be safer until we have a permanent address of our own." It would also ensure they would clear the censor, Marc had cautioned, especially if addressed to him.

"Sometimes you are just too much," Anna exploded. "What are you trying to do? Set up an American home in the middle of Moscow? Next thing you'll want is for Saks to open a branch. I can see the sign now, Saks Red Square. And anyway," Anna continued testily, "from what I read in the papers, the Russian women are out sweeping the streets and building new buildings, not worrying about dirt and glossy magazines. Some communist you'll make."

"Don't be ridiculous," Bluet admonished, determined not to lose her temper on this very last night. "Can you imagine any of our Russian friends cleaning streets? Don't forget I grew up in poverty. It's nonsense."

"But terrible things are supposed to be happening to the people there right now." The pitch of Anna's tone was rising. "It's scary, Mother. I mean . . . what if anything happens to you? What will happen to *me?*"

Bluet dearly wished Anna would not needle her on this point. It reminded her of an odd occurrence only a few days earlier. Dropping in to say good-bye to a woman friend one night (one of the few who knew the truth), Bluet had complained that she would not have another opportunity to go to Stony Point to collect a few final items. Her friend's husband immediately offered to give her a lift in his car. It was an ideal excuse for a drive in the country, he told her. It would get him out of the unbearable heat for a few hours.

Bluet gladly accepted. However, not until they were in the relative cool of the tree-shaded lanes did he start to explain the real reason for wanting to help out. He needed to speak to her alone. A mutual Russian friend—he flatly refused to divulge who it was—had asked him to intercede to warn Bluet to seriously reconsider going to Russia. Was she aware of the precarious political situation at the moment? Stalin had grown immensely powerful in the last year. The GPU, the secret political police, was now firmly under the dictator's control and was making wholesale arrests—from those within the topmost government circles all the way down through the ranks. There had been reports of individuals being shot for hoarding food, slacking on the job, or making a single derogatory remark.

Then he made a curious comment. He asked how well Bluet thought she really knew Marc—really knew him, the man kept repeating.

"Of course, I know him well," Bluet replied defensively. "Or I would hardly be taking such a step. At least, as well as any woman knows any man."

Distraught and bewildered, she said, "If you refuse to tell me what unspeakable thing I'm supposed to know about Marc, then please change the subject right now. You're talking in riddles."

Thinking back over that car ride as she continued to pack her belongings, Bluet became aware that the room had grown quiet. Anna was staring silently at her mother, watching with a wistful expression as Bluet checked off each item on a long list to ensure that nothing was forgotten. The scratching of the pencil across the thin sheet of paper made the only sound. Bluet looked up. Anna's mournful expression, with its pitiful look of abandonment, brought all her own guilt feelings to the surface. Inescapably, there was the subconscious realization that she was abandoning her own child as she herself had been tossed aside as a baby.

She stood up to hug and reassure her daughter and begged, "Don't make it harder for both of us." She lifted Anna from the floor and led her over to an armchair, then added softly, "You know I can't stay here any longer. I promise to bring you over just as soon as possible. Please try to be more grown-up. You have your friends. Mademoiselle is staying on just to take care of you. You won't be alone."

An emotional outburst was the last thing Bluet felt she could handle that night. Finally, after they talked together quietly for nearly an hour, she persuaded Anna to go to bed.

The last item on her to-do list was to complete her personal address book. The task cheered her considerably. Moscow was not exactly strange territory to her. She had visited the city many times with Max. And she had many friends of her own. There were a number of government officials, political couples, and trade representatives she had known during their brief posting in New York, as well as the writers, journalists, and Russian performers Max had brought over for appearances in the United States. She was anticipating an interesting and busy life, just like in New York. She hoped that she could become even more of an asset to Marc than she had been to Max. As a start, she intended to learn the language. She wanted to become involved, not just sit on the sidelines.

The following morning, Anna said a final good-bye to her mother at the house before leaving early for school. They both hugged each other and cried. By this time, Bluet had fully convinced her daughter and herself that it would be only a short while. They would soon be reunited, only this time under happier circumstances.

Taking one final walk through the rooms of her home and running her hands fondly over the familiar furnishings and belongings that she had selected and arranged to her own taste over the years, Bluet felt an unexpected twinge of nostalgia.

The servants gathered in the foyer to see her off. She had thoughtfully prepared a small parting gift for each of them. Then she waved cheerfully and strode forward out the door. However, at the back of her mind was a gnawing doubt that she might never see it all again—that maybe she was, after all, taking a highly impetuous step.

Five

LEANING ON THE SHIP'S RAIL, Bluet was exhilarated by the sea air. She stared down at the changing patterns of white foam—the texture and the color of giant soap suds—that the ship threw out as it cut into the black waters of the bay. Behind her, the silhouettes of skyscrapers receded swiftly into the distance and finally disappeared beneath the horizon. She was more determined than ever to dismiss the previous night's misgivings and think only positive thoughts about her future.

But the reality of actually living in Soviet Russia scared her, despite Marc's assurances. It presented such an ambiguous, mysterious image to the outside world.

To many, particularly historians, writers, social scientists, and left-leaning politicians, it was indeed the dawn of a totally new world order. Books on the emerging Soviet society, written by noted journalists and highly regarded men of letters, were streaming off the presses and making the best-seller lists in France, Germany, Italy, Britain, and the United States. These instant experts on Soviet politics were flooding their readers with praise for Russia's innovative programs, even though most of them had spent only a few weeks touring the country.

The latter part of the 1920s had experienced a virtual explosion of Western tourism to Soviet Russia. It had become a fashionable place to visit, now that the dangers of civil war and upheaval had safely subsided. No writer was worth his prose unless he had visited the new Russia and had come away with at least some socialist thoughts. There was an undeniable fascination for those Dreaded Reds. Despite the contempt for communism among many Western government leaders, Russia was in. Bolshevism was in. These revolutionaries were the brave iconoclasts.

It was the new politics, they all said. Something special to experience. A country where people dedicated themselves to improving conditions for all, instead of working for personal gain (though few paused to consider the stifling effect of removing this most basic of individual incentives). It offered

58

a novel philosophy to examine and consider. Against the all-too-obvious pitfalls of the freewheeling capitalism of the 1920s, after the financial earthquake of the stock market crash had plunged thousands into despair and debt, it presented a viable, challenging alternative. While the West was drowning in an economic whirlpool without a safety net for its citizens, Russia was rushing frantically ahead toward a social paradise. The Marxist dream of utopia on earth was being fulfilled. No compassionate human being could deny it. The contrast was undeniable. Or so it seemed from the outside.

The appeal was so potent that commentators were doing their utmost to ignore or rationalize the atrocities that were occurring. They chose to over-look the late-night visits of fearsome little police wagons—easily identifiable by their telltale rows of air holes near the top—that cruised the streets of cities and towns, rounding up suspected enemies of the state. On a regular basis, the mass of the population was waking up the next morning not know-ing whether friends, relatives, or neighbors would still be free. Arrests—far more prevalent than a few years earlier—were being made on the most trans-parent of pretexts, freezing the popular will to resist. The uncontrolled scope of this terror machine could strike anybody, anywhere, and at any time. Using sweeping powers of summary execution, prolonged prison sentence, or torture, the police were holding an entire nation in the thrall of fear. Why they preferred night arrests nobody quite knew, except that the cover of darkness supplied an added dimension of dread.

This tactic, coupled with Stalin's personal penchant for dealing with high-level opposition through the age-old concept of divide and conquer, put into place the ideal terror machine. Russia—from the innermost offices of the Kremlin down to the most remote villages—was being bullied into submission. The police had established such a ubiquitous network of citizen informers that innocence would be regularly trumped by malevolence. Out of jealousy, revenge, or some trivial personal vendetta, a person's life could be instantly snapped apart like a twig underfoot.

Nonetheless, the apologists were explaining the need for all this human sacrifice and degradation by cataloguing the many enemies arrayed against the young regime: bigoted czarist émigrés scheming to restore the old order; terrified capitalists eager to kill such a noble experiment just to save their own selfish fiefdoms and bloated purses. Besides, they argued, had not bloodshed and terror always been the inevitable bedfellows of revolution, at least at the beginning? The atrocities perpetrated by the czarist Whites had been far worse. The Russian revolution was no bloodier than any other—just the violent birth of a new order.

Look instead, they insisted, at the advances. Look at the way the Bolsheviks have begun educating the illiterate, taking that great leap across centuries by forging an audacious industrialization program that was about to transform the country in the blink of an eye from a backward agrarian nation into a prosperous giant. Look at its laudable aim of giving the working man as big a share as its leaders in the future prosperity of the nation. The laborer was already taking his vacation in the luxurious setting of Livadia palace on the Crimean coast, the summer home of former Czar Nicholas. The trade unions sent him there *free*. Where could a worker obtain a free holiday in America? And was any other society as dedicated to the dignity and the security of full employment?

The Great Illusion was captivating others, too. Physicians were effusive in their praise of the way the Bolsheviks—increasingly called communists—had set up the world's first system of socialized medicine. In intent and scope, it outstripped anything the Western world had to offer. Russian doctors were being welcomed everywhere and encouraged to benefit from the skill and the knowledge of more advanced countries. It was a system that many Western physicians were convinced was so much closer to what a civilized nation should be offering its citizens, regardless of income.

Women leaders in the West were waxing lyrical over advances made by Russian women, which, even forty years later, would not be matched in America: free public day care; free abortion on demand—surely, the ultimate in radical chic—equal pay, with special paid leave for pregnancy and a guaranteed job afterward; simplified and dignified divorce, with no social stigma attached; even communal kitchens. All these were already national policy. The slavery of home care and the confines of motherhood would no longer inhibit the blossoming of the Russian woman. It was the paradise that every former suffragist, every fighter for women's rights (the American woman had won her vote only ten years earlier) had to see for herself, a society where women were appreciated as intellectual and legal equals. The sexual freedoms espoused by Alexandra Kollontai, the renowned Bolshevik revolutionary and a close friend of Lenin, were even outpacing the uninhibited literature and more permissive behavior spreading through the West.

But whether being truly equal was worth it if the opportunity enabled you to sweep the streets—as Anna had remarked—as well as the floors of your own home, and never enjoy the bourgeois pleasure of being pampered and cosseted by a man, was something Bluet would come to ponder in the weeks ahead.

Critics in the West were equally outspoken about the flip side of it all. Some people insisted that Alexandra Kollontai was not merely liberated but was a sexual maniac whose candid pronouncements and behavior made even Lenin blush. Nor did Bluet seriously believe those lurid accounts of how the Bolsheviks planned to "nationalize" women, citing a scandalous Russian news article suggesting that every woman over eighteen should be declared the property of the state and obliged to register at a Free Love Bureau. Conceived in jest, it had been brandished as just a further example of the calamities Bolshevism might bring. The threat of a Free Love Bureau, coupled with startling tales of rampant promiscuity, had become the most potent anti-Red propaganda of the decade. By destroying religion, the anti-Reds argued, the Bolsheviks had removed all moral restraint, tragically breaking up the sanctity of the family unit and the spiritual guidance of a strong church.

For those with greater political sophistication, it was a period when thoughts were centered on the future direction of the Soviet experiment. Lenin's death in 1924 had ushered in an interregnum during which serious news focused on the struggle for power between Trotsky and Stalin and its portent for world communism in general.

On Trotsky's side stood the Old Bolsheviks—international in outlook, idealistic, missionary, and dedicated to creating the new world order. In Stalin's camp were those of a rougher cut: ruthless, tyrannical, uncouth, and fiercely nationalistic. They were the new czars—amoral, tough, and anti-intellectual. They would appeal to a much deeper need among the masses. Harkening back to the old days, they would boast of rebuilding a more glorious and powerful Russia and to hell with the rest of the world. They lusted after power for its own sake, mistrusting and loathing the Old Bolsheviks, who had an intellectual snobbery and an urbanity they could never hope to emulate. By 1930, it would be Stalinists who would win the upper hand. Instinctively, they recognized that the strength of the nation had been sapped by years of war and revolution. The people had no desire to spearhead a drive for international revolution; it was enough to achieve it at home. Or so the new czars told them.

In retrospect, 1928 and 1929—the period when Marc was outside the country—had been pivotal years, a turning point in the Russian experiment. The naive and idealistic Old Bolsheviks were being swept aside by modern-day

Neanderthals, led by a power-mad and paranoid leader named Stalin. He was the only member of the top party leadership whom Lenin, on his death-bed, had warned the others to expel because of an affinity for thievery and brutality for its own sake. Stalin, the Old Bolsheviks recalled, had provided the party with funds in the early days by staging bank hold-ups and other feats of banditry he carried out using his own swaggering troop of loyal hooligans and sycophants.

By late 1928, Stalin had consolidated his position so well that he was able to bring the compromise politics of the New Economic Policy and its fondness for small private enterprise and personal initiative to an abrupt halt. Almost immediately, a brutal program of rapid collectivization and industrialization, designed ostensibly to bring prosperity to all, was insti-tuted without regard to human cost. The new leaders wrapped their edicts of enforcement under the ambitious title of a Five-Year Plan. Completed in four, they said, it would work even better. Old Bolsheviks shook their heads at the potential human cost of such a cataclysmic enterprise. Later they despaired as Stalin's band of personal henchmen flung aside the best and most brilliant of Lenin and Trotsky's original team who had urged modera-tion. In vain. The new Ivan the Terrible was emerging triumphant. The price of this triumph would be incalculable.

Measures that these moderate men had grudgingly accepted as necessar-ily harsh and undemocratic in the early days—to neutralize the threats from counterrevolutionary forces and a hostile West eager to foster their demise—now became simply sadistic. These measures were now being perpetuated, said the moderates, far beyond the original need, employed solely to build a cruel new tyranny.

After a long, drawn-out process of isolation, slander, and expulsion from the party—a strategy Stalin would employ time and again—Trotsky had been deported a year earlier, finally ending up in Mexico. This ushered in a pattern that would continue for decades. Stalin would continue to rid him-self of "unreliables" by removing housing privileges, posting the victim to a lesser job, planting rumors, offering that person a brief period of recall to good graces (a deadly psychological trick to confuse the victim), and ulti-mately putting the individual on trial—the outcome a certainty.

As an avid reader of newspapers and political journals, Bluet worried a good deal about all of this, although her Russian friends continued to dis-miss the stories as the product of antisocialist Western journalists out to malign the new regime. She had sensed a great deal on her previous visits to

Russia, even though the red carpet (a suitable color, she thought) had always been laid out for them, due to Max's efforts to stimulate trade and encourage U.S. recognition. The Rabinoffs had been lavishly entertained at sumptuous banquets and provided with two and sometimes even three limousines for lengthy trips. They were given overnight lodgings at the finest hotels that were fully up to Western standards. Only occasionally had Bluet glimpsed the specter of poverty, hunger, and fear afflicting the country.

Still, she remained uneasy, especially about such basics as food and commodity shortages, which would contrast sharply with the abundance of luxuries available to her on this six-day voyage across the Atlantic—luxuries that complemented the exceptionally high standard of living she had grown to expect as routine.

As she gazed out at the churning waters of the Atlantic, she felt a hand lightly touch her arm. Startled, she turned. One of the stewards, neatly turned out in a starched white uniform and gleaming brass buttons, was apologizing about a mixup over flowers. "Could you come back down and help us sort things out?" he asked respectfully.

"Of course," she smiled. "I'll be down in a minute." She paused just long enough to enjoy a last glimpse of the American coastline, then followed him. As they reached the doorway, she could hear the sound of a high-pitched voice farther down the narrow passage. Another passenger was arguing vociferously with a steward over flowers. Bluet stopped. Out stepped a woman even shorter than she was, but in many ways similar in appearance. The woman also had her hair held back in a chignon and was dressed in a beautifully tailored gray wool suit. Although older and plumper, she looked vaguely familiar. Her features were strong and well-defined.

"Ah!" exclaimed the woman, smiling broadly. "This must be Madame Rabinoff. Madame *Max* Rabinoff?"

"Yes, that's right," said Bluet haltingly, extending her right hand. Naturally, this was no occasion to explain recent events. "I'm sorry, I didn't catch your name."

"Helena Rubinstein," answered the woman. "Surely, you remember me." The empress of the cosmetic world had moved on the fringes of their circle for years. Before Bluet had a chance to apologize for the oversight, Helena was talking again.

"We met in Boston several years ago. You are Max's wife, aren't you? The opera Max, yes," she said, answering her own question. "I'm sure you are. I remember thinking I had finally met someone as short as me." Taking Bluet by the arm, Helena led her down the corridor toward her own cabin. "It looks as if we even have a similar first name ... Helena ... and that's why the flowers were mixed up. Helena R ... it all looks alike on those tiny cards. Please forgive me," she said, "but I have some of your bouquets. And I believe you have some of my roses."

"That's easily settled," Bluet assured her and motioned to the waiting steward to make the necessary exchanges. She stood by the doorway as Helena picked up one of the glass vases and handed it over.

Helena chattered on. "I have always admired Max. He pioneered in music what I have worked to achieve in cosmetics. To create something everyone can afford and enjoy." She paused for a moment and looked at Bluet before asking formally, "It would give me great pleasure, Madame Rabinoff, if you would join me later for coffee in the lounge. I am also alone."

Later, as they sipped their coffee they decided to dine together that evening in the restaurant and they soon became deeply involved in gossiping about a mutual friend—Amazar, a stunningly beautiful Russian singer who had starred in Max's Boston Opera Company some years earlier. Amazar had been the adored mistress of Zinoviev, a leader of the Bolshevik revolution and a close colleague of Lenin.

"Naturally," confided Helena, as they both warmed to a thoroughly satisfying gossip session, "you heard the story of her jewels?"

Bluet nodded. They all knew how Zinoviev had managed to find a way for Amazar to leave for America with the type of gems long since confiscated from private possession. "Today it could never happen," Bluet commented. Suddenly, there was an awkward silence. They were both aware that Soviet Russia had become so desperate for hard currency that it was now confiscating jewelry, silver, and gold from ordinary citizens and even peddling the nation's imperial treasures on the Paris antique markets. Rumors had circulated all summer about discreet overtures being made to Andrew Mellon and other American millionaire art collectors, asking them to buy certain paintings from the Hermitage museum in Leningrad. The hard currency situation had become so acute that eventually a number of paintings would indeed be sold.

"Regardless of her career, it leaves her quite independent," Bluet added, thinking somewhat uneasily that perhaps she should not have been so casual about leaving her jewelry with Max.

"Connections, connections, my dear," Helena said. "Isn't that what it is all about? Amazar understands that better than most." She then confided that Amazar was currently being courted by one of the Gimbel brothers, the famous retailers, and was seriously considering the liaison. "She will do all right for herself," was Helena's final verdict on their friend.

The story reminded Bluet that she knew Zinoviev's sister, who was married to a man named Yonoff, the head of the state publishing syndicate and libraries in Soviet Russia. The Yonoffs had been stationed in New York some years earlier and had grown friendly with both of the Rabinoffs. Yonoff, a great bibliophile, shared Bluet's appreciation of old and rare French books. He told her that he had been working to preserve some of the finest collections from the personal libraries of the old Russian nobility, recounting by name the priceless first editions he had selected from the French revolutionary period. He then arranged for them to be placed in a private library specially built in his Moscow apartment—a privilege, Bluet thought wryly, only the brother-in-law of Zinoviev would dare assume. She made a mental note that it would be important to look up the Yonoffs upon arrival in Moscow. Personal connections were indeed the key, whatever the future might hold.

Bluet and Helena spent many hours in each other's company for the remainder of the voyage. Every morning they strolled briskly back and forth along the promenade deck, sipping mid-morning bouillon and chatting. Helena appeared obsessed with the fact that although she had made a great deal of money, she had never attained the social standing she obviously craved. A year earlier she had sold a portion of her business for a handsome sum. Now the most crucial matter on her agenda seemed to be a socially significant match. If a suitable replacement came along, she assured Bluet, she would divorce her present husband and make the great social leap forward. The difficulty was that all she ever encountered were "fortune hunters, my dear . . . nothing but fortune hunters," she sighed, throwing up her hands in despair.

Since Helena appeared to be the sort of woman who pursued whatever she deemed desirable in a determined manner, Bluet was not at all surprised to read several years later that she had taken a Georgian nobleman as her next husband.

But these conversations were already having a profound impact. Against such an organized life, such an organized set of priorities, Bluet felt a growing sense of personal disorder. As they paced the deck together and paused to glance over the wind-tossed sea, it occurred to Bluet that her own life was now nothing more than the result of a chance encounter emanating from the heart and not the head. That she was impetuously discarding the comfort, the dignity, and the security of a wealthy life with Max simply because she had fallen in love and needed to be loved had to be romantic foolishness.

BLUET SLIPPED INTO LONDON a few days later. In her accustomed manner, she booked an elegant suite at the Park Lane Hotel in Mayfair so that she might complete the shopping that had been the main purpose of her detour. It never occurred to her to live more frugally, now that she and Max were divorced and she was limited to a fixed monthly sum. Soon she would be married to Marc, she thought. She could be as casual about money as she had been before.

Walking into the spacious lobby on the first morning of her stay, she noticed the left-wing *Daily Herald* among the morning papers on sale. It held a special significance in her life. Some years earlier, she and Max had raised money to keep it afloat. Norman Ewer, the British writer and socialist who was their friend, had asked them to do so as a special favor to George Lansbury, one of the founders of the British Labour Party whom they had known for years. She had put Norman's name in her address book, thinking she might look him up. Maybe later in the day, she thought, although she had promised Marc she would travel as discreetly as possible.

She hunted through her purse for some British coins and purchased a copy of the paper, then sat down to glance at its pages. England, it seemed, was in no better shape than America that September. Certainly, the Depression had arrived here, too. The misery in the northern industrial towns was graphically detailed that day in the paper. Perhaps Marc had the right idea after all, she concluded. Glancing around at the elegant women and impeccably clad businessmen in the lobby, she could not believe these troubles even existed.

Out on Regent Street and St. James, it was the same story. There was such a magnificent sense of plenty that the newspaper gloom seemed unreal. Stores were still overflowing with merchandise and the counters jammed with eager customers. It was even so within the exclusive confines of Liberty's where she paused to choose some sweaters for Anna. Her daughter, Bluet thought guiltily, as she asked a salesgirl to ship them to New York, needed to know that her mother was still thinking about her. She scurried around for some warm items for herself, then decided at the last moment to pick up something for Marc, too. Well aware of his obsession with fine clothing, she chose a Scottish sweater and a plain beige wool scarf.

As she wandered around, she could not shake a Cinderella-like feeling. For years, she had traveled surrounded by the noise and the excitement of the endless stream of people who gravitated toward Max. The moment she and Max arrived anywhere, the telephone began to ring, messages piled up, and visitors called. She felt the contrast acutely that first morning, as she completed her shopping and indulged herself in a lunch alone at Fortnum & Mason—food she knew she could not duplicate in Moscow. Later, after making her way into the fashion department upstairs, she chose an exceptionally heavy coat made of blanket cloth. She felt certain she would need it against the upcoming arctic temperatures.

IN THE END, Bluet never did look up any of her London friends. Increasingly, her thoughts turned to Katya. Marc had insisted there would be no problem at all. But Bluet was not as confident as he was. If Katya—a substantial Communist Party member in her own right—chose to make difficulties, would Marc himself have second thoughts? All Bluet had right now was a promise that he would meet her at the border. What if something unforeseen had occurred in the interim? The papers had been full of reports of trouble and unrest.

A few days later she caught the boat train and the overnight sleeper to Berlin. She arrived in the German capital late the next afternoon and checked into the Hotel Adlon, where she had told Marc she would be staying. As she registered at the desk in the lobby, her heart skipped a beat when the man taking the information leaned forward and handed her a small white envelope. "There's a message waiting for you," he said. "I was told it was urgent."

Without pausing even to arrange for her luggage to be taken upstairs or to pull off her gloves, Bluet picked up the note. She opened it nervously. The message was brief. "Please call at the Berlin offices of the Russian Red Cross as soon as possible." There was no signature.

Hurriedly, she left the hotel and headed toward the address Marc had given her prior to his departure. He had told her to contact a personal friend named Dr. Binger at their offices on the Unter den Linden. She hailed a cab but was far too apprehensive to absorb the sights and the sounds of this fast-paced city. She was aware only that daylight was ebbing fast, and it was almost dark. Arriving at the end of the business day, she feared the offices would be closed. Fortunately, the lights were still blazing, and the office hummed with activity.

She asked the receptionist for Dr. Binger. After being told who was waiting, he immediately came out of a meeting. He greeted her with unusual warmth and insisted that she should call upon him for any assistance while in the German capital. "Meanwhile," he added, "I have a note for you from Marc."

He went over to his desk, picked up a small white envelope, and handed it to her. She thanked him and opened it, then glanced quickly at the minuscule, almost illegible handwriting:

> Darling, I hope everything has been fine for you so far and that your journey has been comfortable and not too tiring. We are having some small problems. But I shall tell you all about these when I see you. In the meanwhile could you do some shopping? Buy generous amounts of the following: tea, sugar, coffee, ham, Italian olive oil. Also confirm with Dr. Binger exactly which train you will be taking so I shall be at the border when it pulls in. Let him take care of the visa arrangements.
>
> Look after yourself in Berlin, my darling. Marc.
>
> P.S. Also buy a double bed and have it packed and shipped on the same train. I'll explain.

"Is anything wrong?" Dr. Binger had been watching her closely as she stood there reading the note. Only Marc's persistent predilection for his Italian delicacies in the face of more fundamental needs, and his suggestion about the bed, brought a smile to her face.

"Is anything wrong?" Dr. Binger repeated.

She shook her head. Looking up, she asked, "Just how bad is it in Moscow right now, Dr. Binger?" There had been many critical dispatches in the press concerning—among other difficulties—the chronic food shortages. Stalin had been ruthless in his attempt to drive the peasants off the land and achieve swift collectivization. As a reprisal, the peasants were now refusing to plow or plant. They were even being accused of dumping seed and slaughtering cattle. Rumors also suggested that a great deal of food was being exported to raise the necessary foreign currency to purchase machinery for the Five-Year Plan. These two factors had combined to cause a potentially grave famine.

Dr. Binger shrugged. "The country is going through hard times," he said slowly, seeming to choose his words with care. "It won't be an easy winter."

"For everyone?"

"I can't say. I do know people are lining up all night just for bare essentials." He took her by the arm and steered her to the door. "But I don't want to keep you. I'm sure you have a great deal to do in Berlin."

She folded the note and tucked it into her handbag, then walked slowly back to the hotel. The specter of it all made her again worry about the merits of her decision. All of Europe seemed unstable. Although Berlin, like London, exuded a superficial feeling of riches and ease, she knew that a great deal of trouble simmered beneath the surface. She had been told she should not even be strolling alone after dark. By contrast, Manhattan was still a haven of calm, order, and plenty. She berated herself. She had never been a coward, and this was cowardly thinking. People fell in love, raised families, and cared for each other in times of trouble and famine, as well as peace and plenty.

The shattering of plate glass interrupted her thoughts. Peering down the street, she noticed a crowd gathering. As police sirens wailed, three youths fled down the center of the road. They were running directly toward her. She drew back into the shadow of a doorway. Barely a few yards in front of her, they turned into an alley, followed closely by a squad of riot police on motorcycles. In a panic, she looked around for a taxi to take her the remaining distance to her hotel. But with none in sight, she started to run, trying to reach the safety of her room on foot.

Passing the corner where the incident occurred, she began to understand exactly what had happened. A group of young Nazis had stoned the shop-front office of the Berlin Communist Party. Clearly, Germany was on the brink of economic collapse, and the mood was ugly. One week prior to her arrival, there had been national elections, which had resulted in the current wave of violence, demonstrations, street brawls, and even hand-to-hand fighting, especially among the losers. It had been a campaign characterized by bloodshed and death, rather than by democratic dialogue. Stoking the fires of frustration that September was Adolf Hitler, a relative newcomer. He terrified the voters with the notion that a vote for the republic was a vote for continued impotence, while a vote for communism would be equally as bad—a vote for a loss of national identity in an international movement led by "Jewish Bolsheviks." Only his brand of national socialism, otherwise known as fascism, could rebuild Germany.

Though this was not her battle, Bluet was shaken. The following morning she hastily darted from shop to shop, garnering the provisions that Marc had requested and adding a few items of her own. She also selected the bed, giving the store the exact details of her proposed date and time of departure, so that it could be delivered directly to the station. Later she returned to Dr. Binger's office to initiate the formalities for her visa. She informed him of the train she planned to take into Moscow, and he promised to cable Marc. She was determined to leave Berlin as soon as possible.

A few days later, visa in hand, she packed and hurried to the station. Normally, she would have taken along a new book and a few magazines for the lengthy ride across northern Germany and Poland toward the Russian border. This time she could not concentrate. The activities and the stress of the last few months had worn her out. She had only enough energy to gaze numbly out the window.

Both the German and later the Polish countryside sped by, gray and chilly. The warmth of the September weather she had left in New York was a distant memory. As the train headed northeast, stations intermittently loomed and disappeared with equal speed. She did not notice their names or even what they looked like. She felt curiously apart from it all. Only when the train slowed and kept stopping and starting did she rouse herself to look outside. Groups of harassed people were running back and forth.

They had reached the Polish side of the border. The blinding glare of huge arc lamps on the station platform and the dim ceiling lights that switched on inside the railway coach made her acutely aware that it was already nightfall. The day had disappeared with unusual speed.

"Everyone out!" called a police officer, as he marched smartly along the full length of the train. The passengers slowly filed into the brightly lit customs house—a modern concrete structure that was a sharp contrast to the dreary wooden hut that had stood there the last time she had arrived with Max. Eastern Europe, like Russia, was moving rapidly ahead. The Polish border guards, quaintly outfitted in turn-of-the-century braided uniforms, with ceremonial swords dangling at the side, were so colorfully attired and so perfectly drilled that they could have come out of one of Max's operas.

Clearing the line of passengers with only perfunctory concern, they bantered casually in broken English and German. "Go inside . . . eat, eat," said one of the guards, pointing toward the station buffet. The train, he assured them, could not pull out for at least another hour, as the Russians preferred

Bluet's entry visa to the Soviet Union, 1930

to send their own engine. The veiled message was that food might not be available on the other side.

Feeling more anxious than hungry, Bluet stood by the counter, sipping steaming coffee and nibbling at a buttered roll, without even finishing all that she had ordered. After she returned to her seat on the train, it was not long before they inched out of the station and haltingly covered the next few miles to the border village on the Russian side. She was so excited about the possibility of seeing Marc again that she failed to notice the high watch-towers, the barbed wire, and even the Soviet soldiers with guard dogs. A year from now she would stare at these grotesque symbols in terror.

Now she tugged at the window sash to pull it down. She leaned out to avoid missing Marc on the platform. Up ahead she could see the station looming closer. Knots of people were milling about; soldiers were stomping about in high boots and huge gray greatcoats that reached almost to their ankles. They were slapping their sides with their hands in an effort to keep warm. On their heads were flat peaked caps, each bearing the sign of the hammer and sickle, over which hung a tiny red star. They were a somber group, radically different from the jocular Polish officials.

"Bluet?" The shout came from behind.

Wheeling around, she gasped. Marc was standing in the doorway of her compartment, calling to her. He had jumped aboard the train even before it had come to a halt.

"Oh!" she shrieked in amazement. She turned to rush toward him and knocked over her travel bag. The contents spilled across the floor.

Smiling broadly, his eyes twinkling in delight, he came over to kiss her. "Welcome, my darling," he whispered. "Welcome home."

Aware that tears were welling up in her eyes, she pulled away to kneel on the floor. She gathered up the papers and other assorted items that had tumbled out a few moments earlier. It was an odd reunion, an emotional moment for both of them.

The train jerked to a halt. Russian soldiers jumped aboard and immediately marched through the corridors to make sure all passengers vacated the train and took all their belongings with them for inspection. Marc cautioned her not to do any talking and led the way into a dimly lit customs hall. It was a dreary picture, compared to its counterpart in Poland. From a portrait high on the wall, Lenin glared down like a severe schoolmaster. As they stood on line, she listened apprehensively to an American couple argue over the dollars they were carrying. The official wanted to exchange them all for rubles. The soldiers searched everyone's baggage, item by individual item.

Everybody's belongings but her own. A few words from Marc, and she was required only to show her passport, after which they waved her through with a sharp salute and a gracious handshake. Her luggage had not even been opened. As they walked hand in hand back to the train, Marc casually suggested, "Here, let me take your passport. I have to show it to the authorities in Moscow tomorrow. You won't be needing it for a while anyway." He took it from her and slipped it into his vest pocket.

Admonishing herself for her recent anxieties, she settled down contentedly next to the man she loved. He seemed so genuinely delighted at having her with him once again that she was soon caught up in a similarly joyous mood. It was contagious. There was so much to talk about and plan.

The train moved on, rumbling forward and clacking in a soothing, rhythmic beat. Twilight, which comes early up north and lingers for hours, made the scene outside the window barren, colorless, desolate, and bleak. Inside, an already noticeable silence had replaced the spontaneous chatter that characterized the atmosphere earlier on.

For the two of them, there was no sleep or even much opportunity for intimate conversation in the crowded coach. They just sat quietly in their corner by the window, curled up as close as possible on that chilly autumn night, whispering from time to time.

Marc told her that Dr. Lazareff, a colleague at the Department of Health, had loaned them his apartment in a suburb of Moscow while he was on a medical mission abroad for two months. "We'll have somewhere comfortable of our own, right from the start," he whispered, "and still have plenty of time to find a permanent home together."

She let him know that she had obtained a divorce from Max. "We can get married any time," she told him. "Just as soon as you like."

But Marc did not look nearly as pleased as she had expected, squirming around in his seat as though embarrassed. Finally, he admitted that he had not divorced Katya in the interim weeks. These were matters he just could not explain in the confines of a crowded train. Instead, he assured her in the softest of tones, "You'll be known as my wife. Everybody will understand."

Everybody except her. She could not conceal her disappointment, shifting her body a few inches from his own as a way to express her displeasure. It had not been easy to leave her only daughter and the security of her American life to be told that she had come all the way across Europe alone on a promise that now appeared hollow.

There was an uncomfortable silence. She turned away and stared out of the window at the encroaching blackness. A moment later Marc reached for her hand. She softened. Turning back to look up at his face in the gloom, she reluctantly conceded that perhaps she was condemning the man too hastily. An undercurrent of tension lay beneath his smile and lighthearted banter—enough for her to appreciate that something unanticipated had happened.

She thought of the note he had sent to her in Berlin. She tried to persuade him to explain.

"Not here," he begged, saying that now they were in Soviet Russia, it was not prudent to speak when others might overhear. Finally, just before dawn, weary and thoroughly worn out, she rested her head on his shoulder, tucked her feet on the seat, and fell into a fitful sleep.

$\mathcal{S}\textit{ix}$

IF THE LANDSCAPE FLASHING BY the train window appeared at first glance to be barren and desolate, this was not the case at all. Soviet Russia was buzzing with activity. Factories were springing up where cattle had grazed and trees had clustered. Huge combine harvesters, tractors, and reapers were clattering through muddy peasant hamlets that had never seen anything more modern than an ox cart and an iron plow. A way of life that had been traditional for generations in these villages was being cast aside, supplanted by new approaches to industry and farming and in morals, religion, and behavior.

But such an abrupt change did not come easily to many Russians and was not nearly as welcome as the leaders in Moscow implied. Particularly in the countryside, the elderly deplored the way the central government was instituting its anti-God campaign, sacking churches, persecuting priests, and compelling the peasants to abandon their deeply rooted religious practices in the name of progress. The richer peasants, known as kulaks, resented the barbaric manner in which the recent collectivization decrees from Moscow were being enforced. Earlier that year, they had presented Stalin with his first major political challenge. They stubbornly refused to cooperate. In response, this new czar ordered them ruthlessly suppressed. Total discipline and obedience were required of everyone. And that included recalcitrant kulaks, especially as their small land holdings and the free markets for their goods represented the last vestiges of capitalist profiteering.

By the time Bluet arrived in Russia, scores of railway stations across the nation were witnessing the horror of wholesale arrests, as rebellious kulaks were being rounded up, herded like beasts into overcrowded railway cars, and shipped in prison trains to labor camps. Once there, they became forced labor for lumbering, mining, railway, and canal construction. There were stories of mass suicides as whole families opted for a quick end, rather than endure separation and the inevitable agonies of a prison camp. Closer to the border, they were being slaughtered as they attempted to flee to neighboring countries. At roadsides, in fits of rage and despair, they were butchering their livestock—horses, cows, pigs, and poultry—and burning their own crops, rather than see these confiscated. If they were to go down, said the kulaks, then the entire nation could starve with them. "Neglect of the fields" or "failure to harvest" became grounds for the firing squad.

Stalin's mass collectivization—combining small holdings into larger units and thereby theoretically letting everybody reap the benefits of newly acquired Western farm machinery—had met with nothing but trouble. Even the merciless GPU warned Stalin that he had gone too far. The GPU could not guarantee quiet in the countryside much longer. An entire faction inside the GPU hierarchy was reported to be against collectivization. But eyewitness reports said that Stalin threw these people down the stairs when they came to advise him to proceed more cautiously. He wanted what he wanted.

In the end, five million Russian peasants would die in what came to be known as the liquidation of the kulaks. This was only part of the price of Stalin's impatient "leap across centuries."

By the end of the summer of 1930, the markets and the shops had been stripped bare. Lines were so long outside food stores that people were standing all night for a loaf of bread or a few pounds of potatoes. Poultry, eggs, and meat were unobtainable. Clothing, household items, and basic necessities had also disappeared from the shelves. The scuttling of Lenin's brief experiment in small private enterprise had similarly led to the arrest of the New Economic Policy (NEP) traders. During the early 1920s, it had been these merchants who brought so many of the goods back into the stores. But to Stalin, the NEP men of the city were akin to the kulaks of the countryside and merited the same treatment. First they were taxed to the breaking point. If that did not destroy them, they were arrested. Politicians and officials sympathetic to NEP men and kulaks were denounced for "rightist deviation." There was no other way, thundered Stalin. If the Five-Year Plan were to succeed, it had to concentrate on heavy industry and collectivization, not on consumer items and protection of small holdings.

Parallel treatment was being meted out to the political branch of the nation. When Stalin first emerged as the dominant party leader, most of the major policy positions remained in the hands of the Old Bolshevik intellectuals, many of whom were Jews. His dislike of both intellectuals and Jews meant that he had difficulty tolerating any of them. As a consequence, practically all would be executed or imprisoned during the great purges of the

1930s—an orgy of bloodletting that reached down to all levels of party membership and was not satiated until Trotsky himself was hacked to death in Mexico in 1940.

The third group reviled by Stalin and the ones to come under the most severe pressure during that grim winter of 1930 were the intelligentsia—the nonaligned and basically nonpolitical artists, writers, entertainers, scientists, physicians, teachers, and engineers. Stalin was convinced that a hostile intelligentsia could enlist foreign intervention against him. He viewed the most likely source of this particular attack as an assault led by the czarist émigré groups centered in Paris—or by their friends, the French.

Stalin had reason to fear members of the intelligentsia. Their agitation and debate stirred further discontent among the people. The intelligentsia was also the only group in direct contact with the West, either through professional organizations or through personal association with any number of Western technicians who were being imported to work on huge industrialization programs. To this shadowy man in the Kremlin, members of the intelligentsia were ideal agents for outside plotters.

No wonder the atmosphere among the intellectuals, particularly in Moscow and Leningrad—formerly, St. Petersburg—that winter was bitter and tense. The fear of the notorious midnight knock on the door was beginning to drive many of them to nervous collapse and even suicide.

As if these twin evils of fear and famine were not sufficient to augur a difficult life in Moscow, additional problems were to confront Bluet and Marc as their train hurtled closer to the capital. It was the thorny matter of where to live. Katya, of course, was comfortably settled in the Cheftel apartment. Alternate accommodations had been nearly impossible to obtain.

Soon after the revolution, most Moscow apartments had been carved up into small rooms with communal kitchens and baths. The gracious homes of the rich merchants and the upper classes had been confiscated and subdivided. The original owner of a villa or a mansion was either given a single room or summarily evicted. Later, as pressure increased on an already inadequate housing stock, the rooms were again split up and the occupants confined to narrow spaces separated by crude partitions that often were nothing more than a curtain or a screen. Thousands of Moscovites had to be content with a cot in a corner of a room or simply a space on the floor. The suburbs offered little relief. New buildings resembling concrete barracks had been subdivided into small, vermin-infested rooms. By 1930, the discomforts of Soviet life were being drowned in a sea of vodka, the only panacea in ample supply. It offered a temporary escape from the daily horrors of filth, fear, hunger, overcrowding, and a poverty-level existence.

A handful of highly placed party members, commissars, foreign diplomats, foreign journalists, and, of course, the elite of Soviet society, including favored writers, world-renowned scientists, and the occasional ballerina from the Bolshoi with the right connections, could obtain comfortable living quarters. For everybody else it was impossible to find a room, let alone an apartment.

Since one could not rent an apartment or purchase a home in the accepted Western manner, living quarters were obtained either by currying political favor or through cunning. As Bluet would soon appreciate, one could discover more about a man's current standing with the Communist Party by his accommodations than by his official title. So precious was this most basic of needs that rarely did one hear about couples endowed with attractive living quarters publicly splitting up. Whatever else came between them, the specter of losing their comfortable home became the glue that held the marriage together.

But Bluet and Marc would still have two months before they had to cross that bridge, thanks to the generosity of Dr. Lazareff. They were elated by the prospect of starting a new life together, and their thoughts—as they awoke the following morning a little stiff from sleeping in a railway seat but unbelievably happy just being together—turned to the brighter prospect of the future shape of their lives, the friends they had in common, and the capital in which they would live—at least, until Marc obtained his ongoing foreign assignment.

After all, Moscow was still a fascinating, inscrutable metropolis, a profoundly mysterious blend of East and West.

LYING AS FAR NORTH as Hudson Bay and as far east as Damascus, Moscow had always been a mystical place, steeped in oriental splendor and, during the long winter season, tucked inside a breathtaking blanket of sparkling white snow.

It was founded in 1156 when the Prince of Rostov erected protective wooden walls around a number of vulnerable hamlets at the base of a hill on which stood his own manor house. The settlement quickly grew in importance and size, not only as the royal seat of princes, whose power increased with time and conquest, but because of its strategic position in relation to the commerce of the region. Original track roads from the already-bustling ancient centers of Kiev and Novgorod met at this point, which also happened to be on the shores of the navigable Moscow River, a tributary of the faster-flowing Oka. In time, the manor house became a medieval fortress encompassing other palaces and churches, and the wooden walls were strengthened with stone and brick to produce what eventually became the outer walls of the Kremlin. To further protect the settlement from bands of wandering Tartars and Mongols, outer fortifications and ramparts were constructed, causing it to be dubbed "Holy mother Moscow with White Walls." These rings eventually evolved into the wide ring roads of modern Moscow, as the city slowly radiated out in a circular pattern from the Kremlin.

By the sixteenth century, Moscow had developed into an important royal administrative seat, as well a bustling commercial junction. The city was ready to be placed on the world map as a major metropolis. Strategically, it stood astride vital new trade routes to central Asia and Persia, as well as equally important roads to the West. To commemorate the conquest of neighboring Kazan, the reigning monarch, Ivan the Terrible, further enhanced his capital city by commissioning the construction of an exquisite church beside the turreted walls of the Kremlin. Called St. Basil's Cathedral, it became Moscow's most famous landmark. According to legend, it took a veritable army of masons and carpenters six years to complete, after which the fearsome Ivan ordered the architect blinded so that he could never duplicate his work.

A large open area facing the church already provided old Moscow with a forum, a market place, a public square, and, when occasion demanded, a place of execution. It was here that Ivan and his successors issued their decrees and proclamations before an attentive gathering of anxious subjects. Eventually, this site became Red Square, a plaza so huge that two million people once gathered there on a single occasion. The name had nothing whatsoever to do with the revolution. It had come into being three centuries earlier, rumored to be the result of so many executions.

Although Moscow continued to grow as a strategic commercial center, it suffered a cultural setback a hundred years later during the reign of Peter the Great. Peter decided to construct a brand-new capital, St. Petersburg, several hundred versts to the north (one verst is approximately equivalent to one kilometer). From then on, the Russian nobility rarely spent time in Moscow, preferring the superior elegance of St. Petersburg or their country homes. Meanwhile, the lesser aristocracy and cultural leaders were spending more and more time in Paris—the city of choice for all of them. Some had even purchased permanent homes in France, in addition to a family residence in Russia. Many had become more fluent in French than in Russian.

Nevertheless, Moscow remained the nation's foremost center of commerce. By this time, a plethora of narrow cobbled lanes and passages wove a spider's web between the original ring roads. Neat rows of shops and Russian-style homes—with their railed-in gardens, Moorish window carvings, patterned bricks, and tiled roofs—dotted both the lanes and the boulevards of the city. Craftsmen lent their names to the lanes: Silversmith Lane, Carpenter Lane, Table Cloth Lane. Rows of small shops selling wild fowl, fish, and meats went by the equally logical names of Bread Street, Fish-Stew Lane, Dining Room Lane, or Cook's Lane. At every turn the smaller streets emptied into great cobblestone squares, until Moscow became as renowned for its profusion of spacious open plazas as for its teeming number of churches with their distinctive golden cupolas.

Not even the burning of Moscow at the time of Napoleon in the War of 1812 could lessen the impact of history upon this most oriental of European capitals. From the rubble of those fires, fine new buildings were resurrected in Russian "Empire" style. And in his thunderous retreat from Moscow, Napoleon abandoned hundreds of cannons, many of which would add a picturesque charm to the corners where they stood—ghostly sentinels from a violent past.

Despite these setbacks, Moscow could still boast a goodly share of the nation's creative energy. It continued to provide a home for the Moscow Art Theater, the Bolshoi Ballet, two universities, scientific institutes, colleges, dozens of theaters, and concert halls. At various times it was home to Leo Tolstoy, Anton Chekhov, Tchaikovsky, Mayakovsky and Yessenin (poets of the revolution), and the composer Rimsky-Korsakov.

The threat posed by Western meddling following the Bolshevik revolution forced the seat of government back inside the thick walls of the Kremlin after an absence of four hundred years. It was the same revolution in whose name many of the older wooden houses and pavement blocks would be broken and burned for fuel during the cruel winters that followed. By 1930, this revolution had transformed the city from one of charm and culture into a veritable chamber of horrors. Lubianka prison, its gray stone walls only minutes away from the historic Kremlin, was now the most awe-some landmark in the capital, its cellars ringing in the still of the night with frightful sounds of torture and execution.

THE TRAIN FERRYING Bluet and Marc to Moscow screeched into Alexan-drovsky station in the heart of the city and shuddered to a halt. As the well-dressed foreigners and Soviet officials returning from abroad spilled off this international express, they drew a sharp contrast to the sullen and silent knots of onlookers.

Women wrapped in kerchiefs and shawls were huddled against torn wicker hampers, staring vacantly off into space, while small children tugged at their mothers' skirts. Everywhere, a noticeable absence of men, especially younger able-bodied men, attested to the prodigious amount of blood con-sumed in the name of one side or another during the revolutionary battles of Whites against Reds, as well as those of World War I. As the foreigners climbed down from the train, groups of children rushed forward to block their way and beg for pennies or crumbs (although begging in this "workers' paradise" had been strictly forbidden).

Bluet waited patiently on the platform as Marc rounded up their curi-ous assortment of baggage—the huge cabin trunk, the leather valise, the box of foodstuffs, and even the crated double bed. She felt decidedly out of place in her elegant clothes. It was a long wait, since arrangements had to be made to place the bed into storage while they stayed in their temporary accommodations. There was also considerable controversy over the box of food. For a while it looked as if the box was going to be confiscated, as Marc argued angrily with an official on the platform. Edicts against hoarding were being strictly enforced, and the impasse ended only when Marc drew out a card from his wallet. That seemed to dissuade the man. He let them through with the box.

A car and a driver were waiting to whisk them on to the suburb of Sokolniki, northeast of the city, where their borrowed apartment was situ-ated. Almost everyone else from the train waited with blank gazes in a lengthy taxi line. There were few taxis to be had.

Throughout the city, huge banners and posters flapped noisily in the wind, extolling the virtues of the brave new society. The amount of ongoing construction was remarkable, even by energetic Western standards. Cranes, bulldozers, cement mixers, and scaffolding cluttered the city, as new geometric-

80

shaped office buildings pushed upward, offering a bizarre juxtaposition to the ornate churches, the cobblestone alleys, and the baroque mansions of the older city. As they drove out of the city center, it became apparent that entire neighborhoods of older wooden homes were being razed to make room for dozens of multistoried workers' apartment blocks, with their box-like shapes and crude slab exteriors.

The car pulled up in front of an obviously new but depressingly ugly structure and stopped with a jolt. "We're here," Marc said enthusiastically, opening the taxi door for Bluet with a flourish. As she gazed up at the rectangular lines and endless concrete stairwells—unpainted and semi-finished— that characterized the building, she had difficulty suppressing a sigh. Sensing her disappointment and trying to lighten an awkward moment, Marc explained that even this represented a giant leap forward for many Russians. It had been decreed that indoor plumbing would no longer remain a novelty enjoyed only by the affluent.

When they opened the door, she found herself facing an apartment that was even more grim, sparse, and uninviting than she had feared. Hardly any furniture filled the dreary, narrow rooms. A stained table, two upright wooden chairs, and one armchair with stuffing that oozed from the worn upholstery completed the living room. The bedroom contained nothing more than a single bed and a small chest. A sink, a tap that provided only cold water, a kerosene stove, and a scratched wooden table with one chair furnished the tiny cubicle that served as a kitchen. No oven, no refrigerator, no bath—just a chipped toilet. Not even a closet, a wardrobe, or a telephone. All around were bare plank floors. No one had even bothered to hang drapes to shield the windows and offer the inhabitants a minimum of privacy. The interior concrete walls had been left unpainted and totally bare.

She did not utter a word, thinking of her luxurious home in Manhattan. But she tried to suppress the thought because she suddenly realized how spoiled she had become while living with Max.

"Not exactly Louis the Fourteenth, is it?" Marc quipped with a grimace, trying to break the uncomfortable silence. Realizing even this could not evoke a smile, he continued, "It's not what I would have chosen—for either of us—but it's only for a few weeks. You can't imagine what a struggle it's been to get this."

He called out toward the kitchen. A few moments later, an elderly peasant woman—bloated, shabby, dour, and peculiarly resentful—shuffled grudgingly toward them. With her limited knowledge of Russian, Bluet realized that Marc was asking the woman to boil some water so that Bluet could wash.

Obtaining an occasional servant and even a home of their own in a city where the general practice was for more than one family to share a single room had been a remarkable accomplishment. In all fairness, Marc had warned her in the taxi coming over that housing was such a formidable problem that a weak joke was currently making the rounds. The government—so ran the story—was busy manufacturing mile-long beds and blankets under which all families would soon sleep together in immense communal halls. And since personal kitchens were a bourgeois luxury, along with owning one's own pots and pans, the socialist state would shortly be supplying meals, instead of kerosene or primus stoves, for the entire populace. In fact, so seriously did the authorities believe their own propaganda that newer buildings without any cooking facilities were already being constructed.

Appreciating, as each hour passed, that Marc himself was undergoing a great deal of personal anguish, Bluet gradually accepted these temporary inconveniences without further comment. She kept reminding herself that she had grown far too pampered over the years and was behaving more like a petulant child. After all, she was here to build a new world order with Marc. It was not going to be forever.

By evening she had managed to cheer up considerably, despite her first taste of the local fare—a scanty meal of cabbage, potatoes, black bread, and a morsel of boiled fatty beef served by the servant woman on a haphazard assortment of cracked dishes that had surely seen better days.

$\mathcal{S}even$

THE NEXT TWO WEEKS were spent in a romantic haze that temporarily blotted out the harsh realities, conditions that Bluet quickly sensed were as unappetizing to Marc as they were to her. Even his exceptionally long working hours and one day off each week could not dampen their enthusiasm for just being together. It was their honeymoon, a time when two normally gregarious people wished to be alone with each other.

If young love can be compared to champagne—effervescent, sparkling, and slightly unstable—then their love, the love of middle years, seemed more akin to vintage wine: passionate, yet subtle. Something to be valued with the deeper appreciation of seasoned maturity. She would always regard their lovemaking as the bittersweet essence of ultimate joy combined with ultimate tragedy. What made it magnificent was that even then she sensed that it could not endure. The world has no place for lasting pleasure, she would later say. It is not in the scheme of things.

Whenever they climbed into the creaky, narrow single bed with its coarse sheets and dilapidated mattress, they reached out for each other with such an intoxication that all else faded. And she rested more soundly in that rickety bed than in all the opulence she had shared with Max. She had forgotten, or perhaps had never really known, the simple happiness of living intimately with someone you love. Marc was such a rare and precious lover that she grew more and more attached. As winter cloaked its icy curtain around them, she came to respect that narrow bed as the ideal answer to keeping warm during the freezing nightly temperatures. To cling to each other simply for warmth brought its own special delight.

On Marc's rare days off, they strolled together in the soft autumn sunlight through nearby Sokolniki Park. Originally a pine forest, it had been laid out a century earlier along classical lines, with broad avenues radiating from the entrance. It was here, in bygone years, that the czar himself brought his falcons to hunt game. And during warm spring afternoons, upper-class fathers rode with their marriageable daughters in open carriages along its broad avenues. The hope was that eligible young men of the nobility might see them passing. Then, if one such pretty girl happened to catch the gentleman's eye, he would walk up to the carriage, doff a hat, bow low, and ask to meet the young lady. It was a ritual so graceful and musical that it still warmed the memories of those who cared to remember.

Even their austere living quarters were gradually accepted with better grace and humor. After all, it was only temporary. They felt certain they would soon be posted abroad or offered better accommodations. So they could laugh at some of the irritants: the acrid smell of cabbage soup that floated in from down the hall, the shrill arguments of the couple upstairs that penetrated the thin ceiling. Translated by Marc, these sounded so absurd that tears of mirth would roll down Bluet's face. He was constantly trying to find ways of making it up to her, from the simple gesture of bringing home a small delicacy, whenever he could find one, to taking her letters for Anna personally to the post office to make sure they were correctly registered (and to prevent them from getting "lost").

When exceptionally burdened with work, he brought his papers home. And she would gather pillows to sit down next to him as he worked at the table all evening long, leaning the back of her head against his lap while he concentrated on his reports.

Marc seemed so deeply troubled that she tried not to be critical. Over and over, she heard him mutter to himself in bewilderment, "Madness. It's madness." Through hints he threw out, she gathered that part of his reluctance to divorce Katya had been the housing problem. Such action would have instantly required Katya to relinquish their apartment.

It would take considerably longer before Bluet could appreciate that this new mood of despair had far wider implications. Not for some time would she learn how sickened he was by the lightning sweep of a sadistic tyranny that replaced the optimism that had flowed when he left for New York in 1927. And that he would dearly love to have seized her that day at the border and spirited her away on a train going in the opposite direction. But the ease of movement in and out of the country had gone, too.

Like an anxious newlywed she eagerly listened for the sound of his key in the lock as he arrived home each evening, usually with an overflowing briefcase. He was so much busier than he had ever been in New York. But he could never be coaxed into saying much about what he was doing, except that he was still with the Department of Health and in the foreign division of the Red Cross. Bluet was not accustomed to being left out. She had looked forward to being close, emotionally and intellectually, as she already was physically. She shared his interests. She was ambitious for him. When was she going to be included to support, caution, listen, and advise?

During the daytime, she layered herself with a motley assortment of woolen clothing, along with the handmade shoes and the heavy coat she had selected in London. Then she set out for lengthy walks, striding along in the crisp fall air and watching as the leaves changed to a deep golden glory and then began to fall.

But there was little else to see or do—nothing but endless rows of dilapidated timber houses left to slowly decay from weather and pests while the occupants were caught up in a daily struggle for survival. There was hardly any traffic and few pedestrians—strangely, not even the warm sounds of children at play. Marc had promised her that soon they would be given something nearer the center of the city where their friends lived—people they knew from New York. She was looking forward to that. They had not yet visited anyone. And in Sokolniki she felt isolated, surrounded by silent, shuffling, ghostly people whose gaunt faces reflected little but resignation and exhaustion. Some stopped and stared at her in curiosity, walking on only when she met their gaze. Amid these colorless surroundings, a smartly dressed French woman, unexpectedly slender beyond her years, cut a strange sight indeed. Most people seemed too frightened to talk to her. So she smiled, nodded, and went on her way.

The lack of food troubled her more than anything. It was alarming to pass shops with empty windows and shelves. Sadly, she watched the long lines of silent women, scarves wrapped tightly around their heads, their cheeks crimson against the cold, shivering for hours as icy winds or soaking rain penetrated their endless layers of skirts. Or the men, standing in their threadbare overcoats fastened together with safety pins. There was a scarcity of everything. Any product that needed fat for preparation, such as soap, butter, and even waterproof boots, had disappeared entirely. Meat was a rarity, and, when available, the quality was appalling. More often than not, it was just foul-tasting sausage. Vegetables were limited to cabbage or some bitter greens. The shops had only a few moldy potatoes and sour black bread.

One day she offered to go shopping herself instead of sending the maid, as was the custom, to see what she could find. Marc exploded at the thought.

"Do you think I'm going to let you stand for hours on one of those food lines, only to find there's nothing left when you get inside? Anyhow," he told her, "they will probably pretend they can't understand and push you aside. I'll take care of it in town. I have access to a special store."

There was not much more to be obtained even from his "special store": potatoes, rice, macaroni, cabbage, black bread, and occasionally a few apples, soft and withering, as though they themselves were being drained of strength.

For the first time in years, she found herself very much alone and with time heavy on her hands. Now and then, she broke the monotony by taking a streetcar into the center of Moscow, where she witnessed one of the strangest sights of all: crowds standing patiently in long silent lines outside candy shops. The revolting sweets, composed mainly of soya beans, offered a brief respite from the gnawing pangs of hunger.

And she waited with growing impatience for the upturn in fortune that Marc promised would surely arrive very soon.

A FEW WEEKS AFTER she arrived, Marc came home with some news. "There's a young man helping me out at the office. He's only been in Moscow a short while. He doesn't know many people, and I thought it would be nice if we had him over here tomorrow afternoon. We both have the same day off this week. Remind me to bring home a bottle of vodka."

She was still putting on makeup and combing her hair when the man arrived slightly earlier than expected. She heard Marc slide open the latch and the babble of voices as the two of them began talking in Russian. She glanced at herself in a rusted mirror that hung from a bent nail on the bedroom wall and hurried out to greet her first guest.

He appeared charming enough—a dark, gangly youth with a huge crop of auburn hair and a thin, angular face. Muffled against the early winter chill, he was bundled inside a thick brown coat and a matching woolen scarf wound tightly around his neck. Marc was helping him off with his coat as she approached.

"I'd like you to meet Sasha," he said. "He's just completed his medical studies."

Smiling broadly, Sasha shook her hand. "It was of kind of Dr. Cheftel to ask me here. And you, too, of course. As I always say . . . we members of the GPU," he went on, glancing over at Marc, "we must stick together, don't you agree?"

"The GPU," she repeated, thinking perhaps she had misunderstood.

Sasha frowned quizzically. "Didn't you know? Of course, you did. Marc's one of the senior men in the foreign department. Surely, you must have been aware of that. He was the one who . . . ," he paused awkwardly, adding, "They say he's achieved some amazing things for us abroad. He became a legend in Italy."

There was an uncomfortable silence.

Bluet stared at Marc. He winced visibly, turned away from her gaze, and reached hurriedly for a cigarette from an open pack on the table. He rarely smoked. So it only confirmed what she would have dearly loved to have asked but dared not do so in front of Sasha.

Striking a match, Marc broke the silence. "That's enough explanations for one day, Sasha, don't you think?" he said. Then, obviously anxious to change the subject, he added, "I'm opening a new bottle of vodka just for you. And Bluet saved you some of the ham she brought all the way from Berlin."

Still hugging Sasha's coat, Bluet continued to stare in bewilderment. What the young man had said must surely be the truth. Just the expression on Marc's face seemed to confirm it.

As she stood there in silence, mulling over this odd turn of events, all sorts of seemingly unrelated incidents suddenly fell into place: the warning she had received just before leaving New York; the allegations in the press that she had shrugged aside; the noticeable hush that descended upon a group of their Russian friends whenever Marc walked into a room. Now it all added up. Even the solicitous way the normally ill-tempered border officials handled her papers and luggage.

The only piece that did not fit the puzzle was the man himself. She prided herself on being a good judge of character. Even Max had grudgingly praised her on occasion for cautioning him against dealing with certain individuals, when all she had to go on was intuition. Invariably, she would be proven correct.

Still clutching the coat, she looked over at Marc. He was obviously aware of her thoughts because he kept turning around, beckoning her to join them.

After hanging her guest's coat on a hook by the door, she walked slowly into the kitchen to fetch the cracked plate of ham and black bread that she had prepared earlier in the day. Mulling matters over as she carried the plate back to where they were sitting, she thought to herself that by comparison, the intricate schemes of Max Rabinoff assumed the innocence of a Sunday school production.

There had to be something far more complicated behind the tale of Dr. Marc Cheftel.

Part Two

Marc's Story:
Un Mèdico Benèvolo

Eight

IN THE HEART OF the Cossack country of southern Russia, on the northern shores of the inland Sea of Azov, lies the seaport town of Taganrog. Although situated in the depths of the provinces, Taganrog grew to become anything but provincial in character. By the middle of the nineteenth century, more than half of its 50,000 inhabitants were a cosmopolitan blend of Greek, Italian, Turk, and German. They had migrated there to exploit the seagoing trade and the lucrative sturgeon catch. Prows of tall merchant sailing ships, sweeping up from the Black Sea laden with spices and exotic wares from the eastern Mediterranean, furrowed through the placid waters of the bay, proudly flaunting their billowing white sails in an almost endless parade. They returned to their own native shores carrying wheat and other agricultural products harvested from the rich black earth of the nearby Ukraine.

The Greeks predominated in Taganrog. They were the affluent shipowners and merchants who introduced elegant carriages drawn by thoroughbred horses that ferried them and their families through the muddy streets. Greek money sponsored schools and built theaters and concert halls where Italian opera and first-class stage productions flourished throughout the year, attracting an international array of artists.

Quaint and colorful shops lined the town's main street. They offered such delicacies as Turkish delight, Italian olive oil, homemade pasta, black olives, German sausage, halvah, baklava, dried currants, wine for every palate, and a wide variety of foreign foods whose mouth-watering aromas intoxicated the senses. Early each morning, the women haggled with shopkeepers over wares strewn haphazardly on shelves or stored in warped wooden barrels. And everyone in town scurried about against the backdrop of a cobalt blue sea and tall-masted vessels gently slapping the water—a scene reminiscent of any of the small seaports that rim the Mediterranean.

It was not uncommon to hear four or five languages spoken on the streets of Taganrog. Down at the quay it was German, as the Germans were the dock workers and the longshoremen—industrious, proud, and incredibly efficient.

Of lesser affluence than the Greeks, yet still part of the prosperous community of Taganrog, were the Italians, the Turks, and a smattering of assimilated Jews.

In 1825, Czar Alexander I died under mysterious circumstances at his winter palace in Taganrog. Legend insists that Alexander, a mystical and tormented man, had grown weary of the burdens of the crown. With the complicity of his servants, he staged a bogus death, after which he slipped away to Tomsk, taking over the identity of Feodor Kuzmich, a pious hermit who was treated with peculiar deference by successive czars. Thirty-five years later, in 1860, the writer Anton Chekhov was born in Taganrog.

And it was here in 1884, at the end of the reign of the reactionary monarch Czar Alexander III, that Marc Solomonovitch Cheftel—whose family name was sometimes spelled Scheftel, Sheftel, or Sheftal when transliterated from Russian into Latin letters—was born into an upper-middle-class Jewish family of scholars, professionals, and merchants, with diverse business interests extending over the entire region.

Both his mother, Maria, and his father, Solomon, could trace their origins to families that had attained prosperity and prominence several generations earlier. His parents had experienced only the ease, the comfort, and the security that old family wealth engendered. Their distinctive bearing readily identified them with that elite circle of city dwellers—the privileged Jews. Only a handful of such families existed in Russia in 1884. They were regarded by the Jewish peasants and craftsmen of the nearby Russian Pale of Settlement (the only area of Russia where Jews could officially live) with a mixture of suspicion, envy, and resentment. This was because they were insulated from the depravity and the capricious terror of the dreaded pogrom, that indiscriminate attack against Jewish settlements waged just for sport. In Russian, *pogrom* means "to wreak havoc," and it most assuredly did.

Through adroit and complex manipulations, families like the Cheftels had managed to triumph over the onerous edicts prohibiting ordinary Jews from owning land, as well as the quotas imposed on Jews in education, commerce, and the professions. Some families, like that of Marc's mother, had always enjoyed such privileges. They had emigrated to Russia a century earlier, when the czar was enticing successful Jewish bankers to settle in his domains, offering them every opportunity to prosper as a result of his ambitious projects intended to construct a modern industrial state. But to do so, he also had to make exceptions. And, exempt from the torments inflicted

92

upon the ordinary Jew, they were encouraged to become an integral part of their newly adopted country.

Almost, that is. With a wary eye on history, they never cultivated a true kinship with the Russian people, who they feared would one day vent their anti-Semitic fury with equal zeal upon the rich as well as the poor, should the authorities decide to look the other way.

Solomon and Maria were an attractive couple. Dark and tall, with a captivating twinkle in his eye, Solomon was a perfect complement to his small, vivacious, and dynamic wife, who was high-spirited, headstrong, and unusually intelligent.

Marc, known in the family as Mitia, was the first son, born one year after their marriage. By this time, Taganrog was already slipping into history. Its harbor was slowly silting up, and it had been replaced in importance by nearby Rostov-on-the-Don. Despite its brilliant past, Taganrog bore signs of a decaying future. Life there was already becoming dull, suffocating, and dreary—hardly a stimulating environment for a well-educated and ambitious young couple.

While Marc was still an infant, Solomon and Maria decided to move five hundred versts northwest to Kharkov, a more prosperous and important mercantile center in the heart of the fertile Donetz basin of the Ukraine. Kharkov had developed into the paramount metropolis of the area, due to a combination of rich timber forests, coal deposits, iron mines, and lush farmland. A natural transportation center, resulting from a confluence of rivers, tributaries, and a brand-new rail link into the very heart of Russia, placed Kharkov in a unique position. The quality of the surrounding land was so rich and its grain harvest so abundant, it became known as "The Breadbasket of Russia."

It also contained Kharkov Imperial University, one of the few centers of higher education in the provinces. This provided the area with a student population bursting with ideas, polemics, and the dialectics that were to help spawn the new politics of the twentieth century.

Solomon quickly established himself in the prospering family business— a modest-sized holding of coal mines. Maria's family owned valuable acres of timberlands. Housed in a spacious, well-staffed, and elegantly furnished two-story home in the better section of the city, they and their relatives numbered among the more influential and respected Jewish families of the Ukraine.

Three years after Marc was born, Maria gave birth to a second child, a girl, followed three years later by another son. In such matters Maria was methodical. Then, almost as an afterthought, Maria had a third son a full ten years later.

Despite her keen mind and passionate interests in the outside world, Maria remained first and foremost a devoted mother. An upstanding and religious woman, she kept a kosher home and took great pride in her household. She observed the Sabbath with lighting candles and prayer and raised her children in all the enduring traditions of her people. But her heart was drawn to the salons of St. Petersburg. More than anything else, she loved to travel to the capital and hobnob with the duplicitous power brokers whom she conquered with her quick intelligence and charm. Her excellent connections and influence at court, gained initially through her family, were used for the benefit of her less fortunate relatives and friends. She soon became the unofficial spokeswoman for the simple Jews of the Pale. She interceded to get them hard-to-obtain permits, special favors, or exemption from the unfair and arbitrary local rulings that played havoc upon Jewish lives. She always seemed to accomplish the impossible with such brilliance and flair that she was nicknamed "Catherine the Great" by the good citizens of Kharkov. Maria worked her miracles time and again.

Maria had equally high expectations for her children. She was determined that they be well educated, as well as cultured and cosmopolitan. She exposed them at an early age to the best that the capitals of Europe had to offer. Their intellects were sharpened and shaped in Berlin. Their appreciation of art, music, and architecture came from Italy. Manners and social bearing were learned from the French. Following in the footsteps of the Russian nobility in the way she chose to accomplish these tasks, she carefully selected nurses and governesses from the better-educated families of all these countries. These professionals lived in the household during the children's formative years and provided early exposure to such refinements.

Maria reasoned that this way, her children would grow up with a fluent knowledge of four languages: Russian, French, German, and Italian. They were also taught Hebrew, embracing the standard Jewish curriculum of the day. Indeed, it was through his religious studies that Marc first encountered the world of philosophy that was to electrify and haunt him for the remainder of his life.

From an early age Marc was completely absorbed by intellectual and messianic Judaism, as preached by the prophets, in the discourses of the Talmud, and among the sages of Jewish history. A boy of intense curiosity, he also developed an insatiable appetite for the life of the philosophers. This ultimately attracted him to the writings of Spinoza, the seventeenth-century Dutch Jewish philosopher who was considered the spiritual predecessor of Karl Marx.

Marc was an incurable dreamer, a star-gazer searching for harmony, order, and universal truths in a chaotic and ruthless world. The dreams of the earliest Marxist social revolutionaries fit this vision. He followed their thoughts and actions with increasing fascination. Could they provide the solution where others had failed? The thought piqued and perplexed him.

Since they always spoke Russian at home, Solomon and Maria considered it unnecessary for their children to learn Yiddish, the folk language of the Pale. They were assimilated in every way but one: Maria was fiercely proud of her religion, and while the authorities were vigorously pursuing a campaign to convert the Jews, offering converts the reward of total freedom from persecution and restriction, she viewed conversion as more sinister than anything a pogrom could accomplish. It heralded the end of the Jews as a people.

It was in these early years, while other boys were immersed in nursery rhymes and fairy tales, that Marc spent his childhood listening, wide-eyed and intent, to Maria as she recounted her exploits in St. Petersburg—all that she saw, all that she learned, and all that she experienced in the courtly salons of that distant city. It was his first exposure to political intrigue, graphically illustrated for him with uninhibited honesty by his mother's fine analytic mind. He persuaded her to relate some of her favorite tales over and over. As the years progressed, he would hear firsthand of the decay and the decadence into which the nation was tumbling, the gross corruption of the public officials, and the rigidity and the backwardness of the regime.

Holidays were taken abroad. Summers were spent touring Italy and basking on the unspoiled beaches of the French Riviera. They hiked in the mountains of Switzerland and occasionally stopped in Germany, where Maria liked to "take the cure" in fashionable spas or attend concerts. Maria was determined that the children should appreciate good music and learn an instrument. Marc was offered the violin. He mastered it easily and grew to cherish it as a close companion. The others were taught the piano but preferred the simplicity of their voice lessons.

Maria also had definite plans about their future, insisting upon professions for all her children. A university background was a tradition on both sides of the family. As all Jewish graduates enjoyed immediate exemption from Jewish restrictions, she reasoned that no matter what their financial circumstances in life, they could be spared this burden. Since hardly any places inside Russian universities were allotted to Jews—unless the families could "arrange" a place or afford to educate their children abroad—most of them never overcame this edict. Maria, a fixer par excellence, had the luxury of considering either alternative.

Marc was encouraged to study medicine, a Jewish cliché and a family tradition. There were already as many physicians on Maria's side of the family as there were lawyers and writers among the Cheftels. For her next son and her only daughter, she chose law (Maria flatly refused to differentiate between the educational opportunities for a daughter and those for a son). Finally, having a natural bent toward the sciences, the youngest son became a chemical engineer.

As Maria's own political ambitions had been frustrated by the religious and gender bias of her era, she was delighted to see her eldest son, now entering his teens, exhibit interest in the social revolutionary movement of the day—awakenings that were already unsettling the relative calm of a provincial city like Kharkov. Perhaps, thought Maria, Mitia would inherit all her own unfulfilled political yearnings. And she was not displeased.

Marc initially joined the Social Democrats, the favored party of Jewish youths of southern Russia, since it espoused a program of improved living conditions and equal opportunities for all oppressed minorities. Socialism was the newest and boldest ideology on the horizon, untested and thereby unblemished in the harsh world of reality. It stood for a state-run economy built within a democratic framework orchestrated by the educated middle classes. Aristocratic privileges would be drastically reduced and worker participation increased. The shame of starvation wages, crowded hovels, and curtailed life expectancy would disappear. Needs would be met from cradle to grave.

Like many other Jewish households, the Cheftels supported Marc's earliest endeavors. Their long family history of involvement in political reform and social justice, currently highlighted by Maria's own lobbying activities in St. Petersburg, demanded nothing less. Solomon quietly provided a liberal voice in the business community of Kharkov.

Around them, in the villages and the hamlets of the Ukraine, the first of the most appalling pogroms, fomented and organized by the rabidly anti-Semitic Czar Nicholas II, was creating widespread upheaval, fear, and death.

Terrifying stories of killings, rape, pillage, and plunder—far in excess of anything condoned by the government in the past—reached the Cheftel household from outlying hamlets. The hated *zhid* was now fair game for any Russian thrilled by the sport.

Late into the night and often until the first pink rays of dawn tipped the horizon and cut across the narrow streets of Kharkov, clusters of people gathered in the Cheftel parlor to discuss the most recent of these mindless outrages. Although no pogrom had yet occurred in Kharkov itself or even touched the Cheftels personally, Solomon and Maria nevertheless began to wonder, "Will we be next?"

Decrees of expulsion and a voluntary exodus invariably followed each pogrom. Pathetic bands of Jews packed their meager belongings to seek refuge in the West. The more adventurous embarked for Palestine to join a band of five hundred students who, in 1882, had abandoned the region to spearhead the first mass wave of Jews bent upon creating Zionist settlements in Ottoman Palestine. In those early years, Kharkov had been among the first Jewish communities to recognize Zionism as a serious hope for the future. As conditions grew more and more intolerable, the ranks of its adherents swelled.

Not many miles to the east, in Kiev, one of the earliest leaders, Chaim Weizmann, was already preaching the Zionist credo. The Russians would never change, he argued. Anti-Semitism would thrive under any form of government. The only answer was to build a homeland of their own. "Next year in Jerusalem" was becoming more of a probability and less of a chant uttered at religious ceremonies.

Zionism held little attraction for Marc, not only because it seemed such an improbable pipe dream but also because of its limitations. He could not envision Zionism as a solution to the anti-Semitism that he perceived as the most fundamental Jewish problem. How could a tiny island of Jews possibly survive, surrounded by hostile neighbors and isolated in a remote part of the world? He would champion the cause of those Jews who, like members of his own family, did not care to go to Palestine. Besides, he was interested in altering the foundations upon which all society was built, not merely for the dignity and the preservation of the Jews but for the mutual benefit of all.

Since the growing anti-Jewish bias was already converting many Russian Jews into political activists, rather than into political theoreticians, a point of view merely meant a point of departure. All faced three clear options: join the Zionist movement and build a modern Jewish state on sacred soil in

Palestine; emigrate to the West, preferably the United States, and build a better life for their children; or enlist in one of the revolutionary parties dedicated to overthrowing the czar.

Unlike the indigent Jewish peasant who only had to bundle his meager possessions and move on, Marc and his family had everything to gain by remaining—provided they could replace the present autocracy with a system responsive to their needs and beliefs.

Solomon was the only one who was not interested in participating. He was not cut out for revolutions—for cataclysmic change. He was a peaceful, scholarly man, happiest when surrounded by the warm enduring atmosphere of his family. Besides, he needed to concentrate upon his business interests while everything around them was crumbling. Maria was different. Though she sensed early on that their gracious way of life might be lost forever, she was so captivated by the social possibilities inherent in revolution that it held her in its thrall. But the faction that disturbed her most was the Marxists, the self-professed world shakers. She was far more comfortable with the more benign democratic movements.

Marc was the impatient member of the family—the imprudent revolutionary. He adored the excitement, the intrigue, the secret gatherings in the dead of night, the plotting. He was still the incorrigible dreamer, the quixotic hero. Though his parents were eager to see him make a contribution to a better world, they were more practical. They feared the dangers. And like all parents, they worried. But they failed to dissuade him. The other children were still too young to become involved. Maria was a strict mother, and she made certain that they stayed riveted to their studies. Her daughter and her second son were therefore sent to university locally, and all stayed under her protective wing.

ON A BITTERLY COLD JANUARY DAY in 1905, soldiers fired directly into a crowd of peaceful workers marching with a petition to the czar's winter palace in St. Petersburg. It was a mild petition. It humbly begged the czar, Little Father of all Russians, to help improve their miserable working and living conditions. Closing in upon the palace, hundreds of them were mowed down by the hail of bullets and razor-sharp swords of the czar's mounted guards—their blood staining the white snows an ominous red. Riots, strikes, and mutinies followed. In Kharkov, a general strike was called and demonstrations over the bloody St. Petersburg massacre sparked furious hand-to-hand street fighting.

By this time, Marc had become associated with the Social Revolutionary Party. It foresaw no lesser route to radical change than through lawless and violent acts. Its leadership considered Czar Nicholas unable and unwilling to make the necessary reforms, regardless of his promises. It had run out of patience with his form of government, with his fumbling and corrupt appointees, and with the recent humiliations suffered by all Russians at the hands of the Japanese.

Organized acts of sabotage became a regular part of Marc's life. He helped foment strikes, street disorders—anything that would make the central government aware of the mood of the people and the people aware of their own power.

His conversion was complete. He had become a dedicated revolutionary.

With each success, his party grew bolder. After Grand Duke Sergei Alexandrovich, a senior military commander and uncle of the czar, was blown up on a Moscow street by a terrorist bomb, Marc Cheftel was arrested together with numerous other conspirators.

Livid with fury, the czar sought immediate execution for them all. Not one was to be spared for such a heinous crime, even though the grand duke's widow, a religious zealot, pleaded the Lord's mercy.

Marc was convinced his life was over—the ignominy of death at his first major encounter. If he survived, he told himself, he would abandon any direct involvement with violent groups. He would never repeat the mistake, if only he could be spared.

The news rocked the Cheftel household. At twenty, Marc had become a handsome scholar with a brilliant future before him. He was the brightest star in his parents' galaxy. He was considered an outstanding intellect among his fellow students at Moscow University, the elder brother his younger siblings looked up to with admiration, a gifted politician of whom much was expected.

Not only were the Cheftels completely shaken, their entire circle and community were stunned. Nobody dared visit Maria with petitions and requests. Curtains remained drawn over the windows of the family home, as if the family were in mourning. Servants shuffled noiselessly in and out, like shadowy silhouettes against a paper backdrop. The level of voices never rose above a whisper.

But it was not to prayer, tears, or self-deprecation that Solomon and Maria turned for solace. Maria never did have the patience or the temperament for this sort of response to trouble. The final hour had not yet arrived. Although sentence had been passed on Marc, he was still alive, awaiting the early-morning call of the executioner scheduled for a few weeks hence.

The solid citizens of Kharkov were therefore not surprised when early one morning soon afterward, Maria, accompanied by her personal maid carrying two suitcases—one large and heavy and the other small, shabby, and light—was seen slipping out of the front door, headed for the station.

Drawing her black woolen shawl closely about her against the chill wind and gathering up her long full skirts to avoid the mud of the soggy streets, Maria half-ran toward the railroad station. The maid, hunched over from the weight of the suitcases, tripped and stumbled while vainly trying to keep up with her mistress.

Seeing them pass from a small café on the way, three older men nodded and sighed.

"If she's looking for a pardon for her son," said one, drawing philosophically on the end of his pipe, "she won't get it this time."

"It's a tall order even for Maria," agreed his friend. "Look how pale and drawn she's become."

As Maria and her maid disappeared around the street corner, the other man in the trio shrugged his shoulders and smiled. "Rubbish!" he said, spitting on the ground. "She didn't get the nickname 'Catherine the Great' for nothing."

As the train sped north across the snowy steppes toward the imperial domes and towers of St. Petersburg, not even the czar of czars knew what manner of hurricane was about to strike his capital. St. Petersburg was about to encounter the tenacious fury of Maria Cheftel, prepared to do battle for the life of her firstborn son. All her years of lobbying and plucking favors from the gardens of the czar had been but a prelude to this day.

Maria never did divulge what transpired in St. Petersburg that spring. Whatever it was, it worked. The officials deliberated and argued. Then, about ten days later, Maria was able to return to Kharkov, triumphant. She had worked her miracle. She had achieved the impossible. Marc's sentence had been commuted to life imprisonment.

But if others rejoiced, the Cheftels did not and Maria least of all. She had saved the life of her son, but it was not enough. To endure a living death in the forbidding Siberian prison where it was decreed Marc would now be sent was still too high a price. Her son had played the fool. She could not leave him to rot for that folly.

In those days, political prisoners were still an elite, treated less severely than common criminals. They could obtain visiting permits and other privileges, including an opportunity to receive whatever reading material the prisoner desired. Later, many of the original Bolsheviks would acknowledge that much of their education (and even some of their writing) was made possible because of these reading privileges.

As Marc's initial panic subsided, the period in prison became a time of reflection and self-instruction for him as well. Like most other political detainees, he was convinced that he would ultimately be released. Like the others, he chose the French revolution as his model. But while his comrades focused upon such luminaries as Danton, Marat, Desmoulins, Robespierre, and even Napoleon, Marc studied a far less charismatic individual, yet to him a figure of far greater importance: Joseph Fouché, the shadowy, opportunistic, sinister virtuoso of behind-the-scenes political manipulation and survival.

From the days immediately preceding the French revolution to the restoration of the monarchy, Fouché played the role of master puppeteer. Through threats, bribes, flattery, duplicity, favors, blackmail, and pure genius, he survived, retaining power while comrades and enemies alike either felt the cold steel of the guillotine or disappeared quietly into the mists of history.

Hardly the most admirable character to tread the stage of history, Fouché fascinated Marc. It was certainly not because of his notorious lack of principles or his treachery, for which history has enshrined the man as the archvillain of his era. It was because of his masterly abilities at bending and juggling the power structure to his own will. Others made public orations. Others strutted and waltzed with power. Joseph Fouché, wholehearted disciple of Machiavelli, executed it. A useful man indeed.

In his behavior, Marc would imitate a man who believed in cultivating the technique of silence, the supreme art of self-concealment—a master of psychology. A man who knew how to topple rulers and did, who knew how to muster public opinion and did. Here was someone who watched and waited, knowing that not until the front men of a revolution, the men of passion, had clawed each other to death in the struggle for dominance would the hour strike for the patient and the prudent. Marc noted especially how Fouché appreciated that a revolution never bestows its fruits upon those who begin it, but upon those who bring it to its conclusion. Marc noted these things and in time would use them to fashion his own political life, making sure he was out of the way if and when the Russian revolution took place. Indeed, Marc would stand patiently and unobtrusively in the wings until the "men of passion" had spent themselves, and forces of the revolution were certain to succeed.

Marc noted other useful characteristics about Fouché. How, in his early years in the cloistered life of an ecclesiastic, Fouché developed an iron self-discipline, an exceptional capacity for concealing his private emotions and personal sentiments, waiting patiently for others to make mistakes, others to reach their breaking points.

Fouché, Marc discovered, knew the value of cultivating the image of modesty, subordination, and affability, while in reality delighting in confusion and intrigue and working to manipulate the powers of his time. Fouché's strength lay behind closed doors, in secret diplomacy, inciting and inducing others to act, while he personally remained inscrutable and invulnerable.

Marc noted something else about Fouché that, in its own way, would herald the end of a youthful and hotheaded idealism. Fouché understood better than most that society's values change quickly. Today's heroism can become tomorrow's terrorism. That which is deemed acceptable one day can be judged treasonable the next. And the accusers of one day can quickly become the accused of another. In the final analysis, he learned from Fouché that if any one man values political power, for whatever end, he must abide by all these dictums without deviating, no matter what temptations are placed before him: money, women, riches, or important titles.

As Marc's mood of cynicism grew and, with it, an ambivalence about committing himself wholly and irrevocably to any leader, party, or platform, save for the expediency of the moment, he would henceforth endeavor to live and intrigue by the methods and the maxims of Joseph Fouché, master intriguer of them all.

OF COURSE, the privileges accorded political prisoners were known to Maria. It was not long before she obtained a permit to visit her son, innocently explaining to the authorities how she wished to take him some books.

The prospect of a journey to Siberia was horrendous—a trek clear across the heartland of Russia. Thousands of versts of difficult and uncharted territory had to be crossed, only a portion of which could be made by rail.

The remainder would have to be covered by horse and buggy, steamer, flat board, and sled and even on foot.

Solomon would not hear of it. "Maria," he pleaded. "A woman like you can't make such a journey alone. It's out of the question."

"Then come with me."

"But that would mean leaving for two months . . . maybe more. It's too risky. Wait a little, Maria," he begged, knowing full well the depths of her feelings on this matter. "We have a responsibility to our other children."

Maria was adamant. "Then I'll go alone. I'll take my maid. I'll be just fine." She rose from the table where they were finishing an evening meal and pushed her chair forward with an air of finality.

"Maria," Solomon pleaded yet again. "Come back . . . just a minute."

She stopped and turned around.

"Give me one week to settle things and we'll go together. I promise you."

Maria gathered some books, a box of soap, a hamper of food that she knew would not spoil on the journey, and some warm clothes and boots. After leaving clear instructions at home in case of disorder or violence, the Cheftels embarked on their mission. They were hoping that the spring thaw would reach the northern Siberian wastes in time to shield them from the ravages of cold and frost.

It was a jaunty Maria who returned from Siberia just ten weeks later— a Maria who seemed like her old vivacious self. But she would not reveal why the smile had returned to her face, although her friends could guess. Maria had been up to her old tricks. Whatever it was, Maria and Solomon were keeping it to themselves. Not even the servants could be coaxed to tell.

A short time afterward, it was rumored that Marc was back, squirreled away in an upstairs room at the Cheftel house. The family denied it, and, eventually, the rumors subsided. Marc was not seen again in Kharkov for a great many years—long after the rest of the Cheftel family had left for good.

What really transpired between mother and son on that lonely, snowy Siberian plain? Inside the books that Maria carried to Marc in his arctic prison were gold coins artfully concealed in the supple leather bindings. There were enough coins to induce a guard to look the other way while Marc was out laboring one day with a lumber gang. On foot, across the frozen wastes, Marc hiked and stumbled the many miles to the nearest rail line. Once there, he happened upon a manually operated track man's handcar standing unattended, as if placed there by some unseen friend. He pumped it along the abandoned track to the nearest rail yard, then hid himself half-frozen in the rear of a freight train.

From there, he began the tortuous trek across Russia. Begging, stealing, hiding from the police in haystacks and deserted buildings, Marc gradually made his way home, aided by the poor. Political fugitives were people with whom the poor felt a bond. Many peasant families living in these areas regularly left small offerings of food on their doorsteps at night, in case an escaped prisoner wandered by in the blackness. Hearing the telltale sound of footsteps crunching through the moonlit snow, they would make the sign of the cross and whisper "Godspeed" to these pitiful creatures on their lonely flight to freedom.

It took Marc many months to reach Kharkov and home.

Solomon and Maria quickly set about obtaining false papers to spirit their beloved son out of the country before the police could find him. Marc was anxious to go to Geneva to join those revolutionaries in exile with whom he now felt a kinship: the international socialist groups, with their more disciplined and intellectual approach and their dedication to a world-wide workers' revolution. During all the intervening years, right up to the Russian revolution of 1917, Marc would develop a close bond with many of those who eventually emerged among the top Bolshevik leadership. It was an intimate group, and he would be treated as one of their inner circle, similar to an "old boy" network that nurtured its members early in life and was never forgotten.

Aside from the Russian revolution, the broader Marxist concept of an international workers' uprising was becoming increasingly attractive to him—an interest fostered by a brief friendship with Georgi Chicherin, that aristocratic, highly intellectual Old Bolshevik who later became the first Soviet foreign minister. Through these friendships, Marc grew even more interested in the philosophy of Spinoza.

However, Marc was troubled by a personal dilemma: how to reconcile his deeply religious spirit with the group's tilt toward atheism. He perceived in Spinoza's life the same wrongful excommunication from traditional Jewish blessings that he himself would suffer. And like Spinoza, he never really renounced his Judaism, just approached it in a different way. However, Marc was slowly appreciating the political wisdom of publicly disavowing all religious leanings, in order to remain part of this group. Inwardly, his deep-rooted attachment to Judaism never slackened, although he succeeded, perhaps too well, in paying lip service to the antireligious ravings of his party. Like his fellow Jewish communists, he thereby incurred the wrath of the rabbis and the traditionalists, exactly as Spinoza had done centuries earlier, and was consigned to a Jewish scrap heap. But he candidly admitted that he felt no remorse over the eclipse of the Russian Orthodox Church—that staunch bastion of czarist anti-Semitism.

For now, these Russian exiles, preaching and publishing the radical socialist line across the face of Europe, were relatively unknown—scorned and branded as political eccentrics. Even Lenin found his years in exile depressing and demoralizing, bleating piteously to his wife in their cold flat that perhaps revolution would succeed in at least one European country before he died, if not in Russia itself.

However, unlike so many members of that illustrious group, Marc was unable to give revolution and politics his single-minded devotion. The cold rooms, the Spartan meals, the shabby living, and the endless polemics were not for Marc Cheftel. After all, socialists' chances of winning power were slim at best. He far preferred the role of Renaissance man, captivated by a broader orbit of knowledge, scholarship, wit, beauty, and music—a bon vivant enticed by all the pleasures of the good life that an attractive young bachelor with plenty of family money in his pocket could afford in prewar Europe.

There were his medical studies to resume, and he enjoyed medicine, looking forward with enthusiasm to his future years as a doctor. He was particularly intrigued by the recently published works of Sigmund Freud and the developing medical specialty of psychoanalysis. At the suggestion of his mother's Italian relatives, Marc soon drifted down to Rome, where he could complete his medical studies at one of the better medical schools of Europe.

Within months, he had fallen madly in love with Italy and all things Italian. He was enchanted by its deep-blue skies and silver-green olive groves, whitewashed villas, glorious landscapes, and people so vivacious and fun-loving he could never get enough of them. His gentle, warm personality appealed to them equally as much. The Italians were dreamers. They were romantics. They infused him with a new vitality and an unrelenting love of life.

He devoured it all: its blend of classicism and romanticism, its vibrant lifestyle, its cuisine, its superbly cut clothing, its magnificent music, and its palatial cities crammed with legends from the past. A handsome young physician like Marc Cheftel was not to be denied its sensuous women either. There was something quintessentially feminine about them. They knew how to move, dress, and laugh and, above all, how to love. It was not long before he grew to resemble everyone else in his adopted country in appearance, manner, and bearing. He was affectionately renamed Marco by his Italian friends; it was a simple transition. His upbringing had prepared him for life in a sophisticated capital of Europe.

Inside, however, Marc remained the frustrated revolutionary, fully aware that the exploitation of the poor that he saw in Italy could be every bit as explosive as in Russia. Unlike the highly industrialized nations to the north, Italy closely mirrored conditions in Russia. It lacked a prosperous middle class. There was a widening gulf between the haves and the have-nots, an enmity between the north and the south, and the iron grip of a firmly entrenched elite. If he and his cohorts were to be proven right and the world was ripe for a workers' revolution, then Italy might just fall first—holding out the enticing possibility that his crowd would be at the very pinnacle of power when it occurred.

Such were the possibilities that a political iconoclast like Marc dwelled upon as he hung out his first shingle and opened his doors to patients in Rome. Medicine still came first. There was money and prestige in medicine and none at the moment in political rhetoric, though his thirst for the narcotic of power and political intrigue remained unquenched. So he cemented relations with like-minded socialist agitators, including those who would ultimately form the nucleus of an Italian Communist Party.

Nine

OF COURSE, AS MARC WAS a political exile, it was impossible to go home—a factor that contributed to a degree of loneliness, even for a dapper man about Rome. Though every inch the dashing young bachelor in command of himself and his fate, Marc retained a close affection for his family. He sorely missed them.

After several years in exile, he therefore reached a point where the prospect of matrimony held certain attractions and advantages. He had even met the ideal girl—a fellow medical student and a former classmate. Her name was Katarina Timofeyeevna, though she was always known as Katya. She was two years younger than Marc and came from a similar background in Russia. Also a dedicated revolutionary, she displayed a Marxist zeal much greater than his own. He sensed a kindred spirit. It amused him. She was an attractive girl—tall, slender, dark-haired, and graceful. Her manner was intense and passionate, though that passion would ultimately be consumed by her political beliefs rather than by her sexual desires.

He proposed. She eagerly accepted. Solomon and Maria were ecstatic when they learned about the marriage plans of their son. Perhaps, they hoped, he would now settle down to a more sensible existence. Perhaps he had learned his lesson after his prison experience and prolonged exile. The fact that Katya was Jewish and also a physician made it even more ideal. Double *mazel*.

The wedding of Marc and Katya was a joyous event. The family flocked to Italy. It was a moment for congratulations and a time for the traditional blessings of health, happiness, and prosperity, with many children to enrich their union.

But that was as far as it went. Marc and Katya were more in harmony philosophically than physically. Unlike such distinguished women luminaries of the revolution as Rosa Luxemburg and Alexandra Kollontai, who were as passionate about their lovers as about their socialism, Katya was more the medical and political companion. Marc craved the sexual passion and filled the void by adopting the Italian custom of having a mistress as well as a wife. But he was far from frivolous when it came to the opposite sex. Each time he chose his partner with infinite care and sustained a relationship for a great length of time, savoring the chase as well as the conquest. Three qualities typified them all: physical beauty, elegance, and breeding. It was as if he was seeking in a mistress a gracious reminder of the femininity of the old order, rather than the assertiveness of the new.

If Marc was not a faithful husband, at least he was a respectful one. Unlike Max Rabinoff, who flaunted a mistress in public to demean his wife and advertise his prowess, Marc kept his affairs at a discreet distance. Whatever Katya felt about the matter, she remained silent.

There is no question that in these relationships Marc gave equally as much pleasure as he received, his talents as a lover improving steadily with time and experience. His infectious zest for living never dampened, even into his mellowing years. His appealing looks ripened into a distinguished maturity.

Marc and Katya never did have any children. Yet despite Marc's philandering, they retained a fondness and a respect for each other. Not one person ever recalled a single public display of disharmony. In time they would be described as a team, rather than as a couple. They developed the kind of lasting bond that grows between two people who share the same hopes and aspirations. They became smoothly operating medical associates and a tightly coordinated espionage cell. Katya's quiet support in keeping their medical image alive did much to allow Marc the freedom for more flamboyant activity. Physically, Katya grew plump, dowdy, and rotund early on, like many Russian women. Sparing little time for frivolity, for her appearance, or for play, she totally devoted herself to medicine and politics—the ideal Bolshevik functionary.

As students, they had both made an extensive study of tuberculosis—the scourge of the industrial worker. Shortly after marrying, as might have been expected, they took over a sanatorium of their own, located along the Mediterranean coast at the small resort town of Nervi, near Genoa in northern Italy. They were both innovative, and it gave them flexibility and scope.

Two crucial events took place at that time that also attracted their attention: the unspeakable carnage of World War I and the subsequent period of unrest that would overturn dynasties and alter the social fabric of Europe. Both factors made international socialists like Marc and Katya believe that decadent capitalism was too brittle to deal adequately with twentieth-century problems. As a consequence, their own movement just might have a chance of taking root and, with it, their ascendancy to power. The war was bleeding the monarchies and the oligarchies to death.

As physicians, they became deeply committed to ministering to the war's appalling casualties, which in Italy alone amounted to 600,000 killed, 200,000 permanently crippled, and one million seriously wounded before the last shot was fired. They worked tirelessly with the injured, watching with horror as, year after year, the brightest young men of Europe perished on the battlefield of a purposeless war.

It was during these war years that Marc developed a novel orthopedic device for the knee, to enable people with bone and muscle damage to walk again. Despite his other interests, he remained the conscientious and compassionate healer.

Even so, he could not resist the siren call of politics. The intoxication was too deeply ingrained. For Katya, the allure was more in the humane possibility inherent in change. They became extensively involved as agitators. They were behind much of the pacifist propaganda and the demonstrations that swept Italy, spearheaded by socialist groups, of which their own, on the extreme left, was only one. The senseless war just had to be stopped.

When Russia exploded into revolution in the spring of 1917, they were ecstatic—even more so when the Bolsheviks, most of whom were personal friends, took over from the inept Kerensky government and immediately seceded from the immoral war. Russia was the first country to put the socialist dream into reality. Soon Marc and Katya had an even greater reason to rejoice—one that would cement their allegiance to Bolshevism for years to come. It was actually keeping its promise to the Jews.

They watched with pride as the Bolsheviks immediately freed all ethnic minorities from restrictions imposed by the czar. Publicly proclaiming that hatred against any minority people was shameful, Lenin vowed that anti-Semitism would be banished forever from Russian soil. As promised, anti-Semitism became a criminal act, vigorously prosecuted by the new state. Overnight, Jewish organizations emerged from the shadows, Jewish theater blossomed, and Jewish publications flourished. Those Jews who had been in the forefront of the party prior to the October revolution were given many of the highest posts in the new government. It was a pivotal moment. When the fledgling regime was about to be drawn into a civil war against the White forces intent upon restoring the old order, the loyalty of the Jewish people, who had suffered so much under the czar, went unquestioned. The party went out of its way to utilize their talents, sorely needing skilled and educated men to oil the wheels of a brand-new administration. Educated Jews were the best-prepared, most trustworthy supporters the party could muster.

From their exile in the far-flung capitals of the world, the aristocratic Whites were soon arguing that the Bolshevik success was simply part of a larger Jewish conspiracy to take over the world. They played upon the theme to deliberately fan the anti-Semitic flames of the 1920s and 1930s. Highlighting the campaign was the 1919 publication of a book in Germany entitled *The Protocols of the Elders of Zion*—the alleged minutes of a secret meeting of Jewish leaders aimed at masterminding an international coup. The White Russian perpetrators implied that if events in Russia were indeed the culmination of a carefully laid Jewish plot, then intervention to wipe out the dreaded Bolsheviks should be considered a Christian duty—a modern-day crusade against this most ancient of infidels. Although the episode was later exposed as a fraud, conceived by a former member of the Imperial Russian Secret Police, it accomplished its task superbly well.

THOUGH EUPHORIC OVER the turn of events inside Russia, Marc was in no great haste to return to his homeland. He was well aware that the Bolsheviks held only a tenuous grip on the country. A civil war was brewing between the Reds and the Whites, and from outside, it looked fearfully like the Whites would triumph. Its army was better organized. And it was being equipped and augmented by the Allied powers, who viewed the Bolsheviks and their policy of immediate armistice as a threat to the Western Front. World War I was still raging, and German divisions previously engaged on Russian soil could be unleashed in France and perhaps alter the course of the war. Some Allied officials even suggested that the Bolsheviks were actually puppets of the Germans. If Bolshevism was indeed a contagious disease about to spread westward, it seemed prudent to muster the rest of the anti-German capitalist alliance against this new workers' regime. The Allies therefore landed expeditionary forces on Russian soil. Soon the beleaguered Bolsheviks were facing two enemies simultaneously: the Whites and the anti-German alliance.

Talking it over, Marc and Katya agreed it would better to remain in Italy for a time. It was still too great a gamble to abandon a prospering medical practice for the chaos that now engulfed Russia. So they did not follow their comrades back into the hell and the glory that was the revolution. Marc preferred to wait until he was sure which way the pendulum would swing. Ironically, staying put would provide an excellent cover for future operations. Not returning with the rest of the politically active Russian exiles would naively be viewed by their White Russian friends in Italy as showing lack of interest and support for the new Bolshevik-Communist regime. The Cheftels took advantage of that notion. They promoted and enhanced their image as conscientious doctors, concerned solely with the plight of the Russian people in a humanitarian way, removed from any political involvement—just ordinary physicians.

Marc's affiliation with the Russian Red Cross (secretly used from the outset as an operational center for Bolshevik espionage) did not compromise this attitude. The Russian Red Cross was considered by all Russians, whatever their political allegiance—and, indeed, by foreigners as well—as the one organization that was sufficiently trustworthy and apolitical to handle the variety of delicate negotiations engendered by the internal strife.

Firmly in the hands of the Bolsheviks from the start, the Russian Red Cross did much to foster this attitude, emphasizing the benevolent nature of its work. Ironically, the Bolsheviks had initially recognized the political usefulness of a Red Cross organization by emulating the *Americans*. An American Red Cross mission had been dispatched to Russia immediately following the ouster of the czar in February 1917. Ostensibly, its aim was to offer humanitarian aid to a people suffering terribly from the combined turmoil of a world war and a revolution. In reality, it was a mask for commercial activity. The entire mission had been personally underwritten by William Boyce Thompson, director of the Federal Reserve Bank in New York. Thompson was being urged by his industrialist friends to secure valuable Siberian concessions from the new government before these were given away to anyone else. Thus the mission was stacked with business leaders and Wall Street bankers (using bogus credentials), rather than with medical personnel. It even had the tacit approval of President Woodrow Wilson. Since it immediately tried to curry favor with the new regime by hiring Bolsheviks as translators and was negotiating with officials in the new Bolshevik government, it did not take long for the Russian revolutionaries to figure out what was really going on. They took their cue from this mission.

As the Cheftels had already been effective behind the scenes in the creation of an Italian communist party, the Bolshevik leadership was more than happy to encourage them to remain in Italy. Winning over the citizens of neighboring countries to communism would help secure a communist regime in Russia, isolated as it was in a sea of capitalist hostility. It was also part of the ambitious plan for reshaping world society, underscored by the creation of Comintern, the international wing of the Bolshevik Party in 1919. Comintern—short for Communist International—soon became the most dreaded agency of all, as far as Western leaders were concerned.

Liberal writers looked at it another way. "The springtime of a new world," cooed one excited Western journalist. "The start of a bedraggled but many-splendored thing . . . those young Bolsheviks are so full of hope and faith. . . . What a superb and courageous social experiment," wrote another.

Marc had cleverly placed himself in a position where all of his options remained open. His future was secure, no matter which card he chose to play.

THOUGH INITIALLY BLOODLESS, the Russian revolution soon erupted into a vicious civil war. Communication broke down, disease and famine were rampant, and friend took up arms against friend, brother against brother. Once begun, the internal bloodletting would not abate for years.

Miles from the scenes of the disorders, Marc and Katya grew frantic over the fate of their families. Neither had received word from them in months. Marc became convinced that he should return to the Ukraine and personally assess what was going on. But he preferred to go alone, fearing to take Katya because of the continuing dangers. By 1919, savage fighting between the opposing White and Red armies flared across the face of Russia, ravaging cities as well as the countryside. The Ukraine was engulfed in some of the worst battles. Lurid reports filtered through, of the indiscriminate massacre of local Jews by loosely disciplined White armies and marauding bands of Ukrainians, who used the anarchy and the confusion to slake their age-old thirst for Jewish blood.

The streets of Ukrainian villages and towns were being littered with Jewish bodies. Over 100,000 Jews were eventually butchered. The fetid stench of decaying corpses, the sight of plundered homes and battered women and children had already sent most able-bodied Jewish men (even those with a desire for neither combat nor politics) scurrying to join the Red Army— their one hope of survival. It only fanned the flames. "All Jews are Bolsheviks. All Bolsheviks are Jews!" taunted the White agitators. It was a cry that would echo clear across the world.

When he arrived in Kharkov, Marc heard dozens of eyewitness accounts. Tales of Jews being thrown into cellars and blown up by hand grenades; of bellies being slit open by bayonets and the victims left to rot in the gutters; of hands and noses being chopped off for sport and Jewish women raped repeatedly in the streets. Monstrous stories were circulating of screaming bands of mounted Cossacks shouting, "Kill the Jews to save Russia!" as they thundered on horseback into villages to rob, murder, and plunder. Brandishing their sabers and storming into Jewish homes, they cut down everyone in sight—the old and the crippled, those too scared to flee, pregnant women, and even nursing babies. Cleaning their bloody sabers in the snow, the Cossacks returned to strip the houses bare—breaking doors, smashing windows, tearing up floorboards, and slashing pillows in a rapacious search for hidden money. Clouds of feathers floated over the streets, as frenzied Cossacks dug inside mattresses for buried jewels or gold.

Survivors told of adults and children alike being tied to trees for target practice and women and children being whipped or stoned to death. Feelings ran so high that local non-Jewish doctors refused to tend to the Jewish wounded or sick.

It was always the same story. Only when the Red troops arrived did the terror end.

When Marc reached his parents' home, the doors were wide open and the inside empty. No one could say where the family had gone. Some thought the family members had probably been killed trying to flee north. Even later, after learning that they had managed to reach safety in Petrograd (formerly St. Petersburg), Marc was disconsolate. It was a trauma from which he never fully recovered. He never again was able to say to himself that he had done all in his power to prevent a recurrence of these outrages. And he could never forget that the Western nations had supplied the White armies with both armaments and manpower (the British alone personally trained 1,200 White Russian émigrés).

Ultimately, it was the indiscriminate atrocities of the White armies against the Russian peasantry that soured the interest of a war-weary Western alliance and caused it to withdraw support. But not before the Whites had successfully persuaded one British expeditionary force, headquartered in Taganrog, of the malevolent Jewish involvement in Bolshevism. In the autumn of 1919, the intelligence department of the British Military Mission (South Russia) was specifically requested to prepare a list of all Jewish Bolsheviks in the area, naming as many names as possible. Marked "secret," it buttressed its argument with a liberal sprinkling of alleged Jewish atrocities, all of which, though unsubstantiated, were included. It was later put on public record.

Though Marc's family escaped, his firsthand experience with the ravages of anti-Semitism on the community of his childhood became indelibly engraved in his mind. It provided the motivation for subsequent actions, to an extent that even he refused to acknowledge. From then on, although he would fiercely deny it, revenge played a part.

DEEPLY SHAKEN BY THIS VISIT to Kharkov, Marc was now more willing than ever to offer his services to the Bolsheviks. He placed himself entirely at their disposal. But their primary need was not for doctors, they explained. They were desperately short of influential and valuable contacts stationed abroad. The allied intervention and the economic boycott had created a dire need for clothing, food, and drugs. Lack of even such basics as disinfectants and soap had made the control of typhus impossible. Tuberculosis was endemic. Two highly trained doctors such as he and Katya could be exceedingly useful in Italy in organizing a drive to obtain these supplies. The call was going out to sympathizers everywhere. (Thousands of miles away Max Rabinoff, a man still unknown to Marc, also heeded the call—but for different reasons. Taking time off from a talent search across Europe, he formed a corporation to buy up departing Allied war surplus goods to slip through to the Red Army.)

Since Marc was a physician, the Bolsheviks suggested an affiliation with the Russian Red Cross in Italy. The plan was to bolster the neutral image of this organization by making certain it also assisted the destitute White refugees who were daily pouring onto Italian shores. Explaining the true nature of the game, the Bolsheviks disclosed to Marc that such contact could simultaneously provide an invaluable channel for ongoing information about the Whites. Marc understood. He could be very useful indeed. Moreover, as a Red Cross official, he would be in a position to detail the atrocities of the White armies, without being accused of purveying propaganda. He was eager for the mission.

Within months of his return to Italy, the Italian socialists announced an all-out campaign to win diplomatic recognition for the new Russian regime and the "cessation of interference with the development of Soviet Russia." Having at least one country provide official diplomatic recognition for the new regime—which so far had been rejected by every other nation in the world—could improve the fearsome and negative Bolshevik image. Urged on by their Russian mentors, the Italian socialists even agreed to forge closer ties with the newly formed Communist International and to call themselves communists, not simply socialists. In turn, the Bolsheviks in Russia offered immeasurable help to their Italian counterparts in their own drive for political power.

It was a perfect moment for such an offer, even if it appeared that the new Russian regime had little in the way of practical tools to offer. The Italian scene was poised for change. The government was growing increasingly impotent. National pride had suffered a humiliating blow at the Versailles Peace Conference, following the end of World War I, receiving little in spoils for Italy's sacrifices. Italian workers, unable to cope with the spiraling inflation, vented their frustration in industrial, agricultural, and railway strikes. Communist agitation was particularly strong in the engineering and the metal trades. These companies had earned huge profits during the war and had not passed on any of these benefits to their employees. The communists, by far the most effective agitators, were also gaining support from thousands of maimed and disabled soldiers who were being discharged penniless, crippled, and unemployed from hospitals and left to wander aimlessly through the streets. The gentle Italian spirit was being pushed too far. Genoa, a hotbed of the most extreme groups, experienced the first of the most violent demonstrations.

Unrest reached its peak in Italy in September 1920. Some 500,000 workers took control of factories. A national communist government seemed poised to seize power. Moscow was ready and anxious to provide the know-how needed to tip the balance. The difficulty lay in holding a cohesive group together. Typically, the Italian communists were forever bickering among themselves.

Therefore, as the Bolsheviks organized their intelligence team in Moscow, including the leadership of the much-feared Cheka (forerunner of the GPU and responsible for foreign espionage and intelligence, as well as for internal security against counterrevolution and sabotage), Marc and Katya were recruited as key foreign operatives. They were in an ideal position to help win Italy to the communist camp. They could coordinate propaganda and friendship for the nascent Soviet regime in Russia. They could maintain surveillance over the growing community of White Russian émigrés, who were becoming a dangerous source of counterrevolutionary plots. As skilled physicians, they could infiltrate the Vatican—one of the most influential forces that was determined to crush Bolshevism. And they could compile dossiers on current Italian leaders, with the aim of persuading them to be on warmer terms with the new Russian regime. In this task, they would be aided by the fact that Italy traditionally relied upon Russian raw materials. And finally, the Bolsheviks were in need of a pair of highly trusted operatives to help lead a communist coup in Italy.

As for the local Italian Communist Party, its Comintern representatives demanded total obedience to the bosses in Moscow and complete control over daily functioning. This control was to be vested in a group of hand-picked local envoys. Local communists derisively called these agents their "Russian chaperones" but avoided antagonizing them since the Italian communists' own strength and funds emanated, in these earliest years, from Moscow. These local communists were particularly interested in the tantalizing hoards of imperial jewels that the Bolsheviks were busy confiscating from remaining members of Russian nobility and were smuggling into other countries, to obtain currency to finance their foreign operations.

Marc and Katya were becoming first among equals, as, meanwhile, the entire West seemed on the brink of accepting Bolshevism. Postwar agitation was on the rise in country after country. The Red epidemic was indeed spreading. Katya plunged wholeheartedly into the work. It was her contribution to a new and better world. Marc had additional motives. It was a perfect opportunity to start building his own political future.

THE PICTURESQUE CHEFTEL VILLA and sanatorium, perched on a palm-shaded hillside overlooking the iridescent blue of the Mediterranean, was near the center of the small and sparkling Italian Riviera resort of Nervi. With its bracing sea air, Nervi was ideal for the health of its patients. The Italian Riviera had also become a busy crossroads for all manner of Russian émigrés. It was only about a hundred miles east of the French Riviera, where dozens of White Russians now made their home. Many passed through Nervi on their way to visit relatives and friends in Rome—the most exclusive White Russian community of them all—or to meet these same friends to spend relaxing days together by the sea.

Under the guise of an "associate" with the Russian Red Cross, Marc made sure he was the physician to be repeatedly called upon by White Russian refugees who were still fleeing the Russian homeland. The Whites trusted a Red Cross doctor, a doctor who could speak their own language. They unburdened themselves. When they went to him with medical problems, he learned far more than he needed to diagnose a course of treatment. He learned the names of their leaders, their plans, their liaison activities with the White armies. He learned about their counterrevolutionary teams in Paris and those concealed inside Russia.

Marc listened intently as the White Russians came to tell him about their mental anguish as well—the anguish of the émigré determined to go home. He heard of plots in collaboration with the Paris community to filter agents back into Russia, to harness anti-Bolshevik feeling as part of a plan to return to power (which they were so certain would shortly happen that they squandered their money with foolish abandon). He carefully noted the names of these agents. Later, the émigrés could never understand why so many of their spies disappeared without a trace.

At the same time, he took delight in seducing an exceptionally beautiful member of the Russian nobility. Through her unwitting collaboration, he stole compromising papers that were intended to abort a Bolshevik attempt to sign an important commercial treaty with Italy. The trade treaty, one of the first in Europe, was consummated.

When Vatslav Vorovsky, the first Bolshevik envoy to Italy, arrived at the border in 1921 with a conspicuous trunk filled with imperial jewels to finance propaganda (deflecting its confiscation on the grounds of diplomatic immunity), Marc quietly suggested an ideal hiding place for the gems. Because the fascists were already chasing the communists up and down the peninsula and ransacking their headquarters, it might be safer, Marc suggested, to keep the jewels in a place even the fascist jackboots would never dare to tread: a sanatorium, a sanctuary of healing. The jewels were hidden in a medicine chest labeled "Dangerous Drugs: Keep Out."

Marc was never a man to overlook an opportunity to promote his own political career. So he passed the word to his old friend Chicherin, now the Soviet foreign minister, who was heading the first official Bolshevik delegation to an international conference held in Genoa in 1922, that nearby lived an old comrade. Because of Chicherin's acute hypochondria, it was important that he could avail himself of the services of a local physician who had his own hospital facilities and who was also a trusted comrade. Chicherin was ecstatic. He left indebted to this thoughtful doctor, this dear friend.

At other times, Marc traveled to the sun-drenched piazzas of Rome to slip inconspicuously in and out of the Vatican for more than just medical reasons. Drawing certain cardinals into a carefully contrived spell, he patiently cemented the time-honored bond between doctor and patient so that he could manipulate Their Most Esteemed Excellencies when the occasion warranted. Like the moment when he dropped a hint that perhaps the Vatican was showing a most un-Christian face toward the Russian people by supporting the economic blockade. While conscientiously ministering to an ecclesiastical ailment, he quietly commented that as a member of the Red Cross, he was appalled to see innocent peasants starve. Surely the Catholic Church could not have intended this.

Knowing that these clergymen were mustering all the powers of the Catholic Church to overthrow this new godless regime, he was not going to let them get away with it. History had taught him that popes could topple thrones and make and unmake kings. If he listened carefully to more than just an ecclesiastical heartbeat, if he listened to their whisperings, their deliberations, he could learn before anyone else of their latest plan of assault upon the despised "Bolshies." And he could funnel this information back to Moscow for quick counteraction.

On other occasions, he alerted the cardinals to the danger of interrupting the important medical research work of the renowned Dr. Pavlov, due to a lack of animals on which to conduct experiments. He begged their Most Eminent Sirs to donate hundreds of baboons in the name of science to keep Pavlov's work alive. The baboons were donated. The world heard of how the Bolsheviks were nurturing talent, rather than thwarting it. Surely, they could not be as uncivilized and evil as rumor implied.

Late in 1922, negotiating once again at the Vatican on behalf of the Russian Red Cross, Marc persuaded the Catholic Church to funnel postwar famine relief aid through him, their personal and trusted friend. Having done so, he was now ready for his most audacious coup of all—diverting thousands of dollars' worth of these medical supplies for the direct use of the Bolsheviks. The Vatican had been anxious to spread its influence and undermine the Dreaded Reds by reminding the peasants with each and every mercy shipment that the new regime could not supply their needs. But the Lord and His Church always had the means.

However, in carrying out this confiscation, Marc incurred the wrath of a man he would continue to battle for years—Father Edmund A. Walsh, an American Jesuit priest who became the founder of the renowned School of Foreign Service at Georgetown University in Washington, D.C.

A year earlier, while serving with America's own famine relief administrator in Moscow, Father Walsh had been invited by Pope Pius XI to head an upcoming Vatican aid mission to Russia. He was an ideal choice. Father Walsh never could stomach the Bolsheviks, even from the beginning. The feeling was mutual. They held a profound distrust for one another and not without cause. Walsh had a keen eye, a piercing intellect, and a no-nonsense attitude. He understood the implications of such a regime better than almost any other Westerner. Bolshevism, he concluded, was simply old-fashioned imperialism dressed in a new red coat. What troubled him most was its emphasis on godlessness, an approach that had been designed to free the Russian masses from the clutches of the Russian Orthodox Church and an accompanying aversion to change. But from Father Walsh's viewpoint, it would challenge the centuries-old hold that Christianity had exercised over the uneducated masses.

For their part, the Bolsheviks mistrusted the motives of the Catholic relief effort led by Father Walsh. They fully understood that he was supposed to use his position to lobby on behalf of Catholic properties and interests. But they also knew there was more. The crumbling of the Russian Orthodox Church under the Bolsheviks had provided the Roman Catholic Church with a rare opportunity to increase its influence in a land where Catholicism had ceased its dominance centuries earlier. No envoy could handle this job better than Father Walsh: a tough negotiator, a sophisticated and subtle missionary, and an excellent administrator.

Walsh's encounter with Marc began in the early months of 1923. That was the year the Vatican had agreed to ship a large consignment of medical supplies to the Moscow headquarters of the Soviet Department of Health. It had been agreed in advance that the consignment, to be purchased in Berlin for a million lire, was to be placed directly under the care and the auspices of Marc—a man the Vatican felt by this time it could trust. Upon arrival in Moscow, the consignment was to be divided up into two parts: one half destined directly for Vatican relief stations and other to come directly under the jurisdiction of the Soviet Department of Health, to be distributed where it saw fit, but still with a semblance of Vatican control, and, of course, with the Vatican stamp clearly visible on all the crates.

The Bolsheviks were not wrong concerning the propaganda motives of the Vatican. But they could play the game just as well. And they had their man ready to do the job. By April, a furious Father Walsh was writing to tell the Vatican that half the shipment had been sent directly to such distant places as Daghestan and Kharkov without any of the recipients being aware that it came from Catholic relief services. The half that was to have been sent directly to the Catholic mission in Moscow had never been delivered. But Walsh was still hopeful, he said, that the Russian Red Cross (under Marc's influence) would keep its word.

Come September, Walsh's patience was exhausted. During all this time, the GPU had constantly interrogated members of his household. They clapped his housekeeper in jail, and the authorities were closing him out of a building he had hoped to acquire as a residence and offices in Moscow (and had even paid large sums of money out of Catholic funds to repair). In turn, the Bolsheviks complained to the Vatican that Walsh was rude and intolerant in all his dealings and never tried to understand their difficulties.

It was all too much for the indomitable Father Walsh. Soon afterward, he left Russia—which, of course, was exactly what the Bolsheviks intended all along. Even his negotiations on behalf of Catholic interests failed. The new Soviet government refused to entertain any petitions until the Vatican officially recognized its regime—a move the Bolsheviks felt would go far to influence other nations.

Walsh never forgot his eighteen months inside Soviet Russia. He wrote and preached against communism for the remainder of his life. He was also determined to exact personal revenge on Marc. But he was not in a hurry. He could wait.

Meanwhile, other matters claimed Marc's attention—most especially, the lightning takeover of Italy by Mussolini and his black shirts. Promising to bring order out of the chaos, they had triumphed in no small measure because the local communists had refused to cease their incessant squabbling.

Of broader implication for Marc's personal future was the unexpected death of an important comrade.

ON A RAINY NIGHT IN ROME in May 1923, Marc was awakened from a sound sleep in the small hours by an urgent rap at the door. A colleague from the Russian Red Cross had come to deliver horrifying news. Their good friend and a leading comrade in Italy, the Bolshevik envoy Vatslav Vorovsky, had been shot and killed while attending an international conference in Lausanne, Switzerland.

Vorovsky was dining leisurely with two associates in the main restaurant of the Hotel Cecil in Lausanne, where the participants were staying, when a young man sauntered into the restaurant alone. He inspected them all closely, while glancing repeatedly at a newspaper picture he held in his hand. The man—later identified as Maurice Conradi, a White émigré—sat down not too far away and ordered a glass of brandy from the waiter. At the same time, he inquired whether the three men at the corner table by the window were indeed the three Bolsheviks in the newspaper photo. Examining the photo, the waiter assured Conradi that they were. Conradi gulped down two more glasses of brandy before jumping up and striding quickly toward Vorovsky's table. He drew a revolver and fired six shots at point-blank range.

The first two hit Vorovsky in the head. He slumped to the floor. The next two shots slammed into his companion, Ahrens, chief of the Russian Telegraph Agency in Italy—one bullet in the lung, the other in the leg. The last two hit the third member of the group in the chest—a man called Brilkovsky, who was Ahrens's assistant.

As soon as Conradi fired the last shot, he began walking rapidly toward the exit. "This is my revenge," he shouted. "I have done my task. Now call the police." Whereupon he lit a cigarette and sat down in the foyer to await arrest.

The stunned waiters rushed over to the table and found Vorovsky dead. Ahrens and Brilkovsky were still alive, though lying unconscious on the floor. Ambulances were called, and the two survivors were rushed to hospital. The police arrived and took Conradi into custody. Many people later insisted that there had been collusion between the police and Conradi, since Conradi seemed overly eager to be arrested. Moreover, he was eventually acquitted, even though everyone in the restaurant witnessed the deed.

Back in the restaurant, there was total confusion. The remainder of the Russian delegation alerted both Moscow and the rest of the Bolsheviks' representatives in Italy, fearful that the shooting might be part of a broader counterrevolutionary plot. Marc was ordered to travel immediately to Lausanne; his presence was needed as a trusted physician to help care for his two wounded comrades and to assist with certain other matters—not the least of which was a deposit of 15 million Swiss francs that Vorovsky had just collected from the sale of a remaining trunkload of jewels. Vorovsky had prudently locked the proceeds away in a local safe deposit box before coming to dinner. The money was earmarked for propaganda purposes in Switzerland.

It was pelting rain that fateful night. Marc was drenched by the time he reached the station in Rome. He boarded the first train heading north, not even waiting for an international express. He could find neither a sleeping car nor a swifter train. He had to sit up all night, and it was almost noon by the time he arrived at the hotel in Lausanne.

The rain had not abated, pouring as relentlessly in Lausanne as it had the night before in Rome. What was worse, Marc cut himself twice while shaving with cold water on the bouncing train. Feeling chilled and miserable, he arrived at the hotel to find a photographer about to take a picture of the chief mourners around the coffin. They all looked neat, glum, and dutifully funereal. By contrast, the normally impeccable Marc was a mess. Nevertheless, he dashed into the room to respectfully join the picture-taking session, without even having time to remove his sodden raincoat.

Marc stood there, engrossed in thought. Were any embarrassing papers still in Vorovsky's room in the hotel? What about the safe deposit box? How might he gain access? Even more important, what impact would Vorovsky's death have upon his own future? Could he turn it to some advantage? Or would he be blamed for not having prior knowledge of the murder plot?

Fortunately, he managed to retrieve Vorovsky's papers, along with the rest of the envoy's belongings, before the room was sealed by the police. But the bank notes in the safe deposit box were never recovered. The Swiss authorities refused to allow Marc access, offering a variety of technical legal excuses.

Marc's colleagues pressed him to return to Moscow with the rest of the delegates to take part in an impressive martyr's funeral for Vorovsky. Marc accompanied the entourage on a special train. He knew he should be there in person, in case there was a lot of explaining to do or a vacuum to fill.

It was a grand affair, the most elaborate event of its kind yet staged by the Bolsheviks. By the time the train pulled slowly into the station in the heart of Moscow, the three-mile route leading to Red Square was teeming with people—a crowd estimated at over 250,000. It was a balmy May day and everybody was out, gathering for what promised to be more like a spring festival than a funeral.

So shaken was the regime by the assassination of such a senior official that a statue was hurriedly commissioned to stand (as a tragic reminder of capitalist treachery) in front of the Foreign Office, in a small plaza that would henceforth be known as Vorovsky Square. The sculptor fashioned an unusually sensitive piece of work, portraying Vorovsky with his well-known scruffy appearance, even down to the fine detail of the shapeless trousers he loved to wear and which were forever sagging from a loose belt around his waist.

Marc's trip to Moscow that spring turned out to be more than just a time to pay respects. Dozens of close relatives, former revolutionaries, and friends were rising high and fast in Lenin's government. Political power far greater than Marc could ever wield in Italy now seemed attainable.

He had been right about the vacuum. The civil war had decimated the ranks of the most able and loyal party members, and it had become a problem to find qualified comrades to fill crucial government posts. They needed men like Marc—urgently.

He was not sure. Aside from Germany, no country had formally recognized the Soviet regime. It was still weak. It had many enemies. Vorovsky's blatant assassination was only a small but significant example of this, as was the disgraceful collusion of the Swiss police. Although conditions were improving daily, life remained hard and unattractive, compared to the comforts and the pleasures he enjoyed in Italy. It was still early.

He hedged. He had additional work to complete in Italy, now that Vorovsky was gone. Surely, they did not wish him to leave until he had secured diplomatic recognition—if not from the influential Vatican, then from the Italian government. Mussolini was a pragmatic man, Marc insisted. Despite his hostility to local communists, Mussolini recognized the advantages of making friends with the Soviet regime. He needed the trade and the raw materials. If the local communists could not beat the fascists at this particular moment, Marc pointed out, they could gain some advantage from them— recognition being the ideal. And there was always a chance of a communist countercoup. He did not feel it would benefit the party to leave quite yet.

He was aware that if he returned with either recognition or a communist takeover to his credit, his own position in the party would be greatly enhanced.

He left on the next train, determined to return to Italy. He still could not buy a decent meal in Moscow or have a suit tailored to his taste. A popular joke making the rounds in Moscow that year told about the headquarters of the Commission for the Electrification of All Russia. Affixed to the door to its offices was the following notice: "Please knock. The electric bell does not work." And the beat-up Ford that an influential doctor friend used to ferry Marc to the station had its front doors tied shut with a clothesline.

IN FEBRUARY OF the following year, Italy became the second nation to formally recognize the Soviet government. The establishment of one of the first Soviet embassies abroad aroused wide curiosity in diplomatic circles. What kind of man would the Dreaded Reds appoint as ambassador?

R. Graham, ambassador at the British embassy in Rome, walked cautiously over to take a look and pay his respects. When he later described the newly arrived Soviet ambassador and his entourage in a confidential dispatch to London, Graham observed contemptuously that the ambassador was short and fat and had trouble speaking French, the diplomatic language of the era. Graham was also suspicious of the vast number of clerks and other employees lingering about, most of whom apparently had two or three aliases. And he did not like the fact that they had used their new diplomatic status to raise a large red flag outside the building that had become a rallying point for local communists. The authorities were obliged to ask them to take it down, which they reluctantly did. In short, these Bolsheviks were uncouth and crude in their exercise of diplomatic privilege.

Communist propaganda was also emanating from their embassy, an additional report noted. And the staff mixed freely with members of the local Communist Party. In fact, even the Russian Red Cross moved into the embassy soon after it opened, to do precisely what Graham feared most: foster agitation. The economy had not improved, and it looked as if the fascists might fall.

The climax came only weeks later. On a warm morning in June, Matteoti, a left-leaning leader highly critical of Mussolini, was kidnapped in broad daylight on the streets of Rome by a group of angry young fascists. When Matteoti was found dead some weeks later in a nearby suburb, the fascist plot backfired. The mild-mannered Italians did not care for brutal political murder. Workers demonstrated in an outpouring of rage—encouraged, of course, by the local communists. Mussolini's downfall appeared imminent.

After the Matteoti incident, Mussolini held back no longer. He launched a massive campaign to rid the country of its communist agitators. Nevertheless, the Bolsheviks were jubilant. Within months of Italian recognition, ten other countries followed suit. Even the famine was abating. Economic conditions were improving markedly. Marc was summoned once again to forgo the warm sunshine and the sweet life of Italy for the opportunity to join the party's inner circle in Moscow. His colleagues lured him back with the promise of power and prestige. Marc reconsidered, weighing his decision in light of Mussolini's iron grip over Italy, which now heralded the temporary closure of his nonmedical activities.

He accepted. But he was not at all pleased to relinquish his current mistress—a beautiful, blond-haired member of the White Russian community. He had grown increasingly fond of her. Initially, he suggested that she join him in Moscow, fearing that Bolshevik Russia had little compensatory talent to offer. At first she agreed, but at the last moment she yielded to common sense and family pressure. Her relatives blanched at the discovery of such an insane idea. She had aristocratic blood, they argued. It was certain death!

The Communist Party had been shrewd. It was gaining not one but two hard-working and loyal functionaries. What Marc and Katya failed to perceive was how much they were losing by giving up their Italian base.

Rather, they deluded themselves that Moscow had become a charming and vibrant city. Freed from the constraints of czarism and civil war, the people were flexing their cultural muscles once again. Under NEP, the New Economic Policy—the small private enterprise program that Lenin had temporary enfranchised to quickly lift the country back onto its feet—zest had returned to both city and countryside. Crops were being carefully tended, as peasants leased or worked their own small holdings for personal profit. Eager merchants were packing the stores with attractive new merchandise.

In place of the grass-grown streets, run-down houses, and boarded-up shops of a few years earlier, there was the hum of traffic, the smell of fresh paint and plaster, and attractive new cafés. Markets were filled with fresh dairy products, fruits, and vegetables. In the center of the city, the office buildings again churned with business. The Cheftels could purchase their beloved Italian delicacies and attend the theater, concerts, the opera, and the ballet. They could dine at good restaurants and hear people laugh.

Officially, Marc was given the position of chief of the Bureau of Foreign Information at the Department of Health, a public relations title that would cloak a multitude of GPU tasks. Katya was offered a consulting post at a large Moscow hospital. They were permitted to ship their Italian furniture and belongings—a significant concession, considering the deliberate lack of personal possessions that characterized the households of the early Bolsheviks. Dangled before Marc's ambitious eyes was the promise of higher office, most probably a prestigious posting abroad.

Ten

Every foreigner interested in learning at first hand something of the health work in Russia soon becomes acquainted with the Bureau of Foreign Information at the Department of Health. Its courteous director, Dr. Scheftel [sic], takes great pains to help visitors to understand the organization of Soviet state medicine and to see as many of the Russian health institutions as they wish. But his first duties are really in the reverse direction, for his bureau is the link between the Commissariat of Health and the medical work of the Western World. All the foreign medical journals of importance pass through this bureau. Connections are made with representatives of Russian health work in England, America, Germany, Italy, France and other countries. Foreign specialists and delegations are invited and welcomed to Russian medical congresses. A Russian-German Medical Journal is published in cooperation with a group of German scientists; and membership is maintained in the Section of Hygiene of the League of Nations and other international organizations.

Anna Haines, *Health Work in Soviet Russia*

NATURALLY, ANNA HAINES could not know the true nature of Marc's work. He was in an ideal position to conduct a subtle form of internal counterintelligence, organizing close surveillance and manipulating the goals of all foreign relief groups. Many of these groups were indulging in espionage themselves, using famine relief programs as a political and intelligence weapon against the Bolsheviks. From his position, Marc could also dispatch a variety of undercover agents to foreign shores, purportedly on medical and public health missions. One of the easiest ways to bypass the vexing problem of visas and provide agents with maximum cover was to accept invitations to medical gatherings. It was up to Marc to coordinate these "medical" missions and select suitable candidates for the assignments.

Anna Haines was a lively and dedicated American Quaker woman, a trained nurse from Moorestown, New Jersey. She had come to Russia shortly after the revolution as part of the Russian Relief Mission of the American Friends Service Committee of Philadelphia. She was deeply sincere about carrying out her Quaker beliefs of fulfilling God's purposes on earth through active service to humanity. She had been particularly attracted to the communist creed because of its avowed pacifism and after personally witnessing the senseless slaughter of World War I. She had even been willing to overlook its antireligious campaigns after discovering that the new communist Russia had built the world's first socialized health service. No other nation had come so near, she noted, or so quickly to a realization of these ideals. Plagued by a paucity of funds, an inability to buy costly foreign drugs, and a lack of equipment and facilities, the Bolsheviks had nevertheless forged ahead with their goal of providing health care and education to all Russians, regardless of social class or ethnic group. It was an uplifting contrast to what she saw around her in America, especially in the tenements of the inner city among recent immigrants.

In this respect, the Quaker mission differed from those of all other relief groups. The other groups' activities were generally employed for political ends. Consider the work of the American Relief Administration (ARA), which, like the American Red Cross, was at work in Russia at this time. It fed only children at its designated feeding stations; no adults were included, in order not to keep any adult "Bolshies" alive. No matter that many of these starving adults were simple peasants with scant understanding of politics in general. The ARA, also known as the Hoover Mission, was particularly suspect from the start. Under the guise of a merciful crusade, it was found to be nothing but a smokescreen to infiltrate the country and pave the way for a Bolshevik collapse, after which these American officials would be ideally positioned to ensure the installation of a new regime that would support the profit-centered goals of American capitalism. Moreover, its organizers made no secret of the fact that they blatantly sought commercial concessions in return for large contributions of food and supplies.

By contrast, the Quakers fed and clothed as many adults and children as possible, seeking only to genuinely serve their fellow human beings. So warmly was everyone disposed toward these kindly people wearing gray uniforms—with their nautical flair and the red and black insignias on the left sleeves—that Quakers inspired more admiration than any other relief group.

Quaker beliefs were so closely allied with the humanitarian ideals of communism that the Bolsheviks sought to harness Quaker goodwill; the highly respected Quaker organization could help win friends for their own crusade of diplomatic recognition and international friendship. Maksim Litvinov, later the Soviet foreign minister, suggested to the American Quakers as early as 1919 that they could do more for starving Russians by encouraging the United States to end its trade sanctions and shipping blockade than by all manner of local relief work.

So it was up to the "courteous" Dr. Cheftel to help make friends with the Friends. It was also up to him to encourage and champion those Quaker work projects that particularly fulfilled party needs—at this time playing upon the Quaker penchant for initiating revenue-generating industries by fostering embroidery, weaving, and sewing skills. These articles could readily be sold abroad for valuable foreign currency, which was vitally needed to keep afloat the fledgling republic and Comintern. As Marc's office handled much of the foreign money that came in for relief aid, it was his responsibility to make sure it was distributed to the best advantage of the party. Dozens of foreign medical personnel were seeking visas to enter Soviet Russia, anxious for a firsthand view of the "exemplary" health system. Again, it was up to Marc, as senior GPU man in charge of foreign visitors in the health field, to decide which of them might best serve the interests of the Bolsheviks. The fear of capitalist spies slipping in disguised as medical personnel was widespread.

Sensing a small but ideal propaganda outlet in hostile America, Marc encouraged Anna Haines to prepare her highly complimentary book on the Soviet Health Service. Writing personal letters of introduction, he made it possible for her to enter hospitals, day-care centers, sanatoria, and other medical institutions in the most remote parts of the country. Essentially, he was providing permission that Anna Haines seemed blissfully unaware could only have been authorized and signed by Marc himself in his dual capacity as a senior GPU official and the chief foreign coordinator at the health department.

To Anna Haines, her beloved, soft-spoken Dr. Cheftel always remained a kindly, dedicated doctor and a helpful friend. None of her reports to her superiors at the Friends' headquarters in Philadelphia showed any indication that she suspected more. Dorice White, a fiery Irish Quaker, and Nancy Babb, yet another tireless and enterprising American Quaker working at the combined British-American Moscow offices of the Friends, also seemed to have been captivated by the gentle Dr. Cheftel. He employed his seductive, masculine charms to the fullest with these young women. In due course, they would also serve his personal ambitions.

Over time, an enchanting, irrepressible tease developed between them—a flirtation of the most innocent sort. It was just enough for Marc to win their love, trust, and loyalty but never (ever) anything more. His attitude was consistently one of impeccable manners and scrupulously polite behavior.

They spent a good deal of leisure time socializing—but always in the company of Katya. Visits to each others' homes were frequent and cordial. They discussed the many health problems affecting Russia. The Quaker women told of their difficulties in obtaining supplies and dealing with the bureaucracy. Marc offered to help out, over and above his official duties. It seemed to them as if he took a deep personal interest in their difficulties, using his miraculous ability to cut through bureaucratic red tape whenever the need arose.

Anna Haines chattered incessantly about her pet project—developing a nurses' training school and a children's hospital in Moscow along modern American lines. But the hard-pressed American Quakers, having difficulty raising volunteer funds for their regular Russian mission, were unable to finance the project themselves, though they gave it their full moral backing. Haines hoped that Marc could prepare the way by obtaining the necessary permission. He did. Official approval for a nurses' school came through in the incredibly short period of three weeks from the date of application. However, further agreements and details were held up until the Quakers could sort out their finances.

In time, the Quaker women came to consider Marc a true Friend. Such a close relationship was important. The London Quaker office was uneasy over the possibility that the combined British-American mission would be closed down by the authorities, following a temporary diplomatic schism between Britain and the Soviet Union in the mid-1920s. As a reprisal for a British action ordering all Russian agencies from its soil, the Russians accused the British missions inside Russia of harboring spies—and were shutting these down as a counteraction. The London Quakers were so worried about being expelled that they sent a special appeal to Dorice White, encouraging her to maintain and cement her friendship with Marc. They implied that it might just be an ideal time to offer him a favor in return for his efforts on their behalf.

Marc already knew what that favor would be.

He had realized soon after he returned to Moscow that normalizing relations with the United States was so important to the new regime that a tour of duty inside America could become the ideal route to a higher political office. Besides, it offered an attractive change of scene. What was more, if he needed an upstanding sponsor, then the British-American Quaker mission— increasingly anxious to please him—might just be persuaded to come to his assistance. Its international integrity and standing could open many doors.

For the moment he merely hinted. Were he actually in the United States, he told them, he could probably accomplish so much more for their mission by directly approaching American philanthropists. Perhaps, he added, he could also find a private backer for Anna Haines's school. He confided (the ladies loved a confidence) that he was already working quietly within his department on a plan to send a Soviet representative to the United States to purchase up-to-date medical equipment and supplies. If the department chose him to be that person, he could work simultaneously to promote Quaker interests.

Marc was laying his groundwork with exceptional skill. Artfully, he added a dash of healthy fear. At his home late one night, he confided to the ladies that the Quakers had indeed been placed on the blacklist of British-affiliated organizations slated for expulsion, suggesting that his personal reports to the authorities on the continued value of their mission would do much to sway the final decision. The ladies exchanged doleful glances. They pleaded for help. Any favor they could do for him . . .

His strategy had worked.

The opportunity for enlisting Quaker support for his own needs would not be long in coming.

ABOVE ALL ELSE in the mid-1920s, Bolshevik Russia remained obsessed with its lack of diplomatic success inside the United States. It had failed on all counts. It had failed to win official recognition, already accorded by all the Western European powers and indeed by much of the rest of the world. It had failed in every attempt to organize a viable Communist Party inside America. And it had failed to obtain visas for those representatives it desperately wanted to slip into the country to promote trade, absorb technical know-how, and build the kind of rapport that was necessary as a prelude to recognition.

There was no doubt that the Bolsheviks needed American technology and credits if they were ever going to fulfill the goals of their upcoming Five-Year Plan. They also feared the encroachment of the Japanese upon the Asiatic mainland, if their new regime—and indeed the entire nation—

remained weak much longer. American diplomatic recognition could imply American displeasure with Japan and could compel the Japanese to abort their expansionist activities.

Originally, the Bolsheviks had hoped, somewhat naively, that recognition would come through the lobbying pressure of American workers and their trade unions, anxious to support the world's first workers' government. When this did not materialize, another tactic had to be adopted. The obvious alternative was to gnaw away at capitalism from the other end and to ease into recognition by currying favor with big business. Politics makes strange bedfellows.

Big business, with its voracious appetite for profit, could be seduced into making trade deals with the new Soviet Russia that would require substantial amounts of credit from major American bankers. Out of concern for the viability of such agreements, so the theory went, these companies and their bankers would then exert pressure on Washington for recognition. Only through recognition and the establishment of normal diplomatic relations could such contracts be placed on a sound fiscal basis. For those not swayed by the trade argument, the Bolsheviks would try to emphasize the danger of the Japanese thrust and its possible threat to world peace.

A few Americans had already been active in trying to stimulate trade between the two countries since early in the decade. Prominent among these were Max Rabinoff, with his virtual monopoly on Russian culture and music, and his friend Alex Gomberg. Gomberg had been negotiating for the revival of the cotton trade, so important prior to the revolution. He had organized the All Russian Textile Syndicate in 1923, later to be run by the Russians themselves. But the giant of them all was indubitably Dr. Armand Hammer, the man who had originally gained the pencil concession in Soviet Russia and the one who would eventually win some of the most lucrative contracts and concessions. All three had the ear of industrialists, bankers, senators, and congressmen, many of whom were alarmed at the millions of dollars in trade being lost because of the obstinacy of their own government.

Denied the opportunity to develop legitimate trade or discuss their severe financial problems on a diplomatic level, the Bolsheviks turned in the meantime to subterfuge. In 1922, they set up a quasi-American corporation in accordance with New York State laws—the Amtorg Trading Corporation. Its aim was to secure bank loans and credit denied to a nonrecognized country. Amtorg became the nerve center for all Russian-American dealings, both legitimate and undercover. But it remained a small-scale and even bumbling operation.

Its earliest projects included activity to evade—among other things—the embargo on military hardware that the State Department had put in place to impede trade and prevent technical assistance from reaching the feared Reds—and, more specifically, to foreclose any legitimate opportunity for the Bolsheviks to earn badly needed dollars. Thus the "rackets," as they came to be called, grew year by year. At first, Amtorg employed ordinary circumvention tactics. There was, for example, the contract to purchase four hundred Liberty aircraft engines that were prohibited to them as war material. Originally built during World War I and already considered obsolete, they were of value to the Russians for training pilots. Through collaborating American companies, the government was persuaded to approve the sale on condition that the engines went to a local buyer. This "buyer" then shipped them to a Detroit factory for overhaul and modernization. Afterward, they were placed on a freighter under the guise of machine parts bound for Europe, though they ultimately ended up in the Soviet Union, fully overhauled and ready for use.

Similar plans were hatched for the purchase of other vitally needed products also under embargo. Steel, the Bolsheviks discovered, could also be readily purchased through collaborating Americans, who would ship it to Europe. Such "laundered" cargo would then be slipped piecemeal into Soviet Russia via a variety of European ports.

So-called advertising was a great dollar earner. Any firm doing business with the Soviets was gently advised to advertise its products in Russian publications. The tacit understanding was that should they refuse, the Russians might well take their business elsewhere. Naturally, advertising in a state-controlled economy where consumers had no choice was pure nonsense. But income from the source accumulated substantially. The earnings were retained in the country of origin to finance the printing and the dissemination of propaganda, thus, in effect, making the Americans pay for the subversive literature of a foreign power.

Another excellent dollar source was the Russian people. Scores of frightened Russians with relatives in America were terrorized into writing letters saying that they were starving and destitute and needed any cash the relative could spare. The dollars were then intercepted, remaining inside the United States to bolster its central communist hard currency fund. Only worthless rubles ever reached the relatives in Russia.

Thousands of dollars were also collected from Russian performers living in the West. Compelled to regularly donate a percentage of their earnings, they were warned that unless they paid up, reprisals would be meted out to family members left behind. Chaliapin would be one of the first to cry out publicly at this blatant form of extortion. Artists who toured abroad were never paid in local currency. Instead, a lump sum was collected by the company manager and was transferred once again to the central hard currency fund. The performers were paid in rubles upon their return.

Gold and jewelry squeezed out of Russian citizens by torture, threat, and blackmail—the notorious *valuta* trade—became a particularly fruitful source of dollars. Bags of jewels and diamonds confiscated from individuals were constantly being carried abroad by couriers and agents and sold in the foreign markets for the best possible price. The dealers preferred not to inquire about the origin of the gems.

Some of those connected with the Amtorg trading organization did not even bother to involve themselves in the legitimate end of the business. They were full-time undercover agents with a variety of tasks: intercepting messages between White Russian émigré groups through paid informers inside the telegraph and telephone company, stealing letters from mailboxes, analyzing military information, and using Amtorg's offices as a central command post for Comintern and its underground political activities.

Inventing convincing jobs to obtain the necessary visas that would bring these operatives into the country required skill and imagination. One particular clerk who was needed in the cipher department gained entry as a representative of a phantom sugar trust to make sugar purchases. Another expert in the same department was purportedly a salesman in Russian furs. Yet another described himself as a representative of what turned out to be a nonexistent trade cartel. Then there was the man who obtained entry ostensibly to sign a contract with the Ford Motor Company. Actually, he spent six months touring arsenals and military installations, obtaining blueprints, and recording much of what he saw on film. Aviation and weaponry experts streamed into the United States with requests to study technical engineering on a commercial level.

Lesser intelligence agents, usually women, managed to obtain their visas by insisting they were indispensable to Amtorg as Russian-speaking secretaries.

As soon as the State Department, through pressure from American industry, became more willing to accept these trade envoys, the visas most likely to be granted were those being provided to "buyers" from Soviet Russia, who were presumably coming in with multimillion-dollar orders in their portfolios. This became the favored ruse of the later 1920s.

And when all else failed, there was always the Canadian route. These Russians would arrive by ship in New York harbor and request transit papers to continue by train to Montreal. At one of the stations along the way, they would then simply get off. The authorities rarely checked into these disappearances. Once the Russians were safely inside the United States, it was an easy task for them to disappear into the immigrant community.

By the mid-1920s the concept of normalizing international trade with the Bolsheviks—and reaping the resulting profits—finally attracted the attention of the largest corporations and banks. Henry Ford was eager to supply technical assistance to the Soviet automobile and tractor industries. International Harvester saw a market in farm machinery. Remington-Rand expected a large demand for typewriters. General Electric was in a position to supply the power plants and the hydro-electrification needed for the Five-Year Plan. The Burlington, Chicago, and Quincy Railroad saw a future in improving rail links. The list grew daily. Thus, despite Washington's reluctance and the revolutionary designs of Comintern, as well as the mayhem emanating from Amtorg's offices in New York, it was clearly time for a political change of heart.

But political action in a democracy can move as slowly as rush hour traffic in the city. Meanwhile, the Bolsheviks were getting more and more impatient for action. Whenever they applied for visas for many of the Soviets' lesser trade and diplomatic officials to come to the United States, they were still being turned away by an obdurate State Department, which insisted that without formal recognition, there was no need for envoys. Therefore, the Soviets concluded that a man with a suitable cover would have to be found to coordinate their operations inside the United States, with the immediate aim of steering a carefully chartered course toward recognition. The job required someone with impressive personal credentials and unquestioned loyalty. Someone the Bolsheviks had trusted from way back. But it also had to be someone who could establish a different command center, immune to the suspicion that surrounded their current headquarters in the Amtorg offices in New York.

As soon as Marc heard what was in the wind, he made sure his name was presented for consideration. And due to the friendships he had fostered, even prior to the revolution, he now had just the right contacts in high places. Moreover, one of his close boyhood friends, Dr. Mikhail Gurevitch, was at that moment in New York expressing delight at the possibility of working with such an able comrade.

Working both ends, Marc quietly outlined the reasons why he would be ideal for this post. He was second to none in stealth and intrigue, he boasted, recalling his adroit handling of party affairs in Italy. He possessed an outstanding cover. And he felt certain the Quakers would apply on his behalf, further adding to the credibility of this cover, as this way it would appear as if they were anxious for him to come to the United States to promote *their* interests, rather than it being a regime-sponsored venture.

For weeks Marc lobbied feverishly, making the rounds of all his best contacts. In the end, everyone agreed there were unique advantages in using a man like Marc. Having spent almost all of his adult life in Italy, he was known only as a physician, though he held an excellent reputation among his colleagues as an intelligence coordinator whose information and activities had always been thorough and indispensable. His skill at recruiting local agents and organizing a base for the development of an Italian Communist Party had been recognized as nothing short of genius. His personal GPU appraisal files had proven exceedingly accurate—he had a genuine talent for understanding the motivation of people—so he would be highly useful as a supervisor of Soviet personnel currently in the United States. And his special gifts for subtle political manipulation made him a perfect coordinator for the American recognition drive. Moreover, only someone vested with the supreme authority of a senior GPU official could command the necessary power to redirect all the other U.S. operations to this end—at least, for now.

Finally, at a time when so many Americans disdainfully regarded Bolsheviks as crude upstarts, here was a physician who had the distinguished bearing of a patrician. Posing as a man on a simple humanitarian mission, he could also improve their image immeasurably. And his natural inclination toward the arts made him an ideal emissary at the salon of Max Rabinoff, where bankers, businessmen, politicians, and diplomats, as well as artists and performers, met at the highest level. Marc filled the bill on all counts.

The next challenge was to select the reason why he might be seeking entry right now. Since the Quakers wanted him to purchase medical supplies for their own mission, as did the Health Department, that seemed a perfect rationale. If he added a need to study advanced developments in public health, then the combination would permit him to travel around the country for extended periods of time without arousing suspicion. It would also free him to negotiate with American corporations, persuading as many of them as possible of the value of Russian trade and commerce. These conversations could become an effective form of lobbying. At the same time, his superiors suggested, he could also compile intimate dossiers on influential Americans to see how each one might be engaged more specifically in the recognition effort.

And what about a suitable headquarters? As Marc had been attached to the Russian Red Cross mission in Italy, it seemed natural to attach him to its American counterpart. Since the Russian Red Cross already maintained separate offices in New York City, it could become an ideal command post. Katya could handle the basic medical chores to assuage the Quakers and U.S. immigration. Thus an appearance now and then among the American medical community would be all that was necessary for Marc to keep his cover viable.

The actual work of the Russian Red Cross was being handled at this juncture by a Russian-born American named Dr. David Dubrowsky. Marc was told that Dubrowsky would continue to manage the day-to-day affairs of a mission that, in truth, was just another dollar-earning enterprise. Millions of dollars in veterans' benefits were being collected each year for dependent parents, widows, and children of deceased members of the U.S. armed forces who happened to reside in Russia. Of course, the relative in question would see only a handful of worthless rubles, the dollars themselves having been diverted to the central coffers.

The mission was also relentlessly scrutinizing the obituary columns of all major American newspapers to track Russian immigrants who had died without American heirs. The mission employed an American law firm, then applied for the money in the name of surviving relatives in Soviet Russia. These applications were granted without much delay or difficulty by well-intentioned courts, the relative in question realizing only a nominal payment in rubles. Later, a similar scheme evolved to collect money ostensibly for Russian relatives actually named in wills. Application would be made by a legal representative of the Soviet government on behalf of the relative in question. In the end, the same results would apply. Advertisements were also regularly being placed in newspapers throughout the country, suggesting that immigrants contact the mission regarding the location of lost relatives—in reality, a ruse to smoke out potential future legacies, which indeed it did.

But Dr. Dubrowsky was not pleased to hear that Moscow was sending a high-level GPU agent to use his Red Cross offices as a cover. A senior GPU official hovering about was the last thing Dubrowsky needed, although the man who walked into his offices in February 1928 was as much of a surprise to Dubrowsky as he was to everybody else.

What was kept from Dubrowsky was the principal reason that a man like Marc had been selected. If certain powerful Americans were to be reached, humored, coerced, and even blackmailed for the purpose of gaining U.S. recognition of Soviet Russia, the Bolsheviks needed an exceptional operator who was not inclined to talk too much.

DUBROWSKY'S MISGIVINGS NOTWITHSTANDING, the wheels were set in motion. The only problems remaining were the hard-to-obtain visas for the Cheftels. And that was left to Marc. To win the assignment, he was told that he had to personally obtain the visas.

Anxious to leave as rapidly as possible, Marc wasted no time. He telephoned Dorice White at the small British-American Quaker office in the heart of Moscow. He told her that his Department of Health had approved a proposal for him to personally travel to the United States to purchase medical supplies. And he was hoping that at the same time, he and Katya could study some of the newest American programs in public health. If the Quakers would help him on the small but essential matter of a visa, he would work diligently on their behalf while in America. But he was worried, he told Dorice, because he had recently heard of a Soviet physician being refused a visa for no apparent reason. Therefore, he thought it would be a good idea if the Quakers—with their good name—applied for him. He dropped the tantalizing hint that he would likewise pressure his own government to reopen the matter of Russian visas for Rebecca and Harry Timbres, a Quaker couple recently denied entry.

A delighted Dorice White dashed off an urgent letter to the American Friends' Service Committee at their headquarters in Philadelphia, imploring them to contact Washington right away about visas for the Cheftels. Dorice agreed to personally guarantee that both members of the couple were dedicated physicians. About two months later, she got what she sought. And when she told Marc, she received such a warm hug that it took her quite by surprise.

Miraculously, only the medical backgrounds of these two physicians had been picked up by the American authorities. It helped enormously that Anna Haines—now back in America and about to publish her book on Russia—gave a personal reference. It turned the tumultuous festivities that October, commemorating the tenth anniversary of the revolution, into a personal celebration at the Cheftel apartment. The emergence of Stalin was privately derided as a temporary aberration in the grander Bolshevik scheme of things.

Dorice White (fifth from left), who helped Marc with a visa to the U.S., at a conference of the British-American Quaker mission in the Soviet Union, late 1920s.

Marc and Katya reasoned that by the time they returned to Russia, Stalin would probably be ousted or consigned to an insignificant job.

The following weeks were devoted to exhaustive briefings. The only other outstanding matter was the coincidental arrival of Dr. Alan Gregg, associate director of medical education at the Rockefeller Foundation in New York. Marc had decided that Dr. Gregg could prove valuable in a number of ways. Therefore, he temporarily postponed their departure in order to meet the man personally.

Dr. Gregg, a shrewd and observant administrator, was a respected official of the foundation. Some months earlier, its international board had decided to offer assistance to the struggling people of Soviet Russia. It was up to Dr. Gregg to evaluate the best method of handling such aid, and his recommendations tended to be readily approved. Not a man to be easily fooled, he decided within a matter of days that Marc was "a little too affable" for comfort. But he was sufficiently impressed with the social experiment to suggest how Marc might influence American minds. Marc had wanted to know if printing a promotional brochure would be wise, but Gregg told him not to do so. It would be more effective, he said, to write articles for academic journals and arrange for reprints. Marc, he noted in his journal, seemed in an inordinate hurry to tell him what specific medical help the foundation might provide, which Gregg had found a trifle unsettling. As an aside, Gregg also noted how Marc had rebuked him for using the traditional parting phrase "Adios" in a godless environment.

As usual, Marc obtained what he was really seeking—a promise of an introduction from the Rockefeller Foundation to the American medical community. It would open all manner of doors, as well as cloak Katya and him in an extra mantle of respectability. It would further enable him to personally plead for medical fellowships for his comrades, one of the cornerstones of his program for the United States. Seven fellowships per year, the number tentatively agreed upon by Marc and Gregg, meant the introduction of seven operatives at large in the United States without cost to the Soviets. To enhance Marc's own image and set up his own personal cadre of line agents, the fellowship program would be given primacy over any other aid that Marc requested.

Marc and Katya left Moscow early in December and stopped in Berlin and Paris before boarding the *Paris*, the French luxury liner, late in January 1928, bound for New York. Their Quaker friend Anna Haines offered to meet them when the liner docked. She was anxious to make sure there were no problems.

At forty-three, Marc was in the prime of his political life. If he succeeded at this assignment, he could finally step out from the shadows into the diplomatic limelight. Thus, despite the glamour of the high life he was about to enter, his intention was to remain devoted to the work at hand.

But he knew it would not be easy. They were arriving in America at the tail end of a decade-long party: the era of Douglas Fairbanks, Greta Garbo, Rudolph Valentino, Dixieland jazz, Charlie Chaplin, walking sticks, high hats and spats, wild stock speculation, paper profits, mass motoring, parlor games, bizarre celebrations, the new musical theater, the Charleston, the fox trot, Max Rabinoff, and those magnificent goggled men in their flying machines. Al Jolson had just made the first talking musical. Mickey Mouse was coming to life on the drawing boards of Walt Disney's workshop. Everyone was dancing to the tunes of George Gershwin, Jerome Kern, and Irving Berlin.

For Marc, this hedonistic boom-or-bust society, this overblown pleasure balloon that was about to explode, offered him a chance to enjoy the fun while it lasted. And if and when that balloon burst, there would be a golden opportunity to convert the forsaken American dream into a Bolshevik one.

139

Eleven

DESPITE A BRUTALLY ROUGH CROSSING that confined Katya to her cabin, the first day of February 1928—a gray and bitterly cold morning—found the Cheftels, both early risers, on the windswept deck, eager for their first glimpse of the Manhattan skyline. As they disembarked, they found Anna Haines, as promised, waiting at the pier. She whisked them by taxi to the Park Central Hotel, where they had reservations—made for them by a colleague attached to the Russian Red Cross mission in New York.

Haines was expecting them to move into a rental apartment in Philadelphia near the headquarters of the Friends—an idea Marc had put forward in Moscow to help encourage the Quakers to support the visa applications. So Haines looked dismayed when they told her that Marc had important work to do in New York, and that in the interim his superiors in Moscow had arranged for him to be attached to the Russian Red Cross mission in New York—an already established outpost of Soviet health work in the United States.

Early the next morning, Marc set out to hunt for an apartment for himself and Katya and to visit his proposed offices. Katya remained in bed, regaining her strength after her severe bout with seasickness. In line with the rigid party rules governing all foreign operatives, the Cheftels had to select modest living quarters. They were required to conduct their lives with almost ascetic simplicity: no accumulation of property, no significant acquisitions, aside from personal clothing; and (officially) no dancing and carousing of any sort. The fox trot and the tango, the rage of the decade, were decried in the Soviet Union as "signs of bourgeois degeneracy." They were not even allowed to buy a car; they could only rent one when absolutely needed. To purchase furniture was forbidden, so they had to rent a furnished apartment.

The rule book also required all Soviet representatives abroad to reside in reasonable proximity to one another. In New York, this meant the Upper West Side of Manhattan. The Cheftels rented their first and only American apartment at the northern end of the neighborhood, in a building known as 710 Riverside Drive. Marc made certain they were listed in the telephone book. As soon as the telephone company assigned him a number—in this case, Broadhurst 2579—he notified his comrades and contacts. The Cheftels were pleased and anxious to be recognized as Russian physicians and delighted if anyone chose to contact them in this capacity. Though Marc indulged himself in a chic address with a river view, the apartment itself was simple: a small living room, a dining room, one bedroom, a kitchen, and a bath.

But having a bon vivant like Marc at the head of the political police in the United States meant that the taboo against dancing would never be imposed—at least, not on his watch—nor, for that matter, would any of the other rules forbidding the enjoyment of "bourgeois pleasures." Although he overlooked this paragraph in the code of behavior during his stay, he was adamant about maintaining rigid party discipline. He kept a close eye on Soviet personnel in every other respect. His very presence at a party, a meeting or simply a casual social gathering was known to send shudders of uneasiness throughout the room. Everyone knew that what went into Marc's files and ultimately back to Moscow dictated that individual's future. In some cases, it could even cost people their lives. It became the reason why Max's friends would say that "the Amtorg crowd never relaxes."

Nevertheless, reporting on people was not his style. He preferred a more subtle approach. Since he was as much an advocate of preventing trouble as he was of preventive medicine, he immediately decided to teach at the small Amtorg school where the children of Bolshevik agents were being educated. As it was part of his responsibility to make certain that the children of staff members received regular communist indoctrination, it was viewed as a natural extension of his duties. But it was also an ideal way to learn about the people under him. Since none of the agents would dare voice their feelings openly, even to a friend, the only way he could hope to discover what was really going on—in their homes, as well as in their minds—was from their children. Casually, during their uninhibited banter between each other, the children would reveal what was being discussed in the house. It was an old technique. But he was so convinced of its efficacy that he personally taught classes at the school once each week for over a year.

Within a few weeks, Marc was beginning to administer and coordinate the array of GPU assignments for which trained lower-level operatives were already on the scene: maintaining confidential files on all Russian employees for job efficiency and continued loyalty to the communist cause; and surveillance of the White Russian émigré community, which had been highly successful in forging compromising documents about the Bolsheviks that it would then release to the press. He also had to monitor the behavior of Russian performers and the kickback operation. And he had to transmit to Moscow the reams of information gleaned from numerous military, technical, and political sources gathered through a complex network of couriers, cipher telegrams, and cipher letters. Furthermore, he had to improve the effectiveness of the Comintern operation, with regard to its propaganda activities and goal of increased party membership. And finally, he had to generate a climate that would foster U.S. recognition of Soviet Russia by wooing the political and the business communities.

Though others already on the job would have more specific tasks, in that peculiar Bolshevik hierarchy where the top GPU man wielded power far in excess of all other government departments, Marc Cheftel—for the duration of his stay in New York—was vested with the authority and responsibility for overall control of all covert activities.

Their master spy.

DURING THESE EARLY DAYS, it did not take Marc long to appreciate that his effectiveness could be hampered by a lack of familiarity with the English language and the customs of the American people. While he had moved about with ease in Italy, he felt insecure and inhibited in New York.

He would need help. Two contacts were therefore vital to him. First and foremost was Max Rabinoff, who lived conveniently enough on West Sixty-seventh Street, not too far from his own Riverside Drive apartment. Through Max and his legion of influential friends, admirers, and hangers-on, Marc hoped to ease his way into the American business and political mainstream—quickly. The second was Dubrowsky, whose Red Cross offices were to become Marc's center of operations. A resident of the United States since 1905 and an American citizen who intended to stay in the United States indefinitely (though anxious to serve Bolshevism), Dubrowsky had become the permanent fixture in this Bolshevik outpost. He knew his way around better than any incoming agent like Marc.

Even though Marc realized that Dubrowsky would be of invaluable assistance, the site of the Russian Red Cross offices on lower Fifth Avenue was troubling. It was a defect Marc chose to correct within a month of his arrival. From the very first morning when he pushed his way through the revolving doors of the marble lobby and glanced at the roster of names on the wall directory, he knew he was in the worst possible spot.

He was surrounded by offices of left-wing unions, radical groups, and various other communist agencies. Marc immediately recognized the unfortunate implications of such an address. Worse still, it was constantly being watched by police, as it was on the fringes of Union Square, where the most violent demonstrations had already taken place. This building, along with one used by Amtorg only a few blocks north along Fifth Avenue, had been tagged by the authorities and even lay people as the center for communist agitation and propaganda throughout the entire country. Mulling it over, Marc concluded that it was amateurish to centralize activities in this way.

To become even marginally effective, he had to move to a far less conspicuous location. Besides, the shabby neighborhood did not appeal to him. What he needed was a fashionable Midtown location—an address that mirrored the distinctive manner in which he intended to conduct his mission and his life.

But where?

Since he was also assigned to supervise the surveillance of White Russian émigrés and to monitor the behavior of outspoken Russian performers, it did not take him long to recognize that the most logical spot would be West Fifty-seventh Street. Heart of the concert world and home of the recently opened Russian Tea Room, it was the favored meeting point where White Russian café society hobnobbed with Russian entertainers and certain closet Reds who were playing a duplicitous game—a veritable den of spies, intriguers, plotters, and informers of all persuasions and motivations who swapped stories and information over blinis, zakuski, vodka, and tea. Adjacent to Carnegie Hall, West Fifty-seventh Street was also the hub of Russian cultural and social life. And it was within walking distance from the offices of Max Rabinoff on the fringe of Central Park West. Besides, compared to the factory fumes and the gloom of Union Square, this Midtown street was an oasis of fine restaurants, theaters, and boutiques.

One bright morning a few days later Marc decided to walk the entire length of West Fifty-seventh Street to see what he could find—a hike that soon brought him to the corner of Broadway where he noticed a new multistory building nearing completion. The address: 1776 Broadway. 1776? he mused. 1776? Wasn't that the date of America's own revolution? A highly appropriate address, he chuckled to himself. A quick word with the leasing office led him to understand that many suites were still available. Never having enjoyed the fun of working at the top of a skyscraper, he could not resist the temptation of an upper-floor location. Even the view he chose was pure Cheftel. From the window of suite 1608/9, the one he ultimately selected, he could clearly see the main entrance to Carnegie Hall, watch people stream in and out of the Russian Tea Room, and enjoy the spectacular sweep of the Manhattan skyline. When he felt like relaxing, he could whirl his chair to the side and peer over the lower rooftops to delight in the greenery and the bucolic vistas offered by Central Park just two blocks to the north.

It took only a matter of days to arrange a lease. Soon he was back downtown at the offices of the Russian Red Cross, informing Dubrowsky of the decision.

"Get your hat, Dadzie," he joked with a sly grin, using the doctor's nickname. "Pack everything. We're moving at the end of the month."

"The end of the month? This month?"

"That's right. To a new building opposite Carnegie Hall."

"It will cost double the rent."

"Then you'll just have to raise some extra Red Cross donations."

"And our present lease?"

"Forget it. Revolutions were never won by people who worried about trifles."

The next matter on Marc's agenda during the spring of 1928 was his introduction to the Rabinoff household, which, he had told Dubrowsky—a long-time friend of the Rabinoffs—he wanted to be arranged as soon as possible. Max Rabinoff's house was where Marc intended to exercise his most irresistible charm.

As Max moved seamlessly in both Russian and American circles, no other man provided a better climate for liaison between the two nations. Due to the influential position Max held in the opera and concert world, neither politician, government official, nor corporate executive had to fear for his reputation as being possible "parlor pink" by attending Max's parties. Bankers and businessmen mingled freely with baritones and ballerinas without being stigmatized as Bolshevik sympathizers. Carefully fostered and channeled in the right direction, Max could be the source of a thousand successes. Max's house was also a favorite meeting ground for those artistic émigrés who had White Russian friends. So regular visits could provide a bonanza of information.

The wooing of Max by the Bolsheviks had been a delicate operation from the outset. Max had originally come to the attention of the Bolshevik leadership during the early days of the Russian civil war, and he had profited handsomely from his neat piece of gun running. Acquiring World War I surplus munitions from the departing British and American forces in Europe had been a maneuver that had left Max with considerable wealth, a sense of social accomplishment, and Bolshevik gratitude. Armed with a resulting U.S. government title of "adviser on Russian affairs," he then topped the gun running by becoming one of the Bolsheviks' earliest business intermediaries, entrusted with the first shipment of Soviet gold into the United States; his respected credentials were considered the best way of getting it in.

Max and Bluet's visits to Russia had been carefully stage-managed, so that neither of them had the slightest opportunity to view the unsavory side of contemporary Russian life. Though Max was undoubtedly aware of more than he cared to admit, he was also a businessman. He was smart enough to look the other way and remain prudently silent when his own purse was at risk. He knew perfectly well that his concession for Russian talent and trade could be withdrawn at any moment. He therefore played along, although his garrulous nature and reputation for a violent temper (and scant discretion with women) caused the wary Bolsheviks to restrict their dealings with him. He was too erratic, too talkative, too abrasive. After U.S. recognition of Soviet Russia in 1933, Maksim Litvinov, the Russian foreign minister, declined to have any further dealings with Max. But in 1928, Max was still useful.

Marc was fully aware that Max and his wide circle could provide the key to many important, yet unopened, doors. But just as Marc was setting up channels that would help him accomplish his mission, an unforeseen circumstance threatened to abort his stay in the United States.

Marc's original visa, and that of Katya, had been granted for only six months. It was due to expire at the end of July 1928. Although he had applied as early as May for an extension, he had not been able to obtain the necessary commitments. Visa extensions were not readily granted to Russian officials. By the end of June, he concluded that his best hope again lay with some intervention by the Friends.

He sent an urgent appeal to Philadelphia, bolstering his case by outlining the important conferences that he and Katya had attended and the contacts they had both made in the field of public health. He pointed out that all these meetings were but a prelude to a fuller understanding of recent medical advances, as he and Katya became more familiar with the English language and worked more closely with certain experts. "It is for this reason," he begged, "that I must ask for your assistance in helping me obtain an extension of our visas." He ended by asking them to take up the request directly with the appropriate authorities.

The Quakers were impressed but replied that they could do little to help. Still, trying to soften the blow, they invited the Cheftels to Philadelphia for a few days to take their minds off their troubles and chat about old times. Marc declined, saying that he wanted to send his wife to the mountains as soon as possible because she suffered from heart disease. It was crucial, he wrote, for Katya to leave the city during the very hot months. Immediately after the extensions came in, he said, he planned to put her on the train. Was there nothing more they could do about the visas?

Katya's "heart disease" must have been short-lived because she was known as a robust woman to all her friends and would be appointed the director of a hospital on her return to Moscow—hardly the life of an ailing or frail woman.

As there was still no response on the eve of the date of the visas' expiration, an exasperated Marc sat down in his Riverside Drive apartment to type a personal letter to Wilbur Thomas, director of the Philadelphia office of the Friends. He begged Thomas to send a cable to the commissioner of immigration. And once again, Marc pointed to the medical emergency that could occur if Katya had to linger in the hot city waiting for clearance.

Marc continued to fret for the remainder of the summer while a ponderous bureaucracy deliberated. Not until September did he receive official word that he and Katya could remain for another year, with the possibility of further extensions being more readily granted.

On receipt of the good news, he quickly dashed off a note thanking Thomas. In it, he told Thomas that he had just received word that the Rockefeller Foundation had voted to sponsor a program of fellowships for Soviet medical personnel in the United States. He added that he was now in a position to keep his promise to Anna Haines. He would truly do all he could to develop a training school for nurses in Soviet Russia.

Marc was in high spirits. He had won a double victory that summer. He had overcome his visa problem and obtained the coveted fellowships, despite Dr. Gregg's ambivalence. And the introduction of seven Bolshevik agitators, paid for by the Americans themselves, would substantially burnish Marc's image and career with his superiors in Moscow.

Dr. Gregg had not been fooled, even though he had been overruled. He warned the Rockefeller Foundation officials that they should continue to run the program only while they remained convinced that the Fellows were not indulging in any political chicanery. Though the fellowship program was inaugurated almost immediately afterward, it would flounder three years later. The person who blew the whistle was one of the more conscientious Russian Fellows, who angrily revealed to the American authorities that he had been ordered home early by the GPU because he had concentrated solely on his medical studies and had not carried out his propaganda assignments. The news created an uproar at the foundation.

EVEN MORE IMPORTANT MATTERS absorbed Marc during the fall of 1928 after he overcame the visa extension issue. The lure of trade for the purposes of recognition could not have been developing better. Titans of American industry were falling over one another for contracts. Since larger corporations and certain high-profile banks had given their nods of approval, smaller companies were now anxious to jump into Russian trade. But without a formal agreement between the governments, usurious rates were being charged for loans. Nothing short of full recognition or a formal trade agreement could alleviate the problem.

Though public sentiment in the United States was now running in favor of recognition, there was a clear lack of enthusiasm among politicians, who still fretted over the Red Menace. And President Hoover remained heavily influenced by old friends who were furious that the incoming Bolsheviks had never compensated them for assets lost at the time of the revolution. With the Bolsheviks clearly unable to repay these old debts, Hoover remained adamant, even though they pointed out that the restrictive credit and trade practices being enforced by the American government made immediate repayment impossible. The punitive economic blockade of a few years earlier, plus the resulting famine and the civil war, had bled them financially dry. Besides, they insisted, no government in history that was formed as a result of a popular uprising ever assumed the obligations of its predecessor—and that was even true of the United States after its break with England. Hoover remained unimpressed. A compromise offer to pay the debts off piecemeal as part of a larger agreement was also rejected, with the State Department pointing out that similar promises made by other nations had never been kept.

Among Marc's foremost antagonists and the one most damaging to his cause was Father Walsh. Marc's old nemesis was now back in the United States, running his School of Foreign Service at Georgetown University.

By mustering the power of the Catholic Church, as well as influential political friends, Walsh had become an effective opponent of recognition. Brandishing hair-raising stories about Bolshevik godlessness, the sacking of churches, and moral decay, he crisscrossed America making speeches that railed against the Red Menace and its worldwide ambitions. Father Walsh also had the ear of a well-intentioned young congressman named Hamilton Fish Jr., who led a congressional faction that strongly opposed recognition.

A third faction that widely opposed recognition consisted of women's groups. The women had been outraged by reports giving credence to the fact that the new regime fostered casual sex. They had been appalled by alarming reports of the "Bolshies" promoting such heresies as trial marriage, coed discussions of intimate sexual matters, divorce on demand, abortion, and atheism. The Bolsheviks, they charged, were nothing but a band of sex maniacs—the women worse than the men.

Even the voice of Senator William E. Borah of Idaho, trumpeting the threat to world peace of continued nonrecognition, particularly in light of Japanese expansion and European instability, fell upon deaf ears. The efforts of Senator William H. King of Utah, a friend of the Rabinoffs, urging at least a trade agreement, proved fruitless as well. While big business surged ahead, the political impasse remained.

Marc's summer tour "on organization work for the Russian public health service," as he put it to his Quaker friends in Philadelphia, had actually been designed to ascertain the strength of communist party cells scattered around the country. He was anxious to channel their energies toward recruitment, rather than toward rabble rousing. He was troubled, ironically enough, by the success of the communist agitators in organizing widespread demonstrations. These were gaining momentum due to the developing economic downturn. And they might unfortunately provide Walsh with further ammunition. Such agitation had therefore become counterproductive to the diplomatic climate he wished to foster. His efforts that summer were designed to cool this agitation, gently redirecting communist leaders into a drive to infiltrate their best and most trusted members into the growing ranks of the unemployed and disenchanted groups. Mass demonstrations could be left to a later date.

Marc's further aim was to employ the data he had been compiling on key American figures to point out the hypocrisy of their stand. It was vital that Russian officials and negotiators who came over be armed with the most complete information. Worth noting, as a product of Marc's propaganda work that fall, was a book called *Why Recognize Russia?* by Louis Fischer, the well-known American writer on Bolshevik affairs and an intimate friend of Marc and Bluet. Fischer singled out Father Walsh for an exceptionally bitter diatribe. It was published late in 1931, a little more than a year after Fischer had held a number of meetings with Marc.

But the most compelling argument that began to emerge was the loss of those valuable oil, timber, and fishing concessions in the vast Russian hinterlands. The Europeans were rapidly making commercial inroads in these areas. Even a scandal that suggested that some of the leading senators were being bribed by Soviet agents failed to hold back the momentum. Whatever the truth, big business was desperately in need of new markets. And politicians, worried about their out-of-work constituents, needed to generate jobs. More and more congressional representatives therefore changed their stance and agreed, albeit reluctantly, that it would be worth pursuing recognition for economic reasons alone. The lure of profits and votes, as always, guided politics.

Twelve

BLUET MADE ONLY a minor impression upon Marc when they first met. His energies in the Rabinoff household were focused primarily upon Max. Only later, as he began to know her better, did Marc appreciate what a storehouse of information she possessed on many people—performers, Amtorg couples, bankers, and politicians. It was inside information of the kind that was rarely available. She was indeed a treasure, and Marc was determined to mine that treasure for all it was worth.

So when he first suggested that they meet for lunch, he was happy that she was flattered by the invitation. Her manner led him to believe that she thought it was probably a matter of business. Bluet merely misjudged the business.

Marc did not know much about her then, except that she and Max were apparently having marital troubles. She gave the impression of being deeply unhappy, despite her vivacious personality. He had discovered from mutual friends that although she was a provocative coquette, she was not promiscuous, despite various rumors about lovers circulating from time to time. However, her availability was not his initial concern.

So began the lunches, which Marc never hurried. They were working lunches. Or so he had originally intended. What he had not anticipated was the tremendous sexual allure of this delicate French woman. It threw him off balance. Against his better judgment, against all his inner resolutions to the contrary, he found himself determined to have her. Reason and a well-developed sense of caution should have warned him not to take the risk at this crucial time in his career—to cuckold a valued contact right in the man's own home. He did not even stop to consider the devastating consequences of Max's wrath should Max find out. Marc was now absolutely crazed for Bluet. His emotions had trumped his good sense. But luck was on Marc's side, at least in the beginning. Max was in such deep financial trouble that he was totally oblivious to what was happening. Even so, two problems confronted Marc late in 1929 that would have far-reaching consequences.

The first was his personal bogey—anti-Semitism. Just prior to his departure from Russia, he became conscious of a resurgence of anti-Jewish sentiment. It had been highlighted by the Trotsky-Stalin leadership struggle. Stalin turned the fight into an anti-Jewish slur campaign, and it spread from Trotsky to Trotsky's closest Jewish associates, Zinoviev and Kamenev. The persecution of the small private traders who had flourished in the brief postrevolutionary period of free enterprise (NEP) also took on an anti-Semitic quality. A great proportion of the traders had been Jews.

But its severity did not truly seep into Marc's consciousness until he was personally affected by its onslaught. Always a man of his word, Marc had worked conscientiously for months to help Anna Haines transform her long-postponed dream of a nurses' training school and a children's hospital into a reality. He was determined to ram it through by exercising his full influence as a senior GPU official. After several conferences with Thomas, the head of the Quakers' Philadelphia office, Marc drew up a ten-part contract setting forth the amended responsibilities and obligations of both sides. Within weeks, he obtained the signatures of the commissar of health and the head of the Department for the Protection of Motherhood and Infancy, at whose institute the program would be organized.

It was at this point that news he could scarcely believe reached him in New York. Back in Moscow, Dorice White had been forced to notify both the London office of the Quakers and their Philadelphia headquarters that no Jewish women from America would be acceptable as teachers. "I think this is probably quite wise," she noted, "as there is such a strong anti-Semitic feeling in the Institute that it might add to difficulties if the foreign nurses were Jewish."

For a man as sensitive as Marc to this particular issue, it was a shattering blow. He had never given up his personal agenda for the Jews. He would not lift a finger to help the project after this. Neither the nurses' training school nor the children's hospital ever materialized.

There was no question that the eradication of anti-Semitism had long been a driving force in Marc's continued loyalty to the communist cause. If communism had failed to prevent its resurgence, then perhaps his own future could do with some reevaluation. To find anti-Semitic behavior right on his doorstep, in his own department, was especially chilling.

That concern, together with a certain cynicism for the entire drift of the political scene under Stalin, soon caused Marc to fundamentally reconsider his position. He was appalled by stories of a barbaric upsurge in indiscriminate terror. He was uneasy over the possible repercussions from the murderous sweep of Stalin's collectivization drive. But from a distance, it was impossible to accurately measure the extent of the change. He also feared the implications of the subtle shifts in party positions that had ousted his crowd of Old Bolsheviks in favor of Stalin's hand-picked loyalists. The most ominous sign of all was Trotsky. He had just been kicked out of the country.

By early 1930, Marc was therefore not only laundering Red Cross funds for the Communist Party—a recognized part of his job—but also siphoning off money for an individual "Cheftel Defection Day" fund.

Marc had decided that the hardships he might face, if and when he was posted back in Moscow, were unacceptable. He had expected an easing of the austerity. But colleagues were arriving with alarming stories of a deterioration in housing, food, and lifestyle, particularly with the abrupt end of the NEP. Unless he could be assured of an immediate reassignment to another foreign post, Marc was not certain he wanted to return. But it was not a simple decision. To defect would mean an end to his chances of ever becoming an effective voice in the future of his nation and for the communist movement worldwide. What would he do then? Return to Italy? Practice medicine? With his inside knowledge, he doubted that he would even be left alive.

Making his decision even more tortuous was the recent demise of Grigory Bessedovsky.

GRIGORY BESSEDOVSKY WAS a career diplomat in his late thirties who had recently been appointed chargé d'affaires at the Russian embassy on the Rue de Grenelle in Paris. Very much the social democrat, Bessedovsky had also become alarmed by the direction of Soviet politics.

Like Marc, he was horrified by the latest maneuverings of Stalin, who already showed signs of becoming a latter-day Ivan the Terrible. Though Bessedovsky had led an exemplary diplomatic career, rising from obscurity to his present position in less than a decade, he had a slippery tongue. He was an intellectual and a thinker. Rather than remain quiet about his misgivings, Bessedovsky chose to air his grievances in public among his diplomatic friends. He also complained that some of his diplomatic initiatives, which made superb pragmatic sense for his country's foreign and economic policy, were being dismissed because of an internal power struggle in the Foreign Office back home.

Word soon drifted back to Moscow. His superiors politely suggested that he spend his upcoming vacation in Russia. Sensing trouble, Bessedovsky explained that he had already made other plans. He soon noticed the local GPU agents keeping close tabs on him.

Then early one morning in October 1929, as Bessedovsky was walking through the foyer of his Paris embassy, he spied a pair of enormous trunks being carted through the front entrance. No one seemed to know who had sent them. A few hours later, two men appeared in his outer office, asking to see him. Bidding his secretary to send them in, he quickly realized that they were GPU agents. They had been sent directly from Moscow to bring him back—immediately. He was asked to pack his belongings and leave quietly with them that same day.

Bessedovsky acted swiftly. The trunks he had seen that morning were surely large enough to contain a human body—maybe even two or three. And they could easily be whisked out of the country as diplomatic luggage without being subject to customs inspection. Apparently, he concluded, if he refused to go, the agents had orders to kill him, along with his wife and small son, and return them all to Moscow in those trunks. He knew far too much to be allowed to defect.

He asked the agents to excuse him for just a short while so that he could return to his living quarters and pack his things, then slipped nonchalantly into the foyer and made a dash for the front door. Tipped off by the GPU agents in advance, the doorman barred Bessedovsky's way, explaining that he had orders not to let Bessedovsky through. Bessedovsky turned on his heels and went upstairs to his room. Everyone then presumed he was busy packing.

But Bessedovsky was not yet beaten. Once inside the privacy of his rooms, he slid open a side window. Then he leaped down to an area of the garden where he could vault unnoticed over the embassy wall.

To reach the street, he needed to jump over two parallel walls. He was in such a state of panic that he achieved what he would later consider impossible. Outside the compound, he dashed frantically along the winding streets to the nearest police station. He rushed inside and breathlessly demanded personal protection and a police escort to remove his wife and son from the embassy. At first, the confused gendarme at the desk could not make out what it was all about. By the time an officer realized who Bessedovsky was—at that moment, the acting ambassador of Soviet Russia in France—the police knew they were facing a potentially embarrassing diplomatic incident. They would have to check elsewhere before doing anything.

Bessedovsky grew impatient. Legal matters were all very well, he stormed, but at that moment his wife and child were captive in the embassy and in danger. Would the gendarme return with him at once to save his young family from a fate those trunks assured him awaited them all? The gendarme waved his hands excitedly in the air. He protested that he could not enter a foreign embassy because it enjoyed diplomatic immunity.

Bessedovsky shot back. Surely the Paris police would be within their rights to enter if the lives of a woman and her child were at stake? The gendarme thought it over for a minute and bid Bessedovsky to wait. He hurried toward an inner office, muttering angrily under his breath.

Time was ticking by. Alone on a bench in the station reception hall, Bessedovsky grew frantic. Ultimately, the captain agreed to dispatch one of his men to the embassy for the sole purpose of removing Madame Bessedovsky and her child. The French police then took them all to the nearby Hotel Marigny, where they were held under protective custody.

Moscow immediately demanded the return of the entire family. This was refused. The French government argued that Bessedovsky had become a political refugee and was entitled to asylum. The matter rested there.

But the Russians were uneasy. Bessedovsky could seriously embarrass them if he decided to talk. Their fears proved justified. In December they compounded their folly by sentencing Bessedovsky to death in absentia for embezzling state funds—the classic charge for a defector. It boomeranged. Bessedovsky vowed to seek appropriate revenge. Shortly thereafter, a series of articles appeared in Paris newspapers, later condensed into a book called *Oui, J'Accuse* and translated into English as *Revelations of a Soviet Diplomat.* It was a bombshell—a source of extreme irritation to the Soviet government. In a chapter on Amtorg and the American operation, Bessedovsky exposed Marc. Bessedovsky denounced him as the chief of the GPU in the United States and the coordinator of all covert activities and even described Marc's entry under a false Red Cross cover.

The first American newspaper to publicize the Bessedovsky revelations was the Russian language daily, designed to reach the White émigré community. In January 1930, it published Bessedovsky's full account of Soviet activities inside the United States.

Since Marc regularly read the paper to keep in touch with the activities of the émigré community, he was one of the first to see the article. He was furious. It was just the kind of trouble he had hoped to avoid. Not unexpectedly, by midafternoon the telephones at his office and his home were ringing incessantly. Dozens of American reporters insisted upon interviews. His immediate reaction was to refuse to see anyone, in hopes that the story would die quickly. He instructed both his secretary and Katya to tell callers that he was unavailable.

He badly underestimated the tenacity of the American press, which hounded him as only newspaper reporters can. They turned up at his office and his apartment at all hours, until Marc realized that he had to do something.

He thought the matter over carefully. Several alternatives lay open to him. He could call a news conference and denounce Bessedovsky as a liar, which, he hoped, might close the matter for good. Or he could select a single newspaper and offer its representative an exclusive interview, thus ensuring minimum coverage. After at least one newspaper had printed an interview of this type, others would probably lose interest in the story. The hordes of reporters would be recalled. All Marc had to do was handle one reporter skillfully.

But which paper? In 1930, New York City had more than a dozen. Here again, his skill at intrigue and strategic thinking paid handsome dividends. Several hours of research soon gave him a detailed picture of the readership and the political shade of New York's many dailies. He knew he would have to avoid the serious press—the newspapers most likely read by people who knew him personally. He also feared the sensational tabloids, especially when handling a spy story. Finally, he decided upon the *Sun*, a conservative afternoon paper. He knew it had a far smaller readership than the morning press. The article might just be conveniently overlooked. The *Sun* was recognized for its appeal to middle-income conservatives. Max did not read the *Sun*. Bluet did not read the *Sun*. Neither did the party members nor the important business contacts he had been developing.

Therefore, a few days later, Marc called the editorial offices of the *Sun*. It was the *Sun*, after all, that had given wide coverage to Bessedovsky and the story of his sensational dash over the wall. It had also been hounding Marc more relentlessly than any of the other publications were.

The *Sun* was delighted with the scoop, promising to send a reporter early the next morning. Marc suggested his Broadway offices. This was important.

155

From the outset, he had arranged his office to provide visitors with the best possible image of his work. Medical diplomas hung on the walls. Health journals, magazines, and bulletins were casually strewn on chairs and tables and even on the floor. On his desk were letters, invitations, and announcements from numerous American medical and pharmaceutical organizations. Though Marc was normally a tidy man, that day his office was a concession to studied theatrics.

By the time the reporter knocked on the outer glass door, the scene was perfectly set. Marc graciously extended his hand and invited the reporter in. He motioned the reporter to sit in one of the easy chairs beside his desk. They began talking.

The interview was just what the good doctor had envisioned. After a scathing denunciation of Bessedovsky as a shabby swindler, Marc proceeded to explain in minute detail the importance of his American health mission and how detrimental such calumnies could be. It was not long before the reporter was thrown off track.

Later the next afternoon, picking up a copy of the *Sun* from a newsstand in the street, Marc could not conceal his delight. Tucked away on an inside page of the paper was the following article:

SOVIET AGENT MAKES DENIAL

Dr. Cheftel Not Engaged in Propaganda, He Says.

EXPLAINS NATURE OF HIS WORK

Is Making a Survey of Public Health Field.

Dr. Mark [*sic*] Cheftel, public health representative of the Union of Socialist Soviet Republics, who was named by George [*sic*] Bessedovsky, former Chargé D'Affaires at the Russian Embassy in Paris, as being the head of the Russian secret police in America and a man of mystery, made a public denial today that his mission in this country is one of espionage and propaganda, in an exclusive interview with the *Sun.*

Dr. Cheftel had been accused by Bessedovsky of being one of a series of secret agents who were operating in the United States while ostensibly engaged in innocent commercial missions. Others whom Bessedovsky, convicted of embezzlement by the Soviet courts, named as propagandists were officials of the Amtorg Trading Corporation. They have also denied the charges.

At the offices of the Russian Red Cross at 1776 Broadway, Dr. Cheftel, in the first interview which he has given since his arrival in this country over eighteen months ago, gave an account of his activities in America and described the nature of the public health campaign in which Soviet Russia is now engaged.

Before this, however, he paid his respects to George Bessedovsky. "Bessedovsky," said Cheftel, "is a thief and an embezzler, who robbed his own government and has been convicted of that crime. Must I reply to the charges of such a man? Must I interrupt my work to answer a man who is thoroughly disgraced and discredited by his own knavery?"

Dr. Cheftel paced the little private office excitedly, pausing to pick out of the air terms which might add to his limited English vocabulary in characterizing Bessedovsky. It was an outrage, Dr. Cheftel exclaimed, with some drama to his tones. He had at first decided not to see the *Sun* reporter at all, but on second thoughts had decided to.

"No, I will make no mystery. I will tell you what I do in America. Remember, however, that I am not making a report to you of my activities. I do not have to do that. But I have been so persistently annoyed by these muttered charges that I am a conspirator and a spy that I will answer them just this once," continued Dr. Cheftel.

"First let me tell you something of what public health work in Russia consists of. It is quite different from that which you have in America, where private philanthropy and public projects are found side by side. In its nature you will see the explanation of my mission in this country.

"Russian public health work of the present day is founded on definite principles. The first is centralization. That means that all agencies are under a single department of government, which controls expenditures and initiates projects throughout Russia. There is no duplication, as in America, where you will find, engaged in combating of one disease such as tuberculosis, a national organization, state organizations and city and village associations as well. In addition to these you will find several other organizations whose work touches upon the same disease or problem. In America you have governmental, philanthropic and commercial agencies fighting the same fight. Duplication cannot be avoided.

"In Russia where we have no surplus of well-trained doctors and nurses, we cannot afford to distribute our experts in that way, so we group them together in one governmental agency to fight one disease or to attack a single problem wherever it may arise.

"The second principle in our health work is that of mass participation. In Russia there are no millionaires to carry on the work for the benefit of others, nor are there great insurance companies which as a matter of sound business policy aid public health enterprises. Everyone

SOVIET AGENT MAKES DENIAL

Dr. Cheftel Not Engaged in Propaganda, He Says.

EXPLAINS NATURE OF HIS WORK

Is Making a Survey of Public Health Field. (H)

Dr. Mark Cheftel, public health representative of the Union of Socialist Soviet Republics, who was named by George Bessedowsky, former Charge d'Affaires at the Russian Embassy at Paris, as being the head of the Russian secret police in America and a man of mystery, made a public denial today that his mission in this country is one of espionage or propaganda, in an exclusive interview with The Sun.

Dr. Cheftel had been accused by Bessedowsky of being one of a series of secret agents who were operating in the United States while ostensibly engaged in innocent commercial missions. Others whom Bessedowsky,

From the interview Marc gave the New York Sun *to exonerate himself of charges of being a spy.*

must be made to take an interest. Thus a great part of our work is along educative lines. Russia, building for a new generation, wishes it to be a healthy one.

"Our third great problem is that of prophylaxis. We are doing our best to take care of those who are sick today, but we realize that it is even more important to prevent further epidemics and to remove any conditions which might in future prove to be a bar to a healthy state.

"American doctors have been visiting Russia continually during the past ten years and Russian medical men have been coming here. Most of them have come to study some particular disease. I am making a general survey of the public health field and am particularly interested in selecting hospital equipment and pharmaceutical equipment which can be used in Russia. It is part of my work to select this material which, under our principle of trade monopoly, is bought through the government through the Amtorg Trading Company. I have nothing to do with the actual purchase. I merely recommend what the government should buy.

"This is my only connection with Amtorg, which, I assure you, is not the organization of propagandists that Bessedovsky said it was, but a hard-working group of businessmen. Peter Bogdanov, its new head, is an able and thorough business executive. Any of your American businessmen who know the company will testify to its reputation."

Marc had handled it with finesse and just the proper dose of righteous indignation. He had also been correct. Bluet did not read it. Max did not read it. Nor did anyone else with whom he had dealings. The episode was now closed.

IT IS QUITE POSSIBLE THAT this one small incident would have been quickly forgotten had it not been that soon afterward Marc's name appeared on the front page of every newspaper in the city, along with the names of other Amtorg officials. Grover Whalen, New York City's police commissioner, had called a press conference to make public several purportedly "top secret" documents that were claimed to have been stolen from Amtorg. Though these were later exposed as crude forgeries, they were nevertheless printed by the *New York Times* and other major newspapers on a morning in early May. Marc's name appeared on two of the three documents allegedly sent from Comintern's headquarters in Moscow to its agents in New York.

The atmosphere was heating up. The country was in the grip of mounting hysteria. Communism was feeding on the fertile fields of the growing economic collapse. Right-wing politicians and even moderates were alarmed. Sensing the nervous mood of the public, the House of Representatives quickly passed a resolution setting up a committee under Representative Hamilton Fish Jr. of New York, an arch opponent of the Bolsheviks, to investigate all communist activity in the United States. Twenty-five thousand dollars were appropriated for the task.

Some of the representatives immediately called it a witch hunt, arguing that the money spent on the investigation could better be used to determine ways to correct deficiencies in the system that had caused so much disaffection in the first place.

After an introductory session, committee members agreed to move to New York. The aim was to ascertain the role of Amtorg. Strikes and demonstrations had been especially violent in New York City. And many people believed that these were inspired and organized by communist agents under Amtorg direction. Two months earlier, a demonstration in Union Square of hungry and jobless men demanding work had attracted 50,000 people and ended in a bloody riot.

There was no doubt that Marc's name would eventually resurface. Coming so close on the heels of the Bessedovsky revelations and the Whalen documents, it seemed a certainty. The Russian Red Cross had so far remained unblemished. But Marc's superiors were worried. His cover had worn painfully thin. They did not need further embarrassment. Therefore, they decided to recall him immediately.

Marc resisted. He said that he could easily handle a man like Fish. It would not even be a match, he said. Didn't they remember how he had squashed Bessedovsky's revelations with ease? The Amtorg reply to the charges of the Whalen documents, which he had personally helped put together, had received the best possible publicity. Nobody took the documents seriously any longer.

His superiors in Moscow knew their man. They were clever. They countered with the news that an ambassador's post—most likely, in Japan—was in the offing. Marc's expertise was just what was needed.

Marc took the bait, especially as Katya also played up the possibility of a diplomatic post. She sensed an opportunity to draw him away from his obsession with Bluet. After so many years together, she knew only too well how to handle her man.

But Marc was a satin-smooth operator. He could manipulate as adroitly as he was being manipulated. He was not about to be stampeded.

He played for time. He squeezed several additional weeks out of his superiors by arguing that he needed breathing space to complete outstanding work. Reluctantly, they agreed. But it was not work that Marc had in mind. He could no longer accept losing Bluet. It was not a passing fancy. He had fallen hopelessly in love. He wanted to share his life with her. But not returning while his political star was ascending (or so he thought) was also out of the question. He would compromise. He would go. But he would also take Bluet along.

To take the radical step of abandoning her current life, Bluet would have to be offered marriage and a style of living equal to the one she led with Max. Firmly believing his ambassadorship to be a certainty, and convincing himself in the meantime that daily life in Moscow must surely be an improvement over what he had left in 1927, despite reports to the contrary, Marc put his proposal to her.

He had been right. She was not in a hurry to abandon her home. He explained about the ambassadorship. He gently persuaded Anna of the happiness her mother would find. He applied all the pressure he could. Meanwhile, Hamilton Fish Jr. and his committee were closing in. They had already subpoenaed Father Walsh. Although he had not yet revealed anything about Marc, Walsh was scheduled to testify again soon.

And then, in a move that took them all by surprise, Basil Delgass, a vice president of Amtorg, defected, threatening to expose the whole Amtorg crowd to the Fish committee. As the senior GPU agent in the United States, Marc would need to do some fast talking to wriggle out of this one and still gain his coveted promotion. Luckily for him, Delgass knew the least, compared to other Amtorg executives. He was truly a trade representative. He had never been told what was really going on.

Marc was now out of time and walking on a tightrope. At least, if he were in Moscow by the time Delgass testified, Marc would be on the spot to defuse some of the backlash. He had to leave. He was therefore overjoyed when Bluet agreed to join him and recommended that she follow several weeks later, to allow a reasonable time for him to arrange a divorce from Katya and also find somewhere for them both to live. A separate departure would mean that even Max need not know. And that was now Marc's paramount concern. He was certain that if he and Bluet were already in Moscow by the time Max found out, it would lessen the impact, especially as Bluet would no longer be Max's wife.

But in this regard, Marc made a fatal error. He seriously underestimated Max's wrath and Max's capability for a sustained vendetta.

One final matter remained: Bluet's entry permit. Marc was fully aware that any American requesting a long-term stay in Soviet Russia was being readily admitted, as that person's passport was very valuable. Almost all agents working undercover in foreign countries with assumed names and identities were being encouraged to travel on American passports, which thus gave them unlimited freedom to carry out their work without arousing suspicion. But acquiring these passports for lengthy periods of time was proving difficult.

The only way they could be obtained was through forgery—a risky enterprise—or the surrender of a bona fide passport by an American coming into Russia on a long-term project, such as a technician or an engineer. By 1930, dozens of Americans were seeking such opportunities abroad, as employment at home was drying up.

By bringing Bluet into Russia, he was offering the Soviets an American passport for unlimited use. He was certain that he would face no problem at all.

MARC AND KATYA made the most of their journey back to Moscow. They sailed the Atlantic on a luxury liner. They stopped off in Paris and Berlin for a shopping spree. Katya was in excellent spirits, certain that Bluet would not follow. Marc was equally certain she would. And that, together with the upcoming ambassadorship, convinced Marc that he was indeed the supreme master of his own fate. Nobody else, he assured himself with a certain degree of arrogance, could have possibly pulled off such a coup in face of these formidable odds.

So he was taken by surprise with the scene that faced him when he bounded off the international express in Moscow's central station. He saw nothing but somber faces. Sure, his old friends turned out to meet him. But they seemed anything but happy.

They eyed him up and down, this dapper, ebullient man, who was elegantly outfitted in a fine new suit with a razor-sharp crease in his pants and who was boyishly swinging the soft leather suitcases he had picked up in Paris, as if comparing him to their own stale and careworn selves.

"Great to see you," said one, without even breaking into a smile.

Marc felt a sudden sense of panic. "Why the gloom?" he asked, glancing around.

There was an awkward silence. "Later," they mumbled. "Later."

"Fine," said Marc. "We'll drop off the suitcases and go out to dinner."

They eyed him curiously. Hadn't he heard about meatless days? Ration cards? Executions for hoarding food? About the fact that after the state had resumed control of the restaurants, the service had become appalling and the food nonexistent? "We only go to read the menus," said another, with a hint of sardonic humor. "Each item looks better than the last. But try ordering something . . ."

"Well," shrugged Marc, glancing over at Katya as she chatted with the wives. "Let's go out for a coffee instead."

"Coffee?" said one of the women, raising her eyebrows. "Who has any coffee?"

As they left the station, Marc tried to break the silence with some political talk. "Tell me . . . how are things?" he ventured. There was a look of abject horror and more silence.

One of his friends took him by the arm. "We don't discuss these matters nowadays," the man confided in a whisper, "even among a group of old comrades. Remember your friend Dimitri? He was arrested last week. Nobody knows why. It could happen to any of us now."

"Even us?"

"Even us."

And then it spilled out: the terror; the shortages; the general air of despair; the end of the NEP, which had swept all manner of merchandise from the stores; and the new stringent security measures forbidding travel abroad, even among senior party members, except under exceptional circumstances.

"So what we don't understand," admitted another friend, "is why you're here. We're all scheming to get out. And you two skip airily in. It's not the old days, Marc."

The next morning Marc's thoughts turned to Bluet. He was still in a boastful mood, and he wanted to tell his buddies about his new romance. The reaction was immediate—yet hardly what he had hoped.

"You must be insane!" exploded one old comrade, when Marc mentioned it at the offices of the Health Department. "At a time like this! Where do you think you are? And a woman like that!" The man shook his head. Then he seized Marc by the elbow and began an agitated conversation as they made their way to a meeting down the street.

"Don't you understand what's happened since you left? You fool. Don't you know what's going on up there in the Kremlin?" The man nodded toward the compound's turreted walls. "You'll bring an end to us all."

Pausing to wag a finger reproachfully at Marc, he cautioned, "Two kinds of people are anathema to that man in there. Jews and foreigners. Especially French foreigners. A Jew and a Frenchwoman. You must have lost your head!" He shook his own head violently in disbelief. "I don't even have to stay around for the outcome of this one," he scoffed. "Don't even bother unpacking your bags. But it won't be off to Paris or Rome or Tokyo, my friend. It's madness. It's suicide. Suicide for sex," he declared. "Suicide for sex.

"If it's girls you want," the man volunteered affectionately, "then I'll find you girls. Good-looking girls. Available girls, but local ones. Stay with your wife. Everybody else is playing by the rules. Why can't you? Why do you always have to make rules of your own? Don't bring a piece of French frippery into Moscow now. That lunatic's only looking for an excuse to accuse our whole crowd of treason." He paused for a moment. "And if you expect a woman like that to live in this rot, you are truly insane. She'll walk out— and that will be worse."

Marc shrugged, breaking into a mischievous grin. Suddenly, the man smiled. Enveloping Marc in an enormous bear hug, he chuckled, "What am I going to do with you, you maniac? Welcome back, anyway!"

But after Marc had explained that he was not just bringing in a mistress but intended to marry Bluet and live with her permanently, he sensed a much deeper mood of apprehension. "She's not one of us," he was warned with extreme seriousness. "She's neither a reliable communist nor a party member. Even to be seen in the company of such a woman today is tantamount to a crime. Fraternizing with foreigners . . . you're going to be a very lonely man."

Finally, his friends persuaded him to shelve his wedding plans until it was clear which way the political wind was blowing. The party would need time to evaluate how loyal and sympathetic Bluet turned out to be. Marc was reminded that he would never get anywhere unless he had a loyal wife. At least this way, he could still extricate himself without too much damage. But Marc was not so sure.

For Katya, it was even worse. She now had to face the moment she had been dreading for years. "I want a divorce," Marc told Katya, as they stood in their tiny kitchen one morning a few weeks later, fully aware that Bluet was already on the way and this was no moment for compromise. "It's easy to get, so long as we both agree. Come on, Katya. You know it's all over. It's been over for years."

But Katya was not about to let her man go without a fight. She knew from past experience that he would come back to her in the end. "Give it some time," she begged. "Move out. But don't force me to give you a divorce. They'll take my home away."

She looked him squarely in the eyes, adding, "It's the least you can do for me."

She had him cornered, and he knew it. So he reluctantly agreed not to be hasty and set aside his marriage plans, at least temporarily.

"But where do you two lovebirds intend to live?" asked another friend with a practical turn of mind.

"Don't worry, I'll find something," answered the ever-optimistic Marc. But it was not so easy anymore. He set about using all the influence he could muster. To no avail. An apartment or even a room was simply not to be had anywhere in Moscow that winter. Finally, an idea occurred to him. It had been part of his job, prior to leaving for the United States, to select suitable physicians for visits to medical gatherings abroad. Temporarily, this selection process had been given back to him. One particular research physician, a certain Dr. Lazareff, whom he had known for years, had been begging for an opportunity to attend a medical conference in London. But nobody had been anxious to grant Dr. Lazareff the opportunity and the valuable foreign currency necessary for the trip. Lazareff may have been a good researcher, but he was not an ardent communist. As a dedicated medical man, he had nothing but contempt for politicians—a view he aired too readily.

But Dr. Lazareff was also a bachelor. He lived alone. He had a small two-room apartment of his own—a rarity in Moscow. Marc sensed an opening. He would persuade the GPU to allow Dr. Lazareff to go abroad. In return, Dr. Lazareff promised to lend Marc the apartment while he was gone.

Marc became totally convinced, in the interim weeks, that he would easily obtain a permanent apartment for himself and Bluet. He sat down to write her the note that ended up in the offices of the Russian Red Cross in Berlin. With a mischievous glint in his eye and his mind on priorities, he suggested the double bed and—alarmed at the sight of so many empty shelves and boarded-up shops—some basic items of food.

The same day he set about lobbying feverishly for a foreign assignment, his optimism unflagging. But he soon sensed a chill in the air that had not been there before. It was not only his folly of bringing back a foreign woman. It was something deeper in the body politic. On top of the wider changes, something had happened that suggested he could be headed into personally dangerous waters. Only a few days earlier, he had finally received a copy of the testimony of Basil W. Delgass before the 1930 congressional hearings into communist activities under Representative Hamilton Fish Jr. Unexpectedly, Delgass had revealed some uncomfortable truths that were not going to sit well with Marc's superiors.

Delgass began by explaining that he had become sick of telling lies and wanted no more part of his native country or what was now going on.

THE CHAIRMAN: You resigned of your own accord.

MR. DELGASS: I did. Yes.

THE CHAIRMAN: Because you did not want to testify before this committee.

MR. DELGASS: Because I did not want to testify before the committee and tell the perjury I was told to tell.

THE CHAIRMAN: Were you ever requested to resign from the organization?

MR. DELGASS: I was not requested to resign from the organization. But about a month and a half ago I was advised to go back to Russia. It would be good for me to go back, I was told.

THE CHAIRMAN: But you did not want to go back?

MR. DELGASS: No.

THE CHAIRMAN: Was there a rule or mandate that the children of the employees and officers attend Communist schools?

MR. DELGASS: Yes. There was a senior one and a junior one. There were lectures held by different members.

THE CHAIRMAN: Did you ever hear of Dr. Cheftel?

MR. DELGASS: Yes, I knew Dr. Cheftel. Officially, he came here as a representative of the Department of Health in Russia. But that wasn't his job. For instance, he very often visited these gatherings of Communist Youth and in fact at one time he was in charge of one of the groups.

THE CHAIRMAN: In this country?

MR. DELGASS: In this country. Yes.

THE CHAIRMAN: And he was supposed to represent the Russian Red Cross here?

MR. DELGASS: Not exactly the Red Cross. He represented the Department of Health. He was commissar over Mr. Dubrowsky, the representative of the Red Cross in this country. You see, there is a difference. . . .

THE CHAIRMAN: Let us get this clear.

MR. DELGASS: But I think he has left the country now. Yes, he has left the country.

THE CHAIRMAN: But it is very interesting to find out. Just what was his position?

MR. DELGASS:	Officially, he came here as a representative of the Department of Health of Russia, but at the same time he was commissar—well, I don't know how you say this in English—looking after all the activities here. You know, reporting about these activities to those in Moscow. Dr. Cheftel was spying.
THE CHAIRMAN:	Did you say he also taught school here?
MR. DELGASS:	He was in charge of one of the children's groups for a year.
THE CHAIRMAN:	And do you know what work he did here in the way of the Red Cross?
MR. DELGASS:	None at all, as far as I know.
THE CHAIRMAN:	And did he ever visit Amtorg?
MR. DELGASS:	Oh, he was constantly in conference with Amtorg, especially when Skvirsky [chief of the Russian Information Bureau] came on a visit from Washington. Whenever Skvirsky came for a conference with the heads of Amtorg, Dr. Cheftel would always be present.
THE CHAIRMAN:	And Mr. Skvirsky was in contact with Dr. Cheftel?
MR. DELGASS:	He was in contact with Dr. Cheftel and the heads of Amtorg. In fact, when they were preparing to reply to the Whalen documents, Dr. Cheftel, Mr. Skvirsky, and Mr. Schuster, the company secretary, were all in the room. It was on the eve of the beginning of these congressional committee investigations. I was called that day and told to appear as a witness. I saw these gentlemen preparing the exposé of the documents they had declared to be forgeries.
THE CHAIRMAN:	How many Amtorg officials are part of the GPU, Mr. Delgass?
MR. DELGASS:	I don't know. But I must tell you that such a position as office manager or member of the board or commissar can only be taken by those members of the party who are also members of the GPU or the Central Control Committee.

Marc pondered it all as he sat on the train headed for his rendezvous with Bluet. He worked hard to convince himself that it would all be quickly forgotten, and that no low-bred, humorless maniac, temporarily closeted in the Kremlin, could long thwart the ambitions or inhibit the debonair lifestyle of Dr. Marc Cheftel.

Part Three
21 Bolshoi Lubianka

Thirteen

"YOU NEVER TOLD ME."

"You never asked."

Marc's young medical colleague had just left their borrowed apartment in Sokolniki. And conforming to a ritual Bluet would learn to follow with depressing regularity, they agreed to take a walk to talk things over. From the very first day, Marc had warned her that only casual and inconsequential matters should be discussed indoors, whether at a social gathering or simply between themselves. It was another of those aggravating realities of life in a proletarian paradise that would permeate and poison intimate relationships.

The tension had become so great that even the late afternoon chill could not deter them from going outside. Few people were on the street, and Marc and Bluet's footsteps made a hollow, echoing sound as they strode along. Prudently, they lowered their voices to barely more than a whisper.

"And if I had asked?"

"You know the answer. I couldn't have told you. Even now, there's very little . . . ," Marc's voice trailed off into silence. Try as Bluet might, she would never get the full story out of him.

But she was determined to learn as much as possible. "Then the newspaper stories in New York were true," she ventured, "even though you denied them."

"More or less."

"Those files you've been working on each night. They're about people, aren't they?"

He did not even try to deny it. "We have to know who's loyal. It's the details that count. The details."

"And if they're not . . . ?"

He shrugged. Then he added quickly, "I can't send them abroad."

"You're sending people abroad?"

"All the time."

"Then it's not you who . . . ," she began and then decided to let her comment remain unspoken. She did not want to hear the answer, fearful that he was indeed responsible for some of those midnight arrests, in which so many seemingly innocent citizens had been rounded up and taken away under cover of darkness in recent months.

"No. But I'm a realist. I understand the need for securing the interests of the party so we can get on with the job. Except that it's gone far beyond that today, to something . . . Anyhow, everybody knows where the real political power lies right now."

"In the GPU?"

"Of course. You don't have a voice otherwise. And I've got good connections, so why not use them? I'm also ambitious, if that's a fault. What I've been doing abroad may well decide the fate of this whole experiment. I sent three of my friends off to Africa only this week."

"Africa? Why Africa? Why bother with the African colonies? They're not even independent countries."

"They won't be colonies forever. Not if we can help it. We're sending agents everywhere. Everywhere. We have to train them . . . instruct them in the complexities and the importance of working invisibly and undercover without immediate results. We must think in terms of generations, not weeks or months. There's not one country we've left untouched. Look at Italy. The fascists may be in power now, but we've laid excellent groundwork there. We will succeed in time. You'll see. I have total confidence in the men we chose."

"And the Red Cross?"

"You'll find me there every day," he laughed. "Up in the foreign department, just like I told you."

"And that work?"

"I do that, too. Why do you think I'm so busy? Even in America, I was given enough work for two or even three people. You don't build a new society by punching a time clock. Not in our department, anyway. But it's all part of the same. We don't send anyone abroad on these Red Cross missions unless they have GPU approval. We have to be very careful."

"So it's all in those files you bring home?"

"Much of it." He was not prepared to explain that this was a primary reason why he had discouraged her from learning Russian. By insisting that they would be going abroad again any week, he had pretended it was not necessary. But she viewed it as a question of trust.

"And when they get abroad . . . to these Red Cross missions?"

"Now you're asking too many questions," he retorted with a touch of annoyance. "I'm not part of the excesses that are taking place here, if that's what you're thinking. I haven't turned into a sadistic monster. But I'd be less than honest if I said it didn't trouble me. I'm ambitious, but . . . ," his voice trailed off again.

"Did you know what Sasha was going to say today?"

"It was a setup. I thought you would have understood that. It was time for them to send someone to see what you were like and also . . . they wanted to find out how much I had told you."

"What was his impression?"

"Just what I wanted it to be. It was written all over your face. You should have seen yourself," he chuckled. "At least, they are now sure there's nothing damaging you might have said to any of your friends in America."

"But why worry about me? Everyone knows me. There are people here who have known me for years." She started naming their mutual friends and acquaintances, including prominent members of the government who had spent time in New York and others she had met on previous visits to Russia.

"That's their way. It's different now that you're with me."

"And when you came back? Why were you so baffled . . . so upset?"

"I found a great many changes. Far worse than I'd expected. Our people weren't in power anymore. Too much was happening that was contrary to all I had fought to achieve . . . all that was supposed to be. The change was too abrupt. I was not prepared to believe what I had heard. You leave a place, and your mind plays tricks. You still see it in the way it was when you left. I kept remembering the tenth anniversary celebrations just a few weeks before I came to America. There was so much optimism. So much hope. We all ignored the troublesome signs. You don't want to believe anyone who tells you things are different. And we could change course again. It could just be a temporary setback. That's what I'm hoping."

"What do you think will happen?"

He sighed. "Absolutely anything right now. For me . . . for us both . . . just try to be patient and as silent as possible," he implored her. "I know I've let you down. But I'm a resourceful man. I have a great facility for survival. Just give me time. It's all part of our housing problem as well. But I'll solve that one, too, in the end. Please, not so many questions. A little faith instead. Okay. K.O.?"

"Kayho," she repeated, laughing. It was an inside joke that had originated months ago, when he once tried to express himself colloquially to Anna. He had intended to say O.K., but the expression came out backward. Highly amused, Anna always called him Kayho from then onward.

They walked on in silence. It would be weeks before she would better comprehend what he was really trying to do. Marc remained adamantly opposed to letting her know his secrets.

When they were close to their apartment building, he started to speak again, only this time almost to himself. "It wouldn't have been so bad if it hadn't been for those damned congressional hearings. And Rabinoff."

"Max!" she exclaimed with alarm, "Max Rabinoff?"

"I wasn't going to tell you, but Anna will probably mention it when she writes. I heard that when Rabinoff found out about us, he flew into a rage. He ran around making outrageous accusations. It hasn't done me any good, I can assure you." Marc stopped there. He dared not add the details. Max had accused him of embezzling Red Cross funds, raised substantially through the benefit of Max's good name, then taking the money piecemeal out of the bank for personal use. What even Max could not easily admit, at least in public, was that this money may have also been used to pursue and seduce his own wife—he was the ultimate cuckold. He had simply been insisting to party chiefs that "Cheftel must be punished!"

"What kind of accusations?"

"I don't know," Marc lied. "I was just told he's a great deal angrier than I'd expected."

"I thought Max would be only too glad to get rid of me. He used to enjoy taunting me by saying so."

"He thinks we tricked him. He also found out about my being in the GPU about the same time. Thanks to Delgass and Father Walsh."

"Father Walsh? Who's Father Walsh?"

"You remember those congressional hearings just before I left? Well, Father Walsh was leading one of the famine relief groups that was over here some years ago. He's had it in for me for a long time. We had a disagreement a few years back. I think he considered those hearings a golden opportunity to discredit the whole lot of us. I wouldn't be surprised if he phoned the chairman personally. The committee is supposed to hear from him again in a week or so. And this time it may be about me."

"But why you?"

"I didn't make life easy for Walsh while he was here with his mission," Marc admitted. "We considered him a troublemaker. He was better off out of the country. He also knew I was working hard for American recognition, and he's been campaigning against it for years—making speeches, writing books, articles. The trouble was that by the time I left, more people were listening to our point of view than to his. So he was just waiting for an opportunity to discredit us. And why not name me? He knew me personally. This way, he will be able to accomplish two things at the same time. You know, kill two chickens with one rock."

"That's kill two birds with one stone," Bluet giggled, hugging his arm.

"Well, stones, rocks, chickens, or birds," Marc chuckled. "It comes to the same thing."

"What did you do to him in Moscow?"

"We made it difficult for him to find an office and a place for his staff to live once their famine relief work was over. Without housing, they couldn't stay. He did a good job, but he was constantly creating trouble. It was better for him to leave."

"What has he been saying about you?"

"I don't know. But whatever it is, it's bound to hurt my work. And it doesn't help my personal reputation as a foreign service man. It couldn't have come at a worse time, especially with Rabinoff running around like a madman."

"Max will forget. I know Max. He makes a lot of wild accusations and then forgets just as fast. His pride has been hurt, that's all."

"That's all," repeated Marc, laconically. "Somehow I don't think it's quite so simple." He put his arm around Bluet's shoulder and added, "Come on. It's getting late. I have to be up early in the morning. I'm going to be busy repairing more than one bridge in the next few weeks."

Sokolniki, November 1930

My sweet darling Anna,

You have no idea how happy I was when the postman climbed up two flights of stairs this morning to bring me your letter. I was in the middle of shampooing my hair (we only have a cold tap in the kitchen but I manage somehow), but I was so anxious to read it I just put a towel around my head like a turban and sat right down to open it up. It is wonderful to see you are so busy and happy.

I am glad you liked the little things I sent you from Liberty in London. Did you have to pay any duty? Have you worn any of them yet? I have just started to receive copies of the *New York Times* and some of the magazines that you sent many weeks ago. It was so wonderful to read them. Like this, I can keep up with all that is going on. It makes me feel so much closer to you. Do keep on sending them. Those you have read and anything you can pick up that you think I might enjoy. I have a lot of time to read now and nowhere to find anything in French or English except at the Yonoffs.

Do you remember Yonoff? He's the chief of the State Publishing Syndicate and that includes all the libraries. Well, we met Mr. Yonoff and his wife when we were invited out to dinner at the home of some friends of Kayho last week and I was telling him about my problem with books. He was so kind. He told me I could come to a library he has right in his apartment any afternoon and choose any books I liked. It was quite a treat for me. I went there yesterday for the first time. His wife was so charming. She gave me a cup of coffee—something that is quite rare and precious in Moscow right now. They must be the only household with coffee to spare in the whole of the city! The library was the most exquisite I have ever seen. Dozens and dozens of rare first editions of the French classics and many priceless books from the period of the French revolution. I was almost afraid to touch them. But he left word that I should take whatever I wanted. I chose a first edition of Marat's *L'Ami Du Peuple*. I do not think he finds many people interested in these books nowadays because he was so proud to talk about his collection to me at dinner. It takes an old French woman like myself to understand them, I suppose. Yes, my darling, sometimes I feel very old these days. And I am not even forty!

We are still waiting for a permanent apartment, but I think today or tomorrow will decide the question. In Moscow, my sweet, it is a serious problem not easily solved. In the last few years, they have built many new houses but apparently not sufficient, as the rural population has developed an appetite for city life and industry. These people are especially attracted to the capital with its movies and theaters and possibilities for all sorts of recreation. It is so overcrowded right now, you cannot imagine. Next letter I hope to be able to give you a permanent address and I shall explain all about it: location, the rooms, and so forth.

Do you know that the day before yesterday we spent the entire evening with Nadya? Do you remember her from New York? Nadya came back to Russia right after her divorce and is now living with her family in Moscow. She is trying to revive her singing career over here. She has been going to the opera house and has been auditioning and auditioning. All her family were lovely to me. Her brother is a lawyer at the Foreign Office.

They had all kinds of interesting people for the evening. All of a sudden, right in the middle of dinner, her father, a tall and hefty man who is an officer in the Red Army, walked in looking just like Santa Claus. He was wearing high black boots and he had a huge sack of potatoes slung over his shoulder. He had come directly from the country. We were all given a few potatoes from the sack to take home with us because these things are not so easy to get here. Can you imagine such a thing happening at one of my parties! I expect I will see quite a lot of Nadya in the next few months. We were always good friends.

Tonight we are going to see Regina Gurevitch. Her husband, Dr. Gurevitch, was one of the Amtorg doctors. I expect you remember them, too. Over here, he is the deputy chief at the Health Department where Kayho works. It has been almost two years since they left New York so I will be glad to see them again. They are even closer friends of Kayho than they were of all of us. They have a beautiful apartment, Kayho says. And they have a new baby son. Regina is also busy singing again now they are back. Everyone, as usual, is singing, except me!

We are supposed to go there in a few hours, just as soon as Kayho gets home, but the weather is rather bad. The rain has not stopped all day. It keeps pounding against the window and even trickling through the cracks at the corners. Every so often I get a rag and mop up the water from the floor. The buildings over here are not what we are used to living in, my sweet. Not at all. Today it is so damp and cold that it seems to me the wet comes right through the walls. I hate weather like this, you know that. I shiver so. So we will see later on. Maybe we won't go out after all. We have had quite a lot of snow already, but it does not stay on the ground yet, though it does feel cold enough for a permanent white sheet. The streets are still slushy.

Darling, I forgot to tell you that we met Louis Fischer, the writer, by accident last week while we were out one evening at a movie. He looked so surprised to see us together. It took quite a lot of explaining. I had no idea Kayho knew him, too. I told him I had taken his address with me and that I was hoping to look him up. Anyhow, he was so pleased to see us that he asked us over. We are going there next Saturday. He is expecting quite a few other people and I think it will be another absorbing evening. He knows most of the Western journalists here. There is never much food, but the conversation and the people we meet are the most brilliant I have ever met anywhere. Many of them are the old crowd who used to come to our house. Same faces—different location. I am only sad that with this borrowed apartment so far from anywhere, I cannot reciprocate. I would love to be able to entertain them all. I am sure it would be good for Kayho's sake. Perhaps when we get our permanent address.

Louis said he is going to the U.S. in about a month or so, and I asked him if he would be so kind as to take a small gift for my child. He said he would. I am going shopping tomorrow to see what I can find for you. Do not expect anything special. There is not a lot in the stores. The only thing that catches my eye are dozens of tiny Soudeikine paintings. You must tell Serge! He would be quite astonished. And they are so cheap! I'm sure I will find you a little something. In my next letter I will tell you more . . . when he is coming to New York and so forth.

We are going to the Meyerhold Theater in two days to see a very interesting production. Of course, I shall write to you all about that. For the moment the theater is one of the most exceptional advantages of living in Moscow. It is so exciting and different. They are still doing so many wonderful new things—new staging, new methods that I know you will want to hear all about in detail. We are also going to see the Russian circus. Even that is supposed to be different, very different from what we get back home. You see, I still call it home. Old habits do not disappear so fast. And then we are to see a French play translated into Russian—*Les Marchands de Gloire.* It was taken away from the repertoire of La Comedie Française after a few productions on account of its subject. K.O. tells me it is wonderful so I am quite anxious to see it. I had heard about it in Paris but hardly expected to see it in Moscow.

I see Daddy is giving you a wonderful time and is so kind. This makes me feel very happy, especially because he even took you with him to the opera one night. I am sure he was very proud of you and that you looked very beautiful. What did you wear? I am waiting for that snapshot you promised me. Do not forget. Do not worry that he has been bad tempered lately and upset about Kayho and me. When he says he wants to "bury me" and "kill" Kayho, you must understand that he is saying these things because he feels hurt. He does not really mean them, I can assure you. We all say things we don't mean when we are angry and upset. But it is wrong of him to say them in front of you. That makes *me* angry. No, I am sure it is not you who told him. I am sure you kept your word.

I am writing this letter late in the afternoon, just about the time of day when you and I used to get together before dinner for a chat about what had happened to you at school and what was going on. It hurts every time I think about this time of day because I miss you so much. It is as though there is now a big empty space in the middle of every single day and nobody to fill it. You cannot imagine how much I miss our little talks, my darling. It is the hour when I feel most alone here. I am already beginning to count the months until you will be with us.

Do not worry so much about your studies. I am sure you are doing your best. You are an excellent student, but you cannot be good at everything. So I think your teacher's suggestion about German is the best. Perhaps she will know someone who can help you a few times a week and pull you up to better marks in the language. I cannot understand your D in History of Art, however. I know the subject is one that interests you and that you like it a lot, and the work could not have been too difficult. Anyhow, I am sure this will improve later on in the year. Your compositions are, as usual, most searching and beautifully conceived. But I think you should be more careful with the spelling, writing, and all the decorum in general. Why not devote ten more minutes to brushing up?

It counts, you know. It would help to be just a little more cautious with the technical details. But thank you for sending them to me. Please send as many as you can. I love to read them. Are you making any new friends this year? How is your friend David [*David Rockefeller, who eventually became the chairman and CEO of Chase Manhattan Bank*] and the other friends in the class? Do not forget to give me a sketch in your next letter.

I am well, my love. Do not worry about me. Kayho is taking such good care of me and is kind to me always. Some day you will understand just how much this means. But he has been looking so tired and pale lately that I do worry about him a lot. He does not even laugh the way he used to do when the three of us were together. It is different here. One day I will explain.

You see, my love, how time flies. Almost two months since I left America and you. Keep well, my darling. Wear your rubbers against the damp and keep away from getting wet. Did you get thinner? I hope not. Do not forget that I want to see you beautiful and also strong and principally healthy. Are you going to Mexico for Christmas, as Daddy had planned? If so, it would be a wonderful vacation for you. Take warm clothing with you anyway for the boat and the change of climate and temperature.

Take good care of yourself always and your Daddy, too. Write to me as often as you can. Your letters are just so much sunshine to me, so send lots of them. I miss you and dream about you and seeing you again. I want so much to talk to you and hug you. It seems so much longer than just two months since I said good-bye. Meanwhile, all the best, my dearest. All my kisses to you always.

Maman

P.S. K.O. just happened to come in. He tells me that in three or four days we will receive a nice apartment near the center of Moscow, instead of the two rooms and kitchen we have now, which is really too far from the activities and all our friends. I will be sorry to leave here just the same. In a way I have been very happy here. It was kind of Dr. Lazareff to let us have it. Kayho is now going to add something before I send it off. There is not much room left at the end of the paper, but he will write what he can.

Darling Anna,

I can see that Bluet has written you so many pages that there is not much to say except to tell you that we are always waiting anxiously for your letters. We started our winter season, our theatrical season, on the nineteenth of the month with a Meyerhold play called *The Shot*. It is a satire that many people say is the most important production of the year. We are going to see it in a few days. After that come the many lesser productions in all the other theaters—all of which I know you would like to enjoy with us.

The weather is not too cold yet, and our real winter has not really arrived. Your letters are charming and always so interesting, but you must write more often. Make sure they are especially long letters because your mother needs them so much. It makes her feel so much nearer to you. You cannot believe how happy she is when she gets a letter from you. She reads it over and over. So keep writing!

We have already visited many of our friends, but Bluet tells me she has written to you all about that, especially about those you know. I suppose it is not news to you that your mother loves to sleep late in the morning.

We are receiving both the French and the American papers and occasionally the *New York Times*. It is most important that you send as many magazines as possible just as soon as you have read them because Bluet cannot find enough to read.

My best wishes to Mademoiselle, to your friend Nina [*Nina Fonaroff, who later became a celebrated ballerina*], and to all the other friends whom I am sure have not forgotten us yet. You can continue writing to this address (c/o Lazareff) for the moment. Very soon I hope to let you have the new address.

With loads of kisses,
Kayho

DESPITE THE CHEERFUL TONE of the letter to Anna—necessary not only to avoid problems with the ever-vigilant censor but also to keep Anna from fretting over the safety and the well-being of her mother—the winter forecast was decidedly chilly.

Stalin's desperate (and justified) fear that he was on the verge of being ousted brought forth a wave of tension that pervaded all of Moscow. The more desperate the cornered beast, the more savage his reactions. Daily newspapers featured stories of innumerable arrests of alleged saboteurs and counterrevolutionaries. Professors, engineers, writers, scientists, and even highly placed government and party officials were being summarily dismissed from their posts and hurled into prison. In the space of just a few weeks, the anti-Stalin movement was characterized as an engineers' plot, a Jewish plot, a Red Army plot, an émigré plot, an imminent capitalist assault from abroad, and a plot of Rightist Deviationists. There were even whispers of a plot inside the executive committee of the GPU. All ostensibly had a single aim—to purge Stalin and his ruthless toadies from the Russian body politic. The Western press actively followed the events. On three separate occasions that November, it reported that Stalin had indeed been overthrown.

More remarkable by far was the fact that Stalin survived them all. For regardless of ideology or personal affiliation, no sensitive Russian could remain silent. The human misery wrought by the impossible goals of the Five-Year Plan evoked explosions of outrage. A heroic few were even willing to speak out in public, knowing full well the price they would pay. Some charged with directly enforcing the directives chose instead to commit suicide. They left passionate written appeals, hoping that their sacrifice would encourage resistance. The suicides were reported as terminal illness by the authorities. The written legacies were conveniently lost.

Marc was growing increasingly morose. The scale of national misery was unmistakable, judging from the reports filtering into the Department of

Health. The bulletins showed a country beset by severe dietary deficiencies, overwork, deplorable housing, and mental disorders stemming from the constant fear of arrest. The disruption of normal family life was causing emotional problems. There had been an alarming rise in disease, starvation, homelessness, and roaming orphans. Typhoid was endemic.

Like so many of his friends and other Old Bolsheviks, Marc decided to throw in his lot with the plotters. He could stomach no more. It would become his last desperate effort to salvage the humanitarian ideals of the original revolution. The tension was apparent in his taut, unsmiling expression, in his erratic sleep pattern, in his strange verbal meanderings and preoccupation with death, and in his lapses into prolonged periods of silence.

Early one morning, as he was about to leave for his office, he bent over Bluet while she was still asleep, to shake her gently by the arm and whisper, "I may not come back tonight. Something might happen. If I don't turn up, go to Mika—go to Gurevitch. Go immediately. Do you hear?" The words tumbled out in a chilling monotone. Dr. Mikhail Gurevitch, his boyhood friend, was the only person Marc knew he could really trust. Gurevitch was fond of Bluet and still possessed the influence to spirit her out of the country, out of danger, if anything happened to Marc.

She awakened with a start by the urgency of his message, then begged for an explanation. He refused. "I'm just telling you, that's all," he snapped. "I'm letting you know. Look after yourself. Do as I say." With that, he marched out of the house and shut the door firmly behind him, leaving her alone. She lay on the bed with an uneasy air of foreboding, listening to his shoes tapping their way hurriedly down the concrete hallway.

He came home at his usual time, warm and loving as ever, as if nothing unusual had happened that morning. The incident was closed, as far as he was concerned, but she could not shrug it off so lightly. The omnipresent aura of death and danger had reached into their house, too.

Everyone else seemed frozen by the same tensions. Even Marc's housing request had become bogged down in bureaucratic paralysis. His friends were not about to climb out on a limb for what they considered a romantic peccadillo, particularly now that subtle political maneuvering in the Kremlin had erupted with volcanic fury into a full-scale struggle for power.

Marc's prestige and career had been eclipsed that month for additional reasons. Back in New York, Max's balloon-like ego had been shattered by his wife's desertion. And hell-bent upon revenge, Max was making as many accusations as he could devise about Marc's personal conduct.

To further compromise Marc's position, the true nature of his American mission was being publicly revealed by the defector Basil Delgass and the unforgiving Father Walsh. Comments by both men had already prompted the chairman, Congressman Fish, to contact the State Department for all documents relevant to the Cheftel entry and conditions of stay.

A further round of congressional hearings—this time in Washington—had found Father Walsh bitterly denouncing Marc in thundering pulpit tones. He accused Marc of diverting public property for personal gain (those "lost" medical supplies), as well as of wearing the fake cloth of humanitarianism to cloak his nefarious political deeds.

"I could pick this man out in a crowd," bellowed Father Walsh to committee members. "His activities may have been masked under the heading of Red Cross agent, whereas I can assure you his aim was very different from that. I even discovered him once myself with hands in certain tills where they did not belong. In Russia . . ."

With Marc's international cover blown wide open, the opportunity for another foreign posting was becoming more and more remote, especially as he stubbornly insisted upon remaining with Bluet. The party had already made it clear that it did not trust this pampered, bourgeois French woman. Marc countered with an ultimatum that if the party wanted him, it would have to accept her, too.

The party's retaliation was swift.

Marc came home to break the news. They were not being given the promised comfortable apartment in town after all, at least not for the time being. The fact that Bluet was French had wrought its own unforeseen damage. The authorities had just unmasked a particularly heinous "plot" emanating from an alliance of White émigré groups in Paris, French agents planted inside the Bolshevik infrastructure, and a secret cabal of Soviet engineers who, together with the French military, were conspiring to overthrow the government—the famous Industrial Party Plot of 1930. Every French person in the capital was now under suspicion. Even the French ambassador's wife was accused of diluting the national treasure by secretly moving large quantities of former Romanov jewels out of the country in her handbag. The eight engineers who had allegedly masterminded the scheme were under arrest. They were to be placed on public trial within a few weeks.

No one now dared give special consideration to either Bluet or Marc. National xenophobia had reached fever pitch.

There was more. A note came in the mail from Dr. Lazareff, advising them that he would be returning in a matter of days.

Besieged by problems, Bluet had neither the solace nor the comfort of a real confidante. Though Marc's own friends had been more than kind to her, as had the Bolsheviks who had been posted temporarily to New York, she could not escape the feeling that she remained the suspect stranger in their midst. Not having shared their adventures, their dreams, and their hardships, she sensed that they considered her presence an intrusion. And, as a foreigner, maybe even a risk. All the wives had contributed substantially to their husbands' current success, either by being related to the right party member or by themselves being significant contributors to the cause—like Katya. Bluet had no place in this game of political chess. She was a luxury. And Marc's refusal to discuss ways of easing her into the mainstream of Moscow life only accentuated her feelings of impotence and isolation—though she knew they sprang from an overprotective desire to shield her from the current excesses and intrigues.

Worse, she had nothing to do. She was unable to cook because there was nothing to cook. She was unable to sew because needles, thread, cloth, buttons, and even scissors were nowhere to be obtained. She was unable to socialize, since the allegations against French residents made Marc cautious about the people they visited and made other people cautious about befriending them. He even refused to allow her to contact any of her own Western friends—all except Louis Fischer, who was considered the kind of solid Bolshevik whom Marc was supposed to court. Marc also begged her not to continue spending any of her dollars at the foreigners' store in the center of town. "It's the wrong time," he warned. "It can make trouble for both of us. It will create a bad impression when others can't enjoy such privileges."

Finally, the nagging fear that someone would overhear them restricted conversation to banal small talk. She could sense that he desperately needed to unburden himself, but he dared not allow himself the luxury. And for a man addicted to creature comforts, the physical privations of their lives were maddening.

Slowly, the ease and the pleasure of communication and companionship that marked so much of their joy in each other deteriorated into monk-like silence. Only occasionally, while outdoors, would he beg, "Please try to understand. Please be patient. I know this kind of thing better than you. Wait it out. Just wait. Everything will take a turn for the better. It's just a question of time." It was, however, as if he were trying to convince himself even more than her. The humble pleadings of this proud man saddened her.

She feared that the well of boundless optimism that had always been an integral part of his personality, and the dreams she so desperately wanted to share with him, were fading fast. He was starting to wither—a little more each day. The noble dreams of Marc, son of Solomon, his fantasies and his loves, had perennially held out the hope of renewal as the warm spring invariably chases the winter chill. It was too simple to write off his change of mood as the resignation of encroaching age, even though he had reached that time in life where most men come to terms with the limits of their ambitions and visions. It was more. He could no longer find anything that resembled the kind of society he had intended to create. The tree had nothing left to give. Its fruits had been squandered by lesser men with obscene appetites.

And he had to face a further blow. His delicate cornflower from the Auvergne was withering, too.

Yet unlike other couples who tend to draw apart at their first major obstacle, venting their frustration upon their partners, the opposite prevailed. As the dark and wintry days closed in upon them, Marc and Bluet became so fundamentally sympathetic to each other's problems and needs that they cherished their relationship even more. Marc grew increasingly affectionate, ever more anxious to please, while she returned this love by concealing her disappointment as only a woman can.

Fourteen

The united state political department (GPU) is the most important department of the Soviet system, occupying the entire block between Bolshoi and Malaya Lubianka. The chief building faces Lubianka Square, in the back of which is the GPU "territory" extending to the Select Hotel on Stretenka. The hotel was created for the entertainment of travelers over whom the GPU is thus enabled to exercise complete surveillance. While they are being put to the question, their baggage is similarly but separately being put to the question. Houses on Versonofievsky and Milutinsky Place are occupied by commune barracks for its workers. Thus the entire area between Lubianka and Stretenka is in fact under the control of the GPU.

Notes from the memoirs of former GPU foreign
espionage agent Georges Agabekoff, 1930

Hotel Select,
December 1930

My darling Anna,

When this letter reaches New York, you will most likely be in Mexico. I am delighted that Daddy took you there. The change will be beneficial to both of you, and I am sure you will have a lovely holiday among all the warm sunshine and the glorious flowers. Nevertheless, I shall be very anxious until I hear you have reached New York safely again. Please dear, send me a cable and let me know that all is well. And write a long letter to tell me about the vacation. Did you go by ship or rail? I hope by boat, as the train journey can be very tiresome because it is so long.

I interrupted this letter for over a week. The reasons were numerous. First of all, as I knew you would only be back in New York on the 11th of January, there was no great rush. Then, the day I started to write, we were suddenly told we were being given only a small single room at the Hotel Select (just down from Vorovsky Square and the Savoy where I stayed last year with Daddy) until we receive our permanent apartment.

We left the large luggage in Dr. Lazareff's place. In the hurry I left the writing paper and all the writing accessories behind. We only went back to get them yesterday after a succession of postponements.

The hotel is much better heated than the apartment, and as it is growing colder outside, this is a big plus for me. It is also very central and it is much more convenient on this account. I can get around better. I am able to take the streetcar easily from here, and I am becoming most efficient with all the routes and numbers as I am slowly learning to read a little Russian. I have also made a new friend, and I use public transport particularly when I go and see her. You would like her a lot, I am sure. Her name is Yulina and she is the wife of Sasha Yulin. Her husband is a member of the parliament here and also in charge of industrial development in one of the provinces. They are old friends of Kayho. Yulina used to be a personal secretary to Trotsky. She has been very sweet and understanding. We have no bath here at the hotel, and she insists I come to take a bath at her home whenever I like. So at least that difficulty is temporarily solved until we receive proper accommodations of our own.

You would find the streetcars very old fashioned. Everybody huddles together (they have no heating). But they are usually so crowded, it keeps us all warm. It is so bitterly cold that everybody's breath freezes on the inside of the ice-crusted windowpanes, making them opaque all the way across. I have to scrape away a little opening with my fingernail to see if I have reached my stop. Yulina always laughs at the way I look. She says she can tell when it is Bluet who is coming up the street because I wear two berets, one over the other, and two coats, one on top of the other, because it is so cold.

I know I really should not go around Moscow in such a good fur coat because everybody else has so little. But even that coat on top of the wonderful woolen coat I bought in London does not keep me warm enough. I am bundled up underneath with sweaters, one on top of the other. I look grotesque, but it helps. All except the extremities. My toes become numb inside my shoes after walking only a few blocks, and the tips of my fingers feel as though they are about to fall off, even though I wear a double pair of gloves. After only moments, my breath freezes at the end of my nostrils. Perhaps I will get some of those high felt boots like the Russians wear.

You see, my sweet, Moscow is going through one of her classical winters. It is bitterly cold and there are sudden gusts of wind so strong they churn up the snow. These flurries hit you in the face like ice needles,

187

and you can actually feel the pain. Yesterday was twenty-five below, and today it feels as though it must be even lower.

However, the esthetic part is glorious. All the pristine white snow creaking and squeaking underfoot as we walk along. The sky today is deep blue like a June sky. The sun is so brilliant as it reflects the snow that it makes it all quite dazzling. Moscow belongs in the snow! It is like an enchanted city. The white covers all the roofs and turrets and especially the round domes and cupolas of the churches, so that they look like fluffy white snowballs on top of giant castles.

We took a sleigh ride to visit some friends the other day. The weather was as beautiful as it is today. You would have loved it, my sweet. Such quaint smooth driving and such a picturesque driver. It was still the middle of the afternoon, but the sun was already setting as the days are very short at this time of year. We drove alongside the Moscow River. The sight was as magnificent as I have ever seen anywhere. The floating ice had turned pale pink in the sunset, and as we trotted along, the sun sank even further into the horizon. We watched as gradually the ice changed to a deep orange and then a greenish gray as it reflected the dusk.

Part of our drive took us through a park, where the trees on both sides of the pathway were so heavily weighted with fresh snow that they stooped over to touch in the middle, forming an archway of exquisite snow-laden branches. We were huddled under a thick fur wrap. And with Kayho by my side, the rhythmic clopping of the horses' hooves plus the unbelievable beauty of the trees, it made me believe I was in some kind of magical fairytale. This winter, my sweet, is at once the most wonderful and most difficult I have ever spent. At least for a few hours we forgot our troubles. But I was sorry when it was over. It was like waking up too abruptly from a dream. Quite a little jewel of an outing!

The other evening we saw the historical drama *Peter the Great.* It was a most interesting production. Through it was revealed to me one of the most profoundly interesting epochs in Russian history. Peter the Great was the founder of Leningrad and responsible for the first time in Russia for the importation of European culture. It was also the first time Russia saw any of the Western developments in science and industry. The character of the man was magnificently drawn, and the costumes and the scenery were very authentic. I know how you love historical plays. I told Kayho how much you would enjoy seeing it if it is still on the boards when you get here.

You would love the audiences, too, my darling. The theatergoers wrap themselves in old fur coats, salvaged, I am sure, from the days before the

Revolution. Or they are bundled up to their eyebrows in ancient sweaters and jackets, hurrying so to be sure not to be late. They are most punctual, I must say. You rarely see stragglers coming in late. They are not as tame and polite as the audiences we know in New York. Instead the theaters are packed (they are always packed) with ordinary, simple people, eager and anxious and full of expectation. For many, I think it must be the first time in their lives that they have had the chance to go to a professional production. They look mesmerized, and I think the actors feel the tension because they are so full of enthusiasm, too. For me, it is the quality of the production that is always so great—from the scenery and the mood right down to the most insignificant walk-on role. I only hope it will stay this way although . . . well, I must not talk of such things. For now, the theater is one of the most wonderful experiences this winter in Moscow. So we try to go as often as we can and see all the plays. In fact, Kayho is very understanding. Because we are living temporarily in such a small room in a hotel, he tries to make sure we are out almost every evening. This way, he says, we will not fret over our situation. Either we go to see friends (he has so many friends in Moscow) or it is a concert or a play or a movie. The other evening he took me to a little gypsy café just around the corner and that was fun . . . very lively!

I forgot to tell you that the record you sent of your voice was such an exciting gift for me. It arrived shortly before we moved, and it was something of you at least. We borrowed a phonograph and worked on it until we almost had your natural voice coming over the horn . . . the voice I know so well and love. We worked on it until that machine gave us every syllable and we could catch every word. Please try to make more, and send them as soon as you can. It is like having you next to me.

Another friend of Kayho, Dr. Rabkin, is leaving on a medical scholarship for San Francisco. He is going via New York, and I have asked him to communicate with you on his way. He is coming to see us at 4:30 tomorrow afternoon, and you will probably be hearing from him through Dadzie.

I hope you get this letter on your arrival back in New York. Do not worry, my love, because I am writing letters so infrequently. I shall write far more often from now on because the last thing I want is for you to worry about me. On your side, continue to write to the Red Cross address in Moscow in case we move again in a hurry. Give the same address to any of my friends who still think of me and love me and want to keep in touch with me. I fear they are no longer interested now that my name is not Rabinoff any longer!

Your last letter was very interesting, my sweetheart, and I think your marks for the semester were quite good. After all, you have two A's, one B, one C, and I am quite sure your F in German will not remain an F for long. How are you getting along with Miss Holz? Do you derive any benefit from her, either for raising your grade or intrinsically for the sake of the German?

My sweet, do not worry so much about being a romantic. Of course you are a romantic. First of all, it is because you are naturally so and then also because you will soon be seventeen and a beautiful young woman. That a boy would want to write to you like that is normal, my love. Real love itself will come in its own time and at its own hour, as it has always done throughout the centuries. We shall have a long talk about all of this, my sweet, when I see you again. It is a time for a mother to be with her daughter, and I feel such a longing to be with you. It is an important year for any girl. Meanwhile, tell me all about the class dances, etc. Did you go to the one before Christmas? What happened? We will have so much to tell one another. Letters are so inadequate when people are used to being close and dear.

I shall write again soon. Very soon this time. Meanwhile, look after yourself through the winter weather. Get a hot water bottle for your bed during the cold season, but do not put the water in when it is too hot as it will scald you.

Give my wishes to all my friends and give your special friend Nina a kiss for me. Say hello to all your other friends. Do not worry, my love. Kayho takes as good care of me as he possibly can and is always so thoughtful.

Take care. Eat properly and sleep as much as you can. I worry about you every day, and miss you more and more as each day goes by.

All my kisses, my love. My thoughts are always with you. Always.

Maman

BLUET SIGHED as she stopped writing. Wearily, she laid her pen down on the badly scratched surface of the antique desk at which she was sitting. She glanced around. She could not tell Anna what it was really like to live sealed up for endless days in this not-so-select hotel. A rancid odor permeated the run-down building. Paint was peeling from the walls and the ceiling of the hallway, leaving ugly scars and dark spots. Hallway lighting consisted of a few flickering lightbulbs hanging naked from rusty sockets overhead. Scraps of moth-eaten carpeting crept up the main staircase, stained and threadbare beyond repair. Their room—up a twisting flight of additional steps—was cramped, cell-like, and dim. Paper, hanging forlorn in limp strips from damp walls, was blotched, faded, and torn.

The room itself contained nothing more comfortable than a dilapidated single bed; a heavy armoire that sat uncomfortably on curved legs and wobbled precariously every time someone touched its doors; a beat-up chest of drawers, on which stood a chipped china jug and a basin for washing; plus the curious anomaly of the antique desk and the chair where she was now seated.

The polished floor was the only portion of the room that was clean. But Bluet was well aware that the snoopy women who worked at the hotel were not really there to keep the floors waxed and bright. They were down on their knees to keep a close vigil on whatever was being said and whatever was going on. It was uncomfortable, claustrophobic, and unpleasant in the extreme. For running water or a toilet, it was necessary to use the filthy facilities at the far end of the hallway. Since these were never properly cleaned and were in minimal working order, they added their own nauseating stench to the general odor of decay.

But that was not the worst. Angered over the wider implications of this housing snub, Marc had sarcastically quipped, "Well, at least they provided a room—with a view." Bluet walked over to the small window and immediately realized what he meant. Directly across the street, so close that it was possible to reach out and touch them, were the thick walls of Lubianka prison. Somewhat symbolically, their nearness inhibited even the bravest ray of sunshine from reaching Marc and Bluet's room. Turning her head to one side, Bluet could see the notorious iron gates that swung open and shut throughout each long night—forbidding jaws that swallowed up their fearful cargoes of condemned souls. She and Marc had a ringside seat on death row.

After climbing into bed on their first night, they discovered they had company. Bedbugs, hordes of the little monsters, cavorted in glee, tormenting them as if relishing their role as the repugnant yet irresistible punch line of a cheap, sick joke. Even though it had been nearly midnight when the couple arrived, Marc indignantly marched down to the desk to find the manager. He had had enough! But, of course, nobody was there.

In an insane attempt to get rid of them herself, Bluet frantically rummaged through her valise for the large bottle of Lysol disinfectant she had brought along. Though she appreciated that Lysol would probably be inadequate against these formidable foes, it had proved ideal for another basic

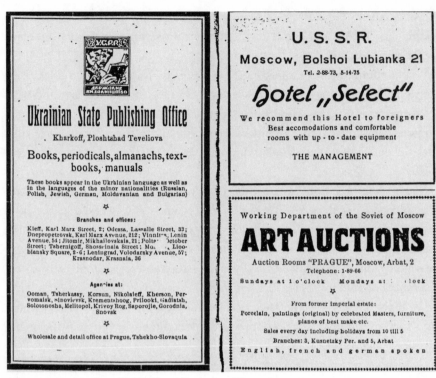

Advertisements from the guidebook Bluet took along with her to Moscow.

problem. From the very first moment she had fully comprehended the uncertainty of her position, she knew that the worst possible complication would have been to find herself pregnant. She was no longer married, and though abortion was readily available under Soviet law, she preferred not to consider it. She had already suffered through this sort of procedure twice in the past and could not have easily tolerated a third.

In previous years she had been a staunch advocate of an old-fashioned method of contraception involving a vinegar douche. It was simple enough to use under normal circumstances. But these were not normal circumstances. Nor did she wish to discuss an alternative with anyone. Therefore, she came to the curious conclusion, based upon a careful reading of the label on the bottle and the usual boudoir gossip, that Lysol was an ideal substitute—if sparingly used.

So far, so good. Now she took out her Lysol to battle this army of insects and rubbed the precious liquid all over the mattress and blankets. "It's ridiculous," she murmured. "I don't believe it. I just don't believe it.

There has to be another way." This latest indignity infuriated her. But, she told herself, nobody would ever accuse her of walking out simply because she refused to confront a Russian bedbug.

Tears were pouring down her face by the time Marc arrived back in the room. He had managed to find two sleepy-eyed porters, and they slouched in behind him. "It won't help," Marc explained, as he took the Lysol from her and capped the bottle. "You're wasting your time." The two men removed the mattress and the bedding and replaced it grudgingly.

But this was not the end of their nightmare. Bluet had almost dozed off to sleep when she was suddenly awakened by a curious popping sound that occasionally punctuated the night silence. At first, she could not readily identify the noise. But lying there, having difficulty sleeping after all that had occurred, she listened to the sound more carefully. It had to be the crack of pistol shots from the prison across the street. She roused Marc, and he whispered, "Don't even listen. Forget about it. Otherwise, we'll both lose our minds."

Yet one basic fact could not longer be ignored. She could never bring her daughter into this living hell. This made her acutely aware that she herself was slipping closer and closer toward an agonizing decision. She could not leave Anna behind forever. Nor could she face abandoning Marc.

As she lay awake that night, weighing the alternatives, an added horror ran through her mind. If it became necessary to go back to her daughter alone, might her departure be interpreted as a sign of treason and jeopardize Marc's life? The authorities could argue that she knew some of his secrets and that she would not hesitate to reveal them once safely outside Russia. On the other hand, she desperately tried to convince herself that perhaps she was being too negative; in fact, her departure might actually help him. It would give Marc the opportunity to return to Katya, live more comfortably, and be reinstated into the good graces of the party. He could rebuild his career and even gain that coveted foreign posting.

It was becoming harder to see him humiliated like this than to accept the discomforts herself—though the specter of continuing much longer under such stultifying conditions did not inspire her. She hated being indolent, not being constructive in any way. Marc would not budge on this point, although he did acknowledge from time to time how deadening such isolation could be for an intelligent, active, and outgoing human being.

And what about the possibility of sudden change? Was there an outside chance that all this terror would soon blow over, as Marc had once indicated, allowing her to pursue a normal life and to consider letting Anna make the trip?

The more she weighed the opposing arguments, the more she appreciated that each solution was no solution at all. Even her ability to reason had become infected with the "paranoia of the proletariat" that paralyzed everyone else. She could no longer view her options from the secure position of the outsider. For better or worse, she was inescapably becoming an active participant. To leave Marc would be heartbreaking. To be responsible for his demise was unthinkable. And having her thoughts interrupted by the monotonous staccato pounding at her from across the street was not exactly conducive to clear thinking.

Damn it! she thought. How could Marc sleep so soundly?

Fifteen

When ruling ideas change there is an accompanying change in the standards by which the deeds of yesterday are judged and this change is perilous to the doers of yesterday's deeds. That which yesterday was regarded as a republican duty and a republican virtue will tomorrow be deemed a crime; the accusers of one day will be the accused of another.

From the biography of Joseph Fouché by Stefan Zweig

CHRISTMAS SNOWFLAKES FELL softly and silently onto the icy streets of Moscow, dusting the shoulders of grim-faced pedestrians, forming gentle mounds atop ragged drunks slumped unconscious in doorways, and blanketing each building in a fresh white cocoon. Nature would not be intimidated from completing her seasonal labors. The sale and the possession of Christmas trees may have been banned by the new regime as a sentimental residue of religious nonsense, but Mother Nature did not heed. She decorated the firs and the pines with her twinkling ice tinsel nonetheless, as if to scoff at nonbelievers.

The epidemic of fear, feeding on the daily lists of indiscriminate arrests, had reached a screaming crescendo in the public announcement of a Great December Show Trial—that supremely Stalinesque circus. Under a leaden sky in the Hall of Columns of the Nobles' Club, the few would publicly confess their "sins" for the consumption and the intimidation of the many.

This trial, among the first of many to come, would serve to lay the blame for the chronic shortages and the ensuing hardships squarely in the laps of saboteurs, rather than on the ineptitude of the dictator. One by one, the leaders of various departments would be forced to play their unwilling roles in these command performances. Ultimately, the trials lasted throughout the upcoming decade of the 1930s and consumed most of the original heroes of the October revolution. These once-respected revolutionaries were forced to degrade and debase themselves, offering monstrous admissions that sickened their comrades.

Their public self-denunciations were understood by outsiders to be the result of deals, whereby the defendants almost certainly traded instant death for the questionable promise of life imprisonment. The mental anguish and the threats against relatives and loved ones that lay behind such public acts of humiliation—only the grim walls of Lubianka would remember. The annihilation of the human personality, the torture, the degradation, the depravity, the slow rotting of the body in the basement cells during the weeks prior to being dragged into the public dock—only the grim, gray walls of Lubianka would remember.

A number of Old Bolsheviks disappeared during this period, without even the benefit of a show trial, giving credence to the notion that only those who agreed to play the roles written for them by their accusers ever saw the blinding arc lamps of the court room. The more stubborn and stouthearted chose instead to retain their honor and dignity, refusing to debase their ideals or prostrate themselves before an ill-bred maniac for whom they had nothing but contempt, even though they knew they faced certain death.

By the end of the 1930s, Stalin reigned supreme, the memories, the sacrifices, and the contributions of the others tarnished or erased forever. A few received the dubious honor of posthumous rehabilitation after Stalin's death, but not many. Some even survived, but not many.

Bread and circuses have long been a favored shibboleth of an autocracy—a tried and true method of placating the people. If bread was now in short supply, then a truly riotous circus was needed as a substitute. And human sacrifice was as potent a form of sport and entertainment in the winter of 1930 as it had been in the forums of ancient Rome.

The show trials eventually made headlines around the world. Members of the Western press descended upon them like starving vultures; this was a perfect opportunity to craft superior prose and win name recognition and prizes. This spellbinding spectacle would sell papers and create instant authorities on Soviet life and politics—a journalist's bonanza.

CLINGING TO MARC'S ARM, Bluet stumbled over hidden cracks and icy mounds in the pavement as they trudged along the snowy sidewalks toward the Hall of Columns. They were on their way to the December trials, too. Marc had insisted that she should be present. At first, he merely suggested she attend. Later he was adamant. "It's important for you to be there," he told her. "You'll be sitting in the GPU box next to me. You must show them you are with us now . . . that you are part of the group. Anyhow," he shrugged, "it will be something to see. You're always complaining that I leave you out. It will be interesting."

So interesting, she concluded wryly, that Marc had been irritable for days. He had refused to speak of anything but the bare outlines of the case as it was being presented to the Russian people. Nevertheless, she was aware that he was far more concerned than he cared to admit. His silences were always more telling than his words.

The charges themselves were simple: Eight engineers were being accused of forming a secret party, the Industrial Party, to conspire with a foreign foe (France) for the purpose of bringing down the government by intervention from abroad and industrial sabotage from within.

As Bluet and Marc entered the hall, they were momentarily awed by the majesty and the brilliance of the setting. The regal, almost medieval, splendor juxtaposed with the grime and the gray of Moscow life seemed incongruous. The ceilings, the walls, and the galleries were a brilliant white, supported by massive Corinthian columns standing like silent sentries from a forgotten age. Each was adorned with a delicate frieze of dancing nymphs cavorting between the tops of the columns and the ceiling. From above, fifty-six blazing chandeliers hung in imperial splendor. The whiteness of the hall was accentuated by the introduction of arc lamps for the convenience of the photographers.

Up on the platform, bright red carpets blanketed the floor, with a matching red cloth covering each of the judges' tables. A contrasting gray cloth draped the prisoners' dock, where the eight accused technicians sat in subdued silence, neatly dressed in business suits, their faces the color and the texture of yellowed parchment.

It was brilliant staging, Bluet observed to herself. And she found herself musing somewhat inappropriately upon Max and his strong belief in the emotional power of spectacular settings. For even the colors had been chosen with meticulous attention to their iconic message.

The trial was already underway as they walked in, and the room was jammed with thousands of anxious and curious spectators. The first few rows were reserved for Russian journalists and foreign press. The rest of the loges around the side had been assigned to members of the foreign diplomatic corps and officials from various Soviet government departments. No one smiled. No one talked. No one relaxed.

197

Marc and Bluet nodded a formal hello to their friend Louis Fischer, the commentator on Bolshevik affairs, who had been invited by Marc to join them in the GPU box and had arrived earlier. They took their places on hard, upright wooden chairs directly to the right of the platform.

Hardly more than an arm's length away sat Professor Ramzin, the chief defendant, after whom the trials would be named. A meek and clean-shaven man in his early forties, he had a curious air of modesty. He was taxing the credulity of spectators by describing the enormity of his "plots" and treasonous deeds.

Normally, when they went anywhere together and the proceedings became too complicated for Bluet's limited understanding of the language, Marc would spend time explaining and translating. Today he remained grave and aloof, studiously training his eyes on the platform.

An extensive knowledge of Russian—after all that she had experienced and witnessed these past weeks—was not needed for Bluet to appreciate that she was witnessing a set-up. The defendants were clearly being railroaded, led through a well-prepared script by Nikolai Vasilyevich Krylenko, the chief prosecutor. He reminded Bluet of a ruddy British country gentleman, suitably attired for fox-hunting. Dressed in a dark tunic, a blue shirt, khaki golfing pants, and high boots, Krylenko had the face of a bulldog and the professional presence of an accomplished actor who well knew how to upstage his fellow performers. His theatrical gestures were mesmerizing.

Yet no Westerner, no outsider, no member of the foreign press—whose faces she instantly recognized but dared not acknowledge—could possibly appreciate the foreboding of those in the audience who knew that they could be the next victims. As she watched the reporters scribble furiously in their notepads, she wondered whether all the Bolshevik sympathizers she knew in America would ever learn the truth, whether something of the tenor of the trials might ever pass the censor. Or would they scoff and say that it was just more of the insidious lies perpetrated by a capitalist press? She had cherished the illusion that the Bolsheviks would indeed build a more humane society. But from inside, it was clear how fast that hope was fading. Marc knew. She knew. She sensed that his friends knew. And Louis Fischer? His face did not reveal a single thought.

She listened attentively as the tale unfolded of how Ramzin and his cohorts were frequently sent to Paris on technical missions. Once there, they contacted the French high command and White émigré leaders, who subverted them with tempting sums of money to build an organization inside

Russia that could overthrow the existing government. The fact that none of the charges were substantiated in the customary manner required by Western courts passed unchallenged. No one on the dais seemed to care.

"The best evidence," declared a triumphant Krylenko, "no matter what the circumstances, is the confessions of the defendants." Each man was therefore given ample opportunity to make statements and even ask questions, though the questions only appeared to further confirm their guilt.

For the record—or, more likely, for world opinion—the defendants were represented by counsel. But these representatives seemed intent upon trapping the defendants into verbally lacerating themselves even more severely.

Several of the defendants made a pitiful stab at a genuine defense, though their statements were directed at obtaining lighter sentences and explaining their motivation, rather than at arguing against the crimes themselves, as confessed. At first, they tried flattery. The great, wise, and compassionate proletariat, they fawned, would surely not be moved to vengeance. "My soul is at peace," admitted Ramzin. "I am happy I confessed."

"Give me a chance to expiate my sins," begged another. "And I will serve the state loyally for ever more. I don't want a traitor's death."

One of the engineers shamefully told of having had a bourgeois upbringing. "A man raised like myself could never understand why the lowly workers should rule," he admitted. "I was unfit to serve."

"I am a class enemy."

"I was bribed."

"We couldn't shake our bourgeois ideology."

"We were wreckers."

Krylenko complained that they could not be heard at the back of the hall. "Speak up!" he commanded.

"We were wreckers!" they shouted.

"Death to the wreckers! Death to the wreckers!" cried the audience.

The horrifying scope of the evil deeds was then revealed in detail. They had installed worn-out equipment. They had tied up capital funds unnecessarily. They had ordered incorrect parts.

"Death to the wreckers!"

The defendants tried to explain that when technical considerations were taken into account, certain goals of the Five-Year Plan made no sense. Why build so many cotton factories before cotton production could be expanded to fill the manufacturing capacity of such factories? Why order expensive assembly-line equipment from America when less sophisticated and less costly British equipment needing more workers (who were available anyway) would do the job at a lower cost?

If they hurried, it was wrecking. If they delayed, it was wrecking. If they shelved a directive entirely because of technical difficulties, it was more than wrecking. It was sabotage. If they allowed equipment to actually break down, then that was sabotage, too.

"Death to the wreckers!"

And what about French intervention to overrun a vulnerable nation now weakened from so much wrecking?

The account of what Western nations planned to do in the rape of Russia appalled the audience. It was civil war all over again, only with a new strategic plan—fuzzy and illogical—but a plan, anyway. Why had the plan not been put into action? The engineers could not explain. No matter. The intent and the collaboration existed. That was enough.

"Death . . . death to the wreckers!"

Ramzin himself raised the most basic, yet compelling, point of all. "The path of wrecking," he said quietly, "is alien to the inner structure of engineering." But nobody cared. It was completely ignored.

Around midafternoon, Krylenko ordered a brief adjournment.

Most of the spectators stood up to stretch their legs or wander outside. Others gathered in tight knots for a conversation with those around them. Marc slipped out to talk to two colleagues. It was then that Bluet noticed Louis Fischer get up, glance nervously around, and approach her cautiously from the rear.

Leaning over her shoulder, he whispered, "Where's your passport?"

"Why?" she inquired. An alarmed look clouded Fischer's normally jovial expression.

"For heaven's sake, where is it?" he whispered urgently. "Tell me."

"I gave it up. I gave it to Marc when I first arrived. Why?"

He shook his head in disbelief. "You shouldn't have done that. You should have kept . . ." He stopped short. Marc reappeared through the doorway and was walking hurriedly toward them. Fischer slipped quietly back to his seat.

"What was that all about?" Marc sensed that he should know.

"Nothing. Nothing at all," she reassured him. "Louis just came over to say hello. He wanted to find out if I understood the Russian. And I wanted to tell him I had that gift ready to take to New York to Anna." Louis Fischer had frightened her. If he, of all people—the man who had defended the

Bolsheviks to a fault—distrusted the new direction, then the situation must have deteriorated beyond repair.

Was Fischer warning her to leave immediately? Not to trust Marc any longer? That she was in danger herself? That Marc was in danger? That Marc might try to hold her against her will for some purpose of his own by not returning her passport? The Byzantine atmosphere pervading Moscow had created a mood where anything was possible. There was no telling how anyone might react where personal survival was at stake.

She resolved to speak to Marc about her passport. But it would have to wait until later, as they had been invited to an important dinner that evening. She was determined not to panic. Panic, she told herself, invariably preceded a foolish error in judgment. How she envied Marc's supreme self-control.

As she sat there watching the crowd of spectators being whipped to a frenzy and loudly chanting with satanic joy, "Death . . . death to the wreckers," she longed to run down to the station, jump on the very next train, and just keep going until she was safely removed from this insanity. In counterpoint to the death song of the audience, Fischer's words rang in her ears. Without a passport or an exit permit, no foreigner could leave the country. There was absolutely no way out. Moreover, she did not want to leave without Marc. She did not want to leave him behind, not even for a few months. Not under these circumstances.

DAYLIGHT WAS ALREADY FADING into charcoal darkness as they left the Hall of Columns and pushed their way through the unruly throngs milling around outside. The proceedings, which would last for several days, were relayed over radio and loudspeakers so that nobody in the capital could shut out this "great event." In the outlying towns and remote villages, those who possessed radios recounted the story to their neighbors and friends. Wide-eyed, they listened to this horrendous plot nipped in the bud in a master stroke by their ever-vigilant government. Miraculously, the Soviet state was still intact. It had survived another thrust from perfidious counterrevolutionaries.

Weaving their way along the crowded sidewalk, the lovers headed back to the hotel to change. They had been invited to the home of their friends the Yulins. That night the Yulins were making a special dinner party for their remaining friends in the Politburo, as well as for commissars and other high-ranking dignitaries who were among their own crowd of Old Bolsheviks.

In honor of the occasion, Marc decided to wear his favorite Donegal tweed suit from Saks. Taking exceptional care choosing just the right tie, he experimented with at least half a dozen different colors and patterns before deciding upon one that satisfied him. Marc did not share the traditional Russian disdain for neckties.

It was a point of contention between him and Bluet. Marc refused to give up his fine Western suits and accessories, disregarding the envy it triggered among his colleagues. "They will resent you," Bluet argued. "It's not a good idea."

"I feel shabby enough," he replied. "Do I have to look the part as well?" He insisted that he was not about to sport a cloth cap, Lenin style. He remained very much the individualist, his sartorial ways being one of them. But Bluet was intuitively aware that it generated an unnecessary risk, even though she also refused to look shabby if she could avoid it. Yet she had made certain compromises, rarely wearing jewelry and purposely dressing in mismatched sweaters and skirts.

It was a savagely cold night and they were already late, but Marc was determined to go. His absence, he explained to Bluet, would have sent the wrong message to his old friends. In fact, the dinner was already in progress by the time they arrived. Still, Yulina greeted them with delight, hugging Bluet and helping her off with her bulky outerwear. Marc shed his coat, hat, and expensive Liberty scarf, rubbing his hands together to chase away the bitter chill.

A long table had been placed in the center of the main living room, with smaller tables set end-to-end to accommodate the anticipated crowd. As the guests arrived, they were immediately ushered to their places and invited to enjoy the "feast." Liberally scattered along the entire length of the table were bottles of vodka, with a reserve stock open and ready on a credenza—the magic potion designed to seduce the crowd, anesthetize the anxious, and embolden the timid. A soup bowl, a plate, slightly stained cutlery, a worn napkin, and a small vodka glass had been set in front of each guest.

Late arrivals simply greeted their friends with a loud and lusty "Good evening" and joined in this makeshift banquet with gusto. Communal self-service, even among the more influential citizens, was the rule in Moscow that winter, a casual reminder of the egalitarian spirit of their revolution.

In the center of the table, pungent and billowy clouds of steam wafted from three huge soup tureens. Each contained a different soup. There was a choice of potato, cabbage, or mixed vegetable broth, in which tiny pieces of fatty meat bobbed up and down or danced in crazy circles as ladles were hungrily dipped in and out.

Yulina had been fortunate that week and, with a wave of her hand and a nod of her head, joyously beckoned the guests to share in her bounty. She looked like a doting mother hovering over a brood of hungry children. Numerous platters of coarse black bread, stacked neatly in mounds of pre-cut chunks, accompanied the soup. Small side plates of thinly sliced cold sausage completed the fare. Butter had long since disappeared from the marketplace. Knowing this, Marc had brought along a small flask of olive oil as a dip for the bread, Italian style, and he graciously offered to share his precious bottle with the guests. "Leave it to Cheftel to beat the system," chided one of his colleagues.

A few of them refused, shaking their heads and waving him off. "Spread oil on black bread?" said one. "I'll accept the system."

"Stalin would applaud your decision," remarked another. The dizzy round of gallows humor, brought on by the events they had all witnessed earlier in the day, was rapidly increasing its pitch.

One guest jokingly suggested that the government import White Russian émigrés, now busy servicing French palates in Paris and on the Riviera, to employ their new catering talents at home in repentance for past sins.

"A magnificent idea," applauded his companion. "But, of course, we'd have to outfit them in red livery."

"Then they'd no longer be Whites!" someone shot back from across the table.

"You see how simple it is to rid the revolution of its enemies," the first man reasoned.

"Have another drink."

"A capital idea."

"Careful of your language, comrade."

The vodka was also beginning to work its mischief.

Conversation turned to *The Shot*, the hit play of the season. A brilliant satire, it portrayed a maverick bureaucrat who had evolved his own style of coping with the system while making a mockery of it. Everyone had expected the play to be quickly closed and the author, Alexander Bezymensky, clapped behind bars to enjoy the "hospitality" of Lubianka prison for such an audacious lampoon. But Stalin had intervened personally to champion its cause. "An ideal vehicle to demonstrate the need for correcting shortcomings . . . in our apparatus," chuckled the wily dictator. As he saw it, the play offered the perfect excuse to accelerate the ongoing purges.

So it had now become a safe conversation piece. Only a few weeks earlier Marc had taken Bluet to see the play, and they had laughed from beginning to end. They both relished the whimsical view of human ingenuity on the loose that Bezymensky had captured.

As the partygoers were a witty, articulate, and intellectually quick group, the chatter grew fast and stimulating. Conspicuously absent was any mention of personal relationships, as even marriage had been relegated to a position of political expediency. The public display of marital harmony had to be maintained, even when there was an absence of love or passion and despite the constant conflict, irritation, and, in many instances, boredom as well. Romantic roundabouts were not for them. Whether for political advancement or personal advantage, these influential citizens recognized the value of retaining the marriage bond in such hazardous times. Marc was an anomaly—the rebellious nonconformist.

As the evening wore on, the frenzied emotions boiling inside each person spewed forth in an excited babble of voices. Everyone chattered away as if a constant stream of words could wash away the tensions. Thick swirls of acrid gray smoke from a variety of cigarettes and pipes overhung and filled the room, blurring the vision and watering the eyes. Vodka glasses were filled and refilled, their contents consumed in rapid gulps. The countless bottles soon stood empty on the credenza.

Marc, alone among these men, alone among these endangered relics of a revolution gone sour, maintained composure, listening and nodding but not really hearing. His thoughts were clearly elsewhere. Occasionally, he glanced over at Bluet and smiled warmly at his cherished French Limoges, so out of place at this table of the damned.

All sought refuge, at least temporarily, from the political storm enveloping them. They knew that Alexi Rykoff, the titular head of government, was soon to be relieved of his post, together with Mikhail Tomsky, the fiery trade union leader, and Nikolay Bukharin, the great Marxist theoretician. Not one person at the dinner that night, despite his or her title or influential associates, could feel secure, linked irrevocably as everyone was with the old-timers. Conversation had an Alice-in-Wonderland ring. They were participants in a Mad Hatter's Vodka Party, a Bacchanalian feast of the condemned. They were paralyzed by the realization that sooner or later most, if not all, of them would be consigned to the scrap heap of the revolution, their destinies subject to the whim of the madman they had been unable to dethrone.

At one end of the table, a plump young man and an elderly commissar assessed the music of Tchaikovsky.

"A petty bourgeois composer."

"Cheap sentimental nonsense."

"Romantic rubbish."

"It should be banned!"

"A bit harsh, comrade. It only needs revision."

"We can't do it."

"Why not?"

"We don't know any revisionists."

"Another drink?" He cursed at an empty bottle in indignation.

"I'll find a fresh one," his companion reassured him.

At another corner of the table, a woman howled in fits of hysterical laughter, while a man at her side continually banged on the table.

Bluet tried to remain calm, chatting amiably with those around her, nibbling at her food, and only occasionally sipping her drink. Her sense of caution restrained her sense of fun—as did Marc's. She was deeply troubled by what they had witnessed that day. However, considering the influential nature of the company and everyone's present state of disorientation, she found it a propitious moment to do a little personal lobbying of her own. Trying to enhance the image of her and Marc as a couple, she gently reminded several guests of her own significant contribution to the Bolsheviks over the years, through her association with Max. As to their current living conditions— well, a word dropped diplomatically to the women who knew best what it meant to be without permanent living quarters was not to be overlooked. When asked several times for her opinion of the trial, she smiled sweetly and explained, "Unfortunately, my Russian was not good enough to follow the proceedings."

For Marc, it was an ideal time once again to reflect upon how his putative mentor—that virtuoso of intrigue and survival, Joseph Fouché—would have reacted and resurrected his personal political fortunes under similar circumstances. Marc was not about to wallow in drunken self-pity, like the others around him, or hide, like Trotsky, who during those long leadership fights always managed to be somewhere else when his followers set the stage for his triumphal return.

In this respect, Marc held a decided advantage over his compatriots, who came directly from the ranks of the old Lenin-Trotsky group. Having operated most of his life in the international arena and lived abroad, he reasoned, he could not be branded with the mark of any one faction. His being a lesser figure, out of the public eye—a behind-the-scenes operative—provided a measure of maneuverability. As all hopes of Stalin's imminent ouster had faded for the moment, perhaps some measure of compromise with the Stalinists was in order. It might earn him an overseas posting, even a very minor one, thus achieving his real goal: to get the hell out for good. For although he was not so foolish as to admit it to anyone, it was patently clear—at least, to Bluet—that he had had enough.

Marc therefore displayed more than his customary composure, nursing only one small glass of vodka throughout the entire evening. He spoke infrequently and then only to make small talk. He would not be drawn into controversy. Any one of these pitiful creatures could drop a word the next day that could make all the difference. No doubt they would do it to each other. It was in the nature of the current struggle. There were few heroes left. Stalin had already seen to that.

Ultimately, it was Yuri Piatakov, Lenin's favorite and an avowed enemy of Stalin, who interrupted the dinner to comment on the day's events. As he became fortified with sufficient vodka, his tongue began to loosen. And with his eyes blazing, he shouted, "They were cowards, the lot of them. They didn't even fight for their lives. They behaved like a pack of sheep! Cowards!" he repeated with disgust and glanced around at the guests seated at the table.

An eerie hush descended over the room.

"They could have at least made an effort," Piatakov thundered on. "They didn't even try to defend themselves."

"They probably knew it was hopeless," muttered someone farther down the table, with more courage than sense. "All Moscow knows what it was really about. Haven't you heard the latest joke? One man says, 'Have they reached the *prigovor* [verdict]?' To which his friend sneers, '*Prigovor?* You mean the *dogovor* [agreement or collusion]!'"

"Like Danton," continued Piatakov, ignoring the comment, while recalling an incident from the French revolution over a hundred years earlier. "I kept thinking about Danton all day . . . sacrificing himself without hardly a murmur . . . not even challenging the guard who refused to let him bid his friend farewell as they rode together in that rattling wagon to the scaffold. 'Our heads will kiss in the basket,' sobbed Danton. Do you remember that? He would not even speak up as one last gesture to his closest comrade. I cannot understand a man like that. If you are going down, then at least go down fighting. These were intelligent men. What happened to them?"

Since Marc had been the only man in the GPU box that day, all heads instinctively turned toward him. If he had any inside knowledge, he was not about to pass it along. "Could have been anything," he shrugged, tossing the remark aside with a casual brush of his hand and a slight furrow of the brow, which was his own peculiar guarded way of registering contempt for the actions of all parties. "And if you will excuse us, we must be leaving. It's been a long day."

He pushed back his chair and motioned to Bluet to fetch her coat. She reappeared a few moments later with her usual extra coat perched neatly over her shoulders on top of the first and began to bid each guest goodnight.

Then it happened.

The rather plump, bull-necked commissar at the end of the table who had banished Tchaikovsky, while pouring profuse quantities of vodka down his throat, leaned forward. With rivulets of perspiration running down his cheeks, he studied Bluet accusingly. "Why all those coats?" he growled menacingly, shaking an index finger at her. "How many coats have you got to wear! Two? One on top of the other? Many of our people have no coats at all! You foreigners are all alike. And what will our people think when one of our own party members goes around with a woman like you?"

There was an embarrassed silence. Such a remark would normally have been tossed aside as the unfortunate blathering of an inebriated clown. But on this night, it electrified and momentarily numbed them all. Yulina stood transfixed in shock. All eyes turned toward Bluet. She looked frantically over at Marc.

Marc placed a hand protectively around her shoulder, stared at the accuser, and drew in a deep breath. Responding quietly but with a contemptuous smile, he reminded the man of a basic tenet of the revolution. "To each according to his needs, comrade. Your pleasure is to shake off the chill with vodka. She prefers an extra coat."

It was a razor-sharp dig.

The commissar continued to stare. Nobody spoke: uneasy guests dropped their gaze to their empty soup bowls. Then, leaning back, the commissar slapped his knee and roared with laughter. "A doctor with a sense of humor.

I like that." He reached over to grab the nearest bottle of vodka to refill his glass yet again and turned aside to continue his conversation with a neighbor as if nothing had happened.

The giddy chatter resumed. Shaking his head, Piatakov sat back in his chair, then stared into space in stony silence.

The vodka had done its work.

Still, Bluet had turned quite pale. Yulina accompanied them to the door. "Don't worry," she whispered. "He's too drunk to even remember what he said. Don't give it a second thought."

For Bluet and Marc, the Mad Hatter's party had ended.

ON A CLEAR MIDWINTER NIGHT, moonlight casts strange and sweeping shadows across the Moscow snow, increasing the size of every building and giving ghostly life to every skeletal tree. Each sudden gust of wind pumps new vitality into these silhouettes, as they dance like well-rehearsed performers in a silent underworld ballet to a backdrop of piercing moonbeams and twinkling star glow. At such times a strange oriental beauty descends upon the old city, transforming ancient stone towers and crenellated walls into shadowy reminders of a dimly remembered past.

The streets, emptied by the lateness of the hour, were strangely silent as Bluet and Marc trudged wearily back through the narrow lanes toward the cramped and threadbare room they called home. The stillness only accentuated the dreamlike revelry of the party. For a time, only the rhythmic sound of the creaking snow underfoot punctuated the silence.

As if to mock the devil himself, whose presence was keenly felt that frigid December night, Marc scooped up a handful of snow and playfully tossed it at her coat. "That's one for the overcoat," he said.

But she was in no mood for fun. She was frightened.

"Marc, I'm no good for you here."

"You're just upset because a crude drunk passed a personal remark. Forget it, like Yulina said. Vodka has been known to addle brains."

"It's not only that. I've felt it for a long time. I wasn't going to say anything, but it's growing worse. Nobody trusts me. I'm hurting you, and that's the last thing I want. I'm in your way. I can't help you. I'm not doing you any good at all. You'll resent me in the end."

"You're doing me a world of good."

"You know exactly what I mean. Your career. I'm no good for your career. And whatever you say now, you're too ambitious to let anyone hold you back for long. I'm not an asset. I'm not Russian. I'm not acceptable."

Everyone told her that Marc had been a key player on the official reception circuit for important foreign visitors before he left for America. The former Cheftel apartment in Moscow had reflected this previous status; it was a spacious and comfortable home designed for entertaining visiting dignitaries, particularly those in the medical field. Indeed, it had been given to them for this purpose. Together with Katya, he had hosted many such occasions and had been among the most important party functionaries at others. No such invitations had been proffered since Marc left his wife and stubbornly insisted upon living with his mistress.

"Maksim Litvinov has a foreign wife," Marc commented. "It's not hurting him."

"She's British and she's been around a lot longer than I have," Bluet argued. "Anyway, they're married. They have children."

"Marriage is a foolish bourgeois relic," he said, grinning with satisfaction at his own joke. He had continued to stall on the question of marriage, offering endless excuses. "Do you honestly believe a piece of paper could make any difference to us?"

She could not agree. She was rather partial to that specific bourgeois relic. There was dignity in it. And she had a great need for dignity. "And children," she said. "I suppose they're a relic, too."

"On the contrary. Don't you know our revolutionary slogan 'Our children . . . The Hope of Our Future.' No country is more child-conscious than ours."

"I'm not even a party member."

"That's true."

"I have an American passport."

"Would you prefer a Russian one? You surprise me."

"Where's my passport, Marc?"

He didn't respond. Instead, he kicked at a mound of snow.

"Where is it, Marc? I'd feel better having it with me . . . just in case I ever need it in a hurry. I mean . . . just in case anything happens to Anna, and I needed to go back quickly."

"I have it, don't worry," he hedged. "I put it away at the office for safekeeping."

"Could you please bring it home as soon as possible?"

"Remind me tomorrow."

"Marc, can't you be serious for a moment?" Bluet was in no mood for this sort of banter. "I mean, about my being in the way. Those wives are flawless party women. They're even related to the right people. What am I? Who am I?"

He thought about that one for a moment. "Someone I want with me more than anyone else. Someone I love."

"That's not the point. I was an asset to Max. Without me, the whole crowd would have drifted apart. Everyone was always blowing up at everyone else and usually at the worst possible moment. I had to smooth things over. I'm sure half his enterprises would have exploded without me. It was like a partnership. Even he appreciated that. I have no real purpose here. I'm an outsider. And it looks like everyone wants to keep it that way."

"You'd prefer a man to put you to work rather than love you? Anyhow," he added, "I'm not sure I want you to be part of what's going on now."

"If I left," she continued, ignoring his comment, "you could go back to Katya. She's the right kind of wife for you. She always has been. You could live comfortably. After a while, everyone would forget what happened. You could pick up as before."

"If that's what I wanted, I would never have brought you here. I'm not regretting my decision. Not for one moment."

They walked on in silence. "Enough for one day," he said wearily. "Relax. And by the way, wear just as many coats as you need. The weather's going to be even colder next month. Wear three coats. That bully! What the hell does he know?"

In the stillness of this strange night, they heard the drone of an airplane flying low overhead. They could see the colored lights on its wing tips, as it swooped and soared over the city, unfettered, and onward into the blackness of the midnight sky. Marc watched it longingly until it disappeared from view. Speaking softly, he said, "It's time for us both to make friends with those boys up there. Now, does that answer all your questioning?"

It did. She had hardly anticipated an admission, oblique though it was, that he was now as desperate as she was to leave. Instead of ridding himself of her, he wanted to go along. There had to be a way, she thought.

Sixteen

Anna, mon trésor,

I am longing to know that you are back in New York. It seems so much nearer than Mexico, my sweet, and so much safer to your old mother. I am sure that you must have had a wonderful time. Tell me all about it.

By the time this letter reaches you at home, you will most likely have seen or heard from Kayho's friend Dr. Rabkin, who was going to stop in New York on his way to San Francisco. If you have not heard, call Dadzie about him. You see, you might have just missed each other, as he was going to reach New York the 10th or 11th of January. Did you receive the necklace I sent you through Louis Fischer? Did he stop in to see you?

Your last letter made me very happy, my love, and your composition was so beautiful that I was very proud. I do not wonder it was the best in the class. It was my Anna who wrote it and it was full of the sweetest, dearest memories. I will keep it and cherish it always.

Kayho is very busy right now, but he gives me all the spare time that he has. We are still at the hotel, as you can see, but I keep hoping it will not be for much longer. It will make you smile to know I have a little friend, a furry little gray mouse who visits me each morning in the hope of some crumbs. He seems to be so hungry, poor thing. He always comes out soon after Kayho has left and I am alone. I'm not a bit afraid. He scampers over to near where I am sitting eating my breakfast (some black bread which I spread with a little olive oil I brought with me from Berlin), setting himself back on his hind legs, rubbing his front paws together and twitching his whiskers as if to say, "Well, what goodies can you spare for me today?" I call him my Romanov mouse because in his own funny way he is so quaint and charming and polite that I have decided he must surely be a relic from the imperial days. He sits

211

chomping away at the crumbs by the carved wooden legs of the beautiful French provincial desk we have in our room, as if to eat in any lesser spot would be a come-down, poor thing.

Thank you again for all the magazines, *New York Times*, etc. I do not know what I would do without them! Kayho loves to read the *Times* each morning while he is having his breakfast in the room before he leaves the hotel. We have both been surprised at the amount of space the paper has been giving events in Moscow. Sometimes he reads certain articles out loud to me while I am still half asleep, especially when it is something he knows I might enjoy. He was making me laugh this morning. He was reading the list of Broadway plays, the concerts and operas and so forth, and asking which we should go and see. Then he started on all the Christmas advertisements from the stores. Everything looks so good this year, but, of course, it's over now. He finished by putting on his best American accent—which you know is really terrible—and read straight through the society news in the haughtiest of tones. It sounded so funny. The tears were rolling down my face by the time he was through. At times like these I do love him so. I was laughing so hard that in the end I had to bury my head under a pillow so as not to make too much noise and wake the other guests. The walls are thin and sound travels right through.

Thank you for the *Ladies Home Journal*, *McCalls*, etc. I cannot look at all those delicious food pages for very long because, my sweet, I cannot get many of those things here at the moment. My mouth waters at the sight of those delicious dishes. Even Kayho glances over them longingly. Reading through those magazines makes me feel like I am on a different planet. But you must keep sending them. I read them from cover to cover! That article in December *McCalls* about Russian women was especially interesting. I shall have to tell some of my friends how lucky they are! I will be interested in reading Part Two next month and Kayho wants to see it because I believe it has something to do with the Health Department.

I still go to see my new friend Yulina nearly every day. Someone gave her some coffee beans last week. Coffee is so difficult to obtain here now and she was all excited. But she did not know what to do with the beans and how to turn them into a cup of coffee. Why she thought I might be able to help, I really do not know, but she called on me frantically. So the other evening Kayho and I went over there, and I started working on those beans. How I worked! I was so anxious to get at least one cup of coffee out of them that without any knowledge of what to do, I just used my imagination and began cooking. I roasted them first of all in a little oil that she had managed to get until they began to give off that wonderful coffee aroma. Everyone crowded around just to sniff that marvelous smell of fresh coffee. Then we discovered we needed a grinder. For a moment we were in a panic because Yulina thought she had thrown her grinder away years before in all the upheavals. Finally, she found it tucked away somewhere at the top of a closet. It looked like an antique (it would have been in the antique stores in New York, I'm sure). But we scrubbed it and put in the beans. Then I boiled some water and a short time later we all sat around drinking my homemade coffee. It tasted so special. When you have not been able to get something for a while, it always seems that much more precious when you have it again.

I am glad that Tessim Zorach [*the son of William Zorach, the noted avant-garde sculptor; Tessim was eventually a respected artist in his own right*] is so friendly with you and sorry because I know your reaction to him. He is a nice young man, though, and it is indeed wonderful for David that they should be friends. They both complement one another perfectly and their friendship should be beneficial to both of them. I also am happy to see that you have renewed your own friendship with David. Are you going out with him or is your friendship localized in school? It would be nice if you could do some of the theaters together. You seem to be seeing more of the girls lately and I am glad of that, too, and that you are keeping up your close friendship with Nina. She has always been a faithful friend. Kiss her for me and tell her to write. Ask her mother to write also, even if I do not always write back. These letters mean more than you can imagine. She is such a dear. I also see that Miss Daringer is giving you a great deal of her time. She is a delightful person and a very good English teacher and I am most grateful. Tell her so and tell her how nice it would be to see her again one day. Say hello also to Miss Eaton for me. She does wonders with that library. I would love to hear from all of them. Do ask them all to write! And always give them the Red Cross address.

I only hope that the trip to Mexico did you a lot of good, and that you rested and that it interested you. Mademoiselle wrote last week to say that Daddy's teeth were bothering him and he was having a pretty difficult time. How is he now? All fine, I hope. Did you go to Dr. Woods yourself? You had better, if you didn't. It is important to maintain your teeth in perfect condition, and I cannot be there right now to make these appointments for you. If you don't want to go to Dr. Woods (I know how you feel about him), then go to Dr. David instead and make sure nothing is wrong.

Tomorrow night we are going to see *La Fille de Madame Argot,* an old operetta that has been very well produced here. I will tell you all about it in my next letter.

My sweet love, I am including a letter for *grandmère* in France. Send it to her as soon as you receive it, and write to her as well so that she receives a letter from both of us. You understand! She is so alone, poor thing. I am terribly unhappy and surprised that she said she was three months without money. Daddy assured me that Miss Rose had cabled for two months before I left. Please, sweetheart, discuss this with Daddy and ask him to repair this error, if error there was, as *grandmère* most assuredly has to borrow money to live. This is most important and makes me very unhappy, but I trust you will attend to it as soon as you receive this letter. Let me know. I shall write to *grandmère* and somehow try to explain the whole situation. I know she is going to be most tragically unhappy. I wanted to avoid giving her this shock, but I suppose I will have to. Do not forget!

Well, my sweet, the first of the year is in a few days. All my thoughts are running with you. All my wishes. All that is best in me is for you. Be patient. Time passes quickly and soon we shall be together again.

Kiss Mademoiselle for me and give her all my wishes for the New Year. Tell her how important her own letters are to me and how much I thank her for taking such good care of my darling daughter.

What can I add about my wishes for you? To see you. I keep your photo near to me and look at it all the time. I have played that record of your voice so many times, I think it is finally wearing out! We will not even be together to wish each other what we feel for the New Year. I have so many wishes for 1931 and for all the people I love. But we cannot look into the future. We can only hope. That is all. Kayho sends you his love, and he still takes such wonderful care of me all the time.

Write again soon. Very soon, my darling. Write to me. I think of you more than you can possibly imagine.

Always,
Maman

Bluet put down her pen, afraid she would run out of ink and not be able to get any more. She felt terribly guilty because Max had apparently decided not to support her mother any longer. This was yet another disgrace, on top of everything else. It made her original decision to leave seem so self-centered and absurd.

A FEW DAYS LATER, Bluet and Marc attended a small New Year's Eve party given by their old friends Mika and Regina Gurevitch. Soon after midnight, they left a rather muted crowd of revelers, and, as they meandered slowly back through the cobblestone passages of the old city, Marc wondered out loud, "Are there really going to be twelve months in this one for me?"

He gazed up at the clear winter sky sparkling with thousands of stars, whose very same lights had shone down on previous generations. Marveling at their longevity, he mused, "They have so much time. Think about it. The ancient sages and all the great figures of history saw the identical stars. Why are human beings given so little time to make their presence felt? I remember growing up believing I had forever. Everything was in the future. The prospects were infinite. Now all I can think about is that it's over. It was too quick. Nothing worked out the way it was supposed to."

"You're becoming unnecessarily morose," Bluet said. "This is not like you at all. Whatever's giving you such crazy ideas?"

"Nothing really. It's just a feeling," he replied. "Maybe it's the atmosphere that's depressing us all. Did you notice how nobody toasted the New Year with much enthusiasm? There are just too many changes. The revolution is starting to devour its own."

"Not you," she assured him. "It hasn't affected you personally. So maybe you're wrong. How do you know that our luck won't take a turn for the better?"

"Luck," he said. "I never used to think about luck. Now I keep looking for omens. I'm getting superstitious, and that's not what a good communist should be doing. We always thought of superstition as the bane of the Russian people."

"And what do you see in the stars for us, my darling philosopher?" she teased.

"I'd rather not say."

For a man who had challenged life with the grace and the bravado of a medieval knight, this was a chilly comment indeed. It was, she thought grimly, as if a shadow were passing over his soul.

Though he never cared to use the telephone in their room, as one could not be sure if it was being monitored, he soon began calling his old Italian friend and comrade Palmiro Togliatti. They had been working together closely in Moscow for several months. At first, it was just to wish Togliatti all the best for the coming year. But it started a trend. The calls became more frequent, and they reminisced in Italian about the old days, though Marc was far too cautious to admit that he missed the easygoing warmth of Mediterranean life.

He became obsessed with the notion that he had a rendezvous with death in the not-too-distant future and that it was waiting in the shadows to cheat him out of seeing the fruits of his labors. But he did not seem to fear death for its own sake. Was it better, he wondered aloud, to champion a cause and die early or to live out one's life solely in pursuit of personal pleasure? He had grasped pleasure and relinquished it for a cause. Had this been a hopelessly romantic illusion?

Suppose he lost his race with time? Who would remember? Katya? He had scorned her. Children? He had none. His beloved Bluet? He had let her down. And anyway, if she ever got out, a woman as attractive as she was would probably find a replacement pretty soon afterward. His was not a name that would be inscribed in the history books. Historians paid scant attention to those who played supporting roles. They focused and refocused their energies on the lives of a handful of the world's most famous leaders. To the Russians, he would conveniently be dismissed as a counterrevolutionary. To the Jews, he would be seen as a traitor who gave the wider world yet another reason to hate them. His original rationale would thus be lost to them. He had tarnished their good name through his association with a movement that was increasingly being identified with brute tyranny. To his friends, he would simply become a misbegotten association.

Although his leisure reading had previously centered on practical needs— newspapers, periodicals, and occasionally a book from abroad on foreign affairs—it now included Jewish religious texts. It was as if Marc, son of Solomon, were searching for a pathway within his own Judaism that held the promise of influencing and seeking a closer union with Divine Providence. It was the way he had always approached his life, believing that there was no obstacle that could not be overcome, as Spinoza pointed out, with superior knowledge and understanding.

If it were preordained that he should die prematurely, then at least he should try to discover the reason. Perhaps then he would be in a position to alter his fate? It was an audacious concept for an audacious man who now saw a need to approach his dilemma on a spiritual, as well as on a temporal, plane. Not only did he fear losing control of his own destiny, he was also grasping for an understanding of why the movement had soured. Perhaps

God, in His infinite mercy and wisdom, might provide the necessary assistance or at least an explanation. Besides, Marc was not an atheist. He was a paladin, a champion, an adventurer. A true socialist society could still salve the wounds of its people. He retained that belief. Perhaps to cleanse the wounds, one must scourge the soul. There was an answer to it, somewhere.

Though floundering in spiritually muddy waters, Marc repeatedly refused to discuss his Judaism. Significantly, it was the one topic upon which he never gave free rein to his irrepressible wit. He was too emotional about it. Much of it ran counter to his supposedly communist beliefs. But Bluet was learning that he could never totally deny his ancestral faith. He could not operate purely as an ethnic Jew. He was too sentimentally attached to the old ways; too theosophical for that.

Bluet might have treated this as a passing phase, the reaction of a cerebral, innately mystical Russian to extreme pressure. She would have felt presumptuous interfering (though she did question how prudent it was for him to keep such books around) had he not embarked upon a far more perilous course for both of them.

In the midst of that savage winter, in the middle of that period when the Stalinists were determined to crush nonconformity, particularly among party members, in the middle of the winter when Stalin personally renewed his attack on all vestiges of religious practice (requiring prayer books of any denomination to be turned in and demanding curtailment of public worship), Marc insisted upon attending clandestine Jewish religious services—not occasionally, but regularly.

Bluet might have never found out had she not noticed him remove a tiny white prayer cap and a fringed shawl from his suitcase on certain mornings and stuff them hurriedly into his briefcase when he thought she was not looking. After he dropped the cap by accident one morning, they stared at each other in awkward silence.

"Don't worry. Nobody knows," he whispered, as he snatched it from the floor and left the room. But that was not enough. Bluet knew only too well that there was hardly anything about anyone that ultimately did not find its way to the authorities in the end.

She had been careful. She had not attended Catholic Mass at Christmas, an absence that troubled her considerably. She even kept her feelings to herself the day that Marc introduced her to the founder and the creator of the Museum of Anti-God—an exhibition of blasphemous cartoons and desecrated icons. They had met the man by chance on the street. And from Marc's warm and friendly attitude, she had the impression he had rediscovered a long-lost comrade. That was the trouble with Marc. It was impossible to tell what he was really thinking. That museum, which she had visited at the beginning of her stay, made her wonder more than once whether perhaps there might just be some justification to the notion of divine retribution. Did this ever occur to the founder of the museum, too? Might he also recite prayers on the side, as Marc did . . . just in case?

She felt compelled to caution Marc but was determined to wait for the right moment to discuss it. She chose an evening when they decided to eat nearby at their favorite little gypsy café. The nightly fare at the Hotel Select, a minuscule portion of leathery chicken, accompanied by congealed rice, served tepid on a greasy plate, had never once varied in all the months they spent there. Still, they were lucky to have any sort of meat, and this was only because the Hotel Select was primarily a GPU billet. To help cement loyalty, the GPU maintained special farms where it raised livestock and poultry.

Luxury though it may have been, by prevailing standards, the food was so unappetizing that they tried to eat out as often as possible. The menu at the café was not much better, but at least it offered a change of scene and some variety.

It was, in fact, a squalid basement eatery located five worn stone steps below a row of tumbledown shops. Red and white checkered cloths, sticky and crudely patched, covered the small rectangular tables that were clustered together to provide space for the nightly hordes, who were anxious to escape their dreary, overcrowded lodgings. Dim lightbulbs, hanging low under burgundy tassel shades, masked the stained, flaking plaster walls. A group of upright chairs, each supporting a guitar, had been set up on a low wooden platform in the center of the room. Soon after eight o'clock, gypsy singers, outfitted in multicolored costumes fashioned after the traditional layered and embroidered regalia of their forebears, pranced onto this makeshift stage with much clamor and ado to chant their soul-stirring melodies, accompanied by the frenzied strum of their guitars and the jangle of tambourines.

These gypsies were a colorful group, with their brazen makeup, blackened hair, and arrays of ill-assorted necklaces and bangles that clanked and clicked in rhythmic counterpoint to their music. All evening long, these provocative performers weaved in and out of the tables in wild revelry, jousting playfully with the audience. Meanwhile, harried waiters performed their own strange ritual, swerving with masterly precision to avoid the dancers, while balancing a tray on high with a forefinger and a thumb. The audience, starved for a song and a few hours of release, usually burst into a spontaneous, rowdy mixture of carousing, clowning, and laughter.

Bluet and Marc munched on pieces of bitter sausage and sipped their grease-laden vegetable "borscht" with disfigured spoons. Chunks of coarse black bread and vinegary Caucasian wine rounded out the meal. As regular visitors to this bizarre subterranean refuge, they often brought their friends. Tonight they were alone.

It was therefore an ideal place and time to talk. The clamor made eavesdropping impossible. Continually taking walks to engage in real conversation was impractical and irritating, considering the arctic temperatures at that time of year.

At first Bluet hesitated, waiting for Marc to mellow after drinking a few glasses of the wine, eating a little food, and listening to the music. There was something special, he told her, about those lyrical and sensual melodies. That evening he was particularly captivated by the words of a haunting song, translating it for her and telling her the Russian folk tale upon which it was based. As the story wound toward its conclusion, he said unexpectedly, "We've let them down. We've let them all down."

He stared into his empty glass. "I remember," he continued, "right at the beginning the peasants expected great things. Now what's happened to them? They've been driven off the land. Collectivized. But are they better off? Is anyone better off? We thought we could achieve something. We gave them hopes and aspirations that are never going to be fulfilled. You cannot believe the real mood of the people. The bitterness. The despair. They're looking for someone to blame, and they're already starting to say it's our fault, just like in the old days."

"I don't understand."

He groped for a way to explain. "You see, in some ways it's similar to when I was growing up. I can feel it. I've come back to a Russia that's as bigoted as ever. We thought communism was going to eliminate all that, but it hasn't. It's still here. Anti-Semitic incidents are already being ignored in the smaller towns, even though these are supposed to be vigorously suppressed. It's become a low priority. The practice is too deeply ingrained in the Russian soul. I should have understood it all along. Stalin intuitively recognized this and has been capitalizing on it. He's cunning. He understands. To them, we will always remain the despised *zhid*. You can't alter centuries of hatred overnight.

"I remember, just about the time I left for America, there was a big ideological fight going on. Trotsky, Zinoviev, and Kamenev—the foremost Jews in the leadership—were locked in a power struggle with Stalin's inner group. All sorts of grotesque cartoons appeared in the papers, jeering at the three of them for being Jews. 'Oh, no,' the Stalinists insisted. 'We're fighting them because they're opportunists.' Yet the newspapers kept reminding the public that the leaders of this so-called opportunist clique were Jews. It helped the Stalinists enormously.

"There are too many of us at the top today, and we're going to pay the price. Look what happened to Kaganovitch. He was put in charge of the Ukraine four years ago. He was genuinely a man of the people. Crude, perhaps, and far too much of a sycophant. But he was not criticized for his character, only because he was a Jew. The Ukrainians spread vicious propaganda against him. It was unthinkable, they said, to accept a Jew as their leader. They made such a fuss that Kaganovitch had to be recalled to Moscow.

"And that's only the beginning," Marc continued. "They've already started to go after our children." He told her how earlier that month in the Kizel coal mining region, a group of Jewish schoolboys had been attacked and beaten, specifically at the instigation of the director of the school. Almost immediately, it had provoked a further episode involving some youths who were part of Komsomol—the organization that trains young people for party leadership. Hearing about the other incident, the youths thought it would be fun to devise something of their own. Cornering one of their Jewish comrades in the schoolyard, they poured icy cold water over the boy and then dripped liquid candle wax all over his body.

Bluet and Marc were both silent for a while. It triggered a memory. "Has this anything to do with the brutal way you treated that priest?" she asked, recalling an incident that had astonished and angered her shortly after she arrived. A Russian Orthodox priest had knocked at their door, begging for a few slices of bread, while they were still at the apartment. Many priests were left destitute after the communists destroyed their churches. It became a common sight to see a begging priest. Marc had lost his temper and his customary self-control. Shaking with rage, he shouted, "We don't want your kind around here," after which he slammed the door in the priest's face.

Now he said, "You would have had to witness the horrors of a pogrom to really understand. It was always the priests with outward displays of Christian charity and compassion who whipped up hatred among the people. How could I feel pity for the man? Maybe I should have, but I couldn't.

I certainly wasn't inclined to share our few slices of bread with him. If the positions had been reversed, he'd have taken great pleasure in watching me starve to death."

"You don't truly believe that?" Bluet sounded horrified.

"Yes, I really do. Perhaps that's why I feel so despondent. What did we fight for? A new czar? A new Jew baiter? We're going down again. I'm certain of it."

"Then why," she began, sensing the ideal moment to mention her primary concern, "are you putting yourself personally in danger by . . . well . . . the cap . . . "

He did not answer.

"Is it such a good idea for someone in your position?" Bluet continued. "Especially at a time like this?"

In a whisper, he told her, "That was something else many of us thought would not go this far. We knew we had to break the power of the church, the political power, the ignorance, the superstition, and the prejudice that organized religion fostered. But for a while back there, we overlooked a lot once the organized aspects of the religion and the leaders were under control.

"Even Lenin appreciated that the religious fight had to be waged with special skill and delicacy, or the people wouldn't accept it. The sacking of churches will have to die down again, just like after the French revolution. It will have to stop. You can't wipe out religion overnight, especially in the villages. It will only go underground. We're seeing it already. It's neither good politics at this point nor good sense. This year's banning of Christmas trees was petty and foolish. They could have reached a compromise."

"And you?" she asked, bringing him back to her original point.

"Don't worry so much. I'm not the only one, by any means, if that's any comfort to you. We had a report just the other day. It amused me. Religious icons were discovered in the home of the secretary of the local League of Militant Atheists. Of all people! We found out that he had secretly baptized his children, too. You see what I mean? So I'm not going to give up something I want to keep. Don't waste time trying to persuade me. I know what you're going to say. It's far more dangerous for someone in my position. But you must understand. There are certain things that are fundamental to all of us. I feel I have to draw the line somewhere. But," he added, patting her hand, "I can assure you I'm not putting either of us in any danger."

Then he added, somewhat curiously and in a manner that gave her no initial idea that there was a close relationship between the matter of religious observance and the upcoming statement, "We've been invited next week to the home of a family I think you will like. The Abarbanels. There are two brothers and they are partners. They're in banking. They both came to America on a small matter just before I left last summer. Maybe you remember. I took them out to Brooklyn, to Seagate, for a swim one Sunday."

He stopped momentarily, looking up as one of the singers brushed past their table. He waited for her to saunter on before continuing his story. "It was strange, now that I think about it. While we were sitting on the beach, they tried to explain to me that life here had changed radically in the three years I had been abroad. Perhaps none of it was for me any longer, they hinted. I could not tolerate it, they said. But I must have been a blind fool. I certainly wasn't wise enough to appreciate that they were begging me not to come back. But," he added thoughtfully, "you don't easily discard an idea you've nurtured for a lifetime. Or even a career. You delude yourself. 'It's a temporary setback,' you say. 'It won't last.' Now I'm not so sure."

"Wasn't it dangerous for them to open up like that?" Bluet asked. "I mean, unusual . . . saying something like that to you . . . in your position?"

He chuckled. "Coming from anybody else, you might have been right; from them—no. We are too close. We've gone through too much together. It's not the first time they have tried to help me. They were very close to my mother. The family has always looked out for my welfare. Maybe I never stopped to appreciate it."

"What kind of people are they?"

"Oh . . . a very old and wealthy family. They still live better than almost anyone in Moscow. Because of their international banking contacts, they were left alone. You'll love their apartment. Very bourgeois, just like a home from the old days. And we'll get a real dinner. I suspect they will probably have meat and perhaps even dessert for a change. You can dress for this one. It will be quite different from anywhere we've visited so far."

THE ABARBANELS WERE an ancient and distinguished Jewish family that first rose to prominence in Spain and Portugal, where successive generations served as financial experts to various medieval kings. This paved the way for their role in banking and politics at the highest levels over subsequent centuries. After the expulsion of Jews from the Iberian Peninsula in 1492, they moved to Italy. Gradually filtering into the mainstream of Italian life, they assimilated into the very heart of the Italian establishment. In time, the family spread even farther afield. One branch arrived in southern Russia in the mid-nineteenth century, when the czar, seeking outside capital and financial know-how to help build his backward nation, called upon such bankers for assistance.

It was to this distinguished family that Marc himself now turned in his own hour of greatest need. On a practical level, the Abarbanels could become a potential route out. They still had leverage with the party (in its own way, a latter-day royal court). He was hoping they could get him that ambassadorship or something similar. He was playing all possible angles.

But it did not work out the way he had hoped. Though the dinner provided a respite from the harsh conditions that enveloped their lives, the climate was deteriorating too fast. Marc's gentle pleas generated no more than polite acknowledgment. Like many of his other influential friends, the family was reluctant to get involved. It was far different to obliquely suggest to Marc while he was still abroad that he might not find Soviet Russia to his taste any longer. It was far worse to foster a foreign assignment for a man who might do something that could compromise the family members personally or their immediate group. It was already clear that under Stalin, it was foolhardy to put one's name to any initiative or recommendation. These were, after all, the descendants of a family that had learned over the generations the best way to steer a steady course through the shifting sands of court life.

Seventeen

Hotel Select,
January 1931

My Anna, my darling,

I received your letter from the Yucatan, dated December 30. Thank you, my love, for this lovely letter that is complete harmony with all the love that I feel for you. How I am waiting to see you, to talk to you again, and to be with you again. Only you can guess and comprehend what this means to me. Meanwhile, we must both be brave and patient until the summer vacation. My sweet, you are *always* with me, *always* near me, and I follow you in my thoughts everywhere I go. Tears fill up in my eyes whenever I see a girl of your age who is a little like you. I cannot live long without my darling Anna somewhere nearby. I am finding that out.

I began this letter quite some time ago because I was waiting for another letter from you before finishing it. But I waited in vain. I asked the man down at the desk each morning if there was a letter for me, just in case you might have decided to use the hotel address instead of the Red Cross address. But each morning he said no. He knows me so well by now that we always have a little chat. He is charming. He is a young man and recently his wife had a baby—their first. Poor things cannot get enough sweet soap for the baby at the moment so I have been giving them small pieces of my good Palmolive. He is so thankful and grateful. And now he looks out carefully each morning for any letters that might come to the hotel for me. Yesterday, he came upstairs just to bring me a letter from your teacher, Miss Daringer. It was a charming letter. She is a love. It was so revealing and so explicit of all that I wanted to know. Tell her that I understand and that someday I hope to be able to see her again personally and tell her myself how grateful I am for her kindness and interest in my daughter.

I suspected you did not write because you had to catch up on all your schoolwork after you got back. And that, I know, is always disagreeable and irksome. Did you miss many days of school? I only hope it did not prove too discouraging and make for too many difficulties. I am longing to hear more about your trip and particularly if it did you any good. I hope so.

Yesterday Kayho came home from his office with a few magazines that you sent before you went away—the *Nation, Literary Digest, Scientific American*, etc. He was so glad and so grateful. If it is not too much trouble, my darling, please send as much literature and reading matter as you can after you are through with it. *Anything!*

The winter is in full swing, and somehow or other I manage to keep warm. I have not had a cold yet, which is quite an achievement for me. Do not worry, my sweetest, Kayho still looks after me so magnificently that I am quite overcome by all his attention and kindness. I am beginning to get spoilt! Moscow remains very beautiful under the snow. The trees are just so much lovely lace; white, with intricate, delicate designs. Well, two more months of this, then I understand the temperature will quickly get milder.

I have seen quite a lot of my friend Nadya lately. We meet in a park not far from here and take a walk together in the middle of the day when the brilliant sunshine makes it all feel so much warmer. At least it gets me out of doors for a while and for some exercise. Everybody asks after you, and I think they all understand what it is like to be away from one's own for a long time.

Last week we were invited to dinner at some friends of Kayho called Abarbanel. I do not think you met them. What a wonderful home they have. It was such a delicious meal and elegantly served in the old-fashioned way. The other guests were such interesting people that in the end we stayed so much later than anywhere else we have been so far. Kayho was in excellent humor and we all had a wonderful time. It was a comfortable home and furnished with many of those French antique pieces you know I like so much. It made me a little sad. I kept thinking of our own living room in New York.

You see, my love, we did not get an apartment yet. But we are still hoping to do so very soon. Meanwhile, we remain at the hotel. The best I can say is that it is so centrally located that I can walk to all the shops, theaters, etc. In fact, almost anywhere I wish in a matter of minutes.

So you are reading Balzac this quarter. I can fully understand why you do not like his style of writing. His details, it is true, are a little tiresome and unnecessary. But remember, it was written when the tempo of life was much slower. It is also more difficult for someone of your generation to understand a man like Balzac. There remains so much in his writings that was annihilated by the war and all its natural aftermath and consequences. As a stylist, I believe he will remain one of the masters but never be considered the greatest of his contemporaries. He is more of an illustrator of an epoch, faithful and brilliant, and as such he is a document to appreciate rather than enjoy. *Les Chouans* is not his masterpiece, but what I liked about the book were the descriptions. Anyhow, it was beautifully written, if a little lengthy. If you approach it this way, then I think you might have an easier time.

Mr. Yonoff just let me have all of O. Henry's works yesterday evening when I went over there to choose some books. I am sure I will find them amusing. He sends you his love. Please darling, could you send the new biography of Fouché? Kayho and I were just talking about Fouché this week, and Kayho said he thought he had seen something about a new book in the *Times*. I must have thrown away the issue because I could not trace it. Maybe it came out just before we left. I do not know the author, but I am sure Scribner's would know. Could you call them or go there when you have time and arrange this for me? Send it to the Red Cross address. Don't forget!

Our friends Mika and Regina Gurevitch have left for London again. I do not know how long they will be gone. They left their son Jack in care of his grandmother, as they could not take him along this time. It is not permitted any more. The officials must now leave their children behind. I am sure the authorities are only considering what is best for a child. He is still very young and it is such a long journey.

Well, my love, I must say goodbye to you once again. I kiss you my darling. Look after yourself. Try not to catch a cold, as I worry so about illness at this time of year.

I am waiting . . . waiting for the day you get here.

I kiss you always.
Maman

P.S. Kayho is writing asking you questions about your coming here. Answer them all, my sweet, then I shall answer right away with all the instructions, details about the journey, passports, etc. Reply at length if you will. I think it would be better to thrash everything out with Daddy as soon as possible so that I may know the decisions and we can act accordingly. It is certainly not too early to start. February is a short month and by the time we exchange a few letters, it will already be getting on toward April and May, and you finish school in June.

I quickly end this letter now, as Kayho is going to post it as usual and I am anxious for your reply. I read in the papers that there has been quite a lot of flu in New York this winter. Do take extra care. I worry so.

I kiss you again, my darling.
Maman

DESPERATE THOUGH SHE WAS to see her daughter, Bluet had no intention of allowing Anna to make the trip, at least not for the present. But she was compelled to frame her letter to Anna in language calculated to mollify the ever-vigilant censor.

She had tried to warn Anna on several occasions, asking her to keep her "feet dry" and not "go near any water." But Anna had not picked up the signals. Telling her point-blank not to make the trip that summer could devastate an already lonely and emotional teenager. Anna would interpret the message as an indication that she was no longer wanted by the mother she truly adored, no matter what fable Bluet concocted to dissuade her from coming.

But even fables were impossible because Marc was now continually writing to Anna and pleading with her to join them. Long before Bluet herself was consciously aware of the problem, Marc realized that she might be compelled to choose between her child and him. So the sooner Anna was with them, the better. Besides, Bluet was so anxious to see her daughter that nothing could be lost by proceeding with the formalities. And if the situation really did change for the better, Anna could safely make the trip by June.

And it was still possible. Earlier that month, Marc had been unexpectedly summoned by Stalin to several personal meetings. Stalin wished to discuss the unresolved question of American recognition. Perhaps, they were both hoping, these meetings would result in a new overseas posting.

Aware of Stalin's inherent loathing for anyone with natural eloquence and a nonproletarian background, Bluet cautioned Marc on each occasion to cool his hauteur—to find a temporary substitute for his Western suits, as well as for his sophisticated use of language. There was no need to antagonize a man who had gained a notorious reputation for exploding into unexpected fits of rage. "Speak simply, dress simply . . . be humble," she implored.

These sessions could not have gone well because they plunged Marc into further despondency. One day Bluet overheard Marc discussing the meetings with a friend. Throwing caution to the wind, he ridiculed Stalin's coarse demeanor, his yellowed teeth, his sneer, his beetle eyes, his sweaty palms, his shapeless outfits, his limited vocabulary, his stunted speech, and his aston-ishingly myopic view of the outside world.

Not surprisingly, therefore, the possibility that these meetings might earn Marc a new foreign assignment failed to materialize. Marc was no longer trusted as in the old days, not only because of "that bourgeois French woman," but because he personified the hated Old Bolsheviks. Even if Bluet quietly departed, it would serve only to confirm those long-whispered rumors of her innate treachery, making it even worse for Marc.

What was even more troubling, Bluet discovered that she was now being followed.

She had, of course, recognized from the start that she had to tread a delicate path if she wanted to avoid making trouble for Marc. But even this might not be enough to dispel suspicion. By January, she was certain that regular surveillance had been placed on her. She learned of it quite by acci-dent. While taking the streetcar one afternoon, she observed the same "stranger" climbing off and on at stops identical to hers. At first, she thought it was a coincidence. Then it happened once too often.

She became convinced after a series of visits she made to a nearby park with her friend Nadya. Day after day, she noticed the same shabby and dour-faced gentleman wrapped in a gray padded coat. Perhaps, she mused, the more skillful agents were being assigned to higher-priority targets, because he was not very subtle. He hovered around like a hungry bear in search of honey. With a newspaper tucked rather too obviously under his arm, he quickly glanced in the opposite direction if she looked his way. He had such a pathetic stare that even though she was the quarry, she nevertheless felt pity for him. What he needed, she concluded, was an indoor job, a desk job, during such cold weather.

The man continually wiped his nose from the same soiled rag he drew out of a torn pocket—so often that she was tempted to offer him a good handkerchief of her own or at least a hot drink. She would have to speak to Marc about it, she thought impishly.

"See that fellow over there," she confided one day to Nadya, as she watched him take out his rag yet again and trumpet into it, shaking violently as he did so. "He's following me, I'm certain of it."

"Surely not," Nadya scoffed, as they walked toward a pond frozen hard enough for skating.

"Watch. You'll see I'm right," Bluet insisted. "We'll experiment. You go round the pond one way. I'll go the other. See which direction he takes and we'll know," she announced. They were standing next to a tall fountain, icicles dangling from its spout. Just as they were about to begin, Bluet collapsed in a paroxysm of laughter. Nadya grew uneasy.

Bluet explained. "It reminds me of when I was growing up. We used to get up to all sorts of mischief like this at the convent. I must be giddy from all the pressure because I agree it isn't funny. Anyway," she added, "if he's clever, he'll just stand there and not even move. He could always catch up later."

Her shadow could not have been too alert because he did follow. It prompted Bluet to suggest, "Let's walk around and around the pond today. If we can't get rid of him, at least we'll make him dizzy."

"Do you know any good pet names?" suggested Nadya, glancing warily back at their companion.

"Why?"

"Doesn't he remind you of a pet hound?" she observed. "Faithful and drooling, well-trained and obedient."

"I must bring him a bone the next time I take him for a walk in the park," giggled Bluet.

"I was hoping you'd ask him home for tea."

"It's a thought. We do have a doghouse right next to our hotel. A most secure one."

Yet despite the frivolity, the episode had clearly disturbed and frightened her friend. As they said good-bye, Nadya looked uncomfortable, almost embarrassed. "I'm going to be busy rehearsing during the next few weeks," she explained. "I won't be able to meet you for a while."

Bluet understood. Nadya was afraid to be seen with someone who was suspect. Bluet was losing even the handful of friends she had left. And it did not end there. Toward the end of the month, one of the maids at the hotel asked if she might borrow the large portrait photo of Bluet that Marc kept in a silver frame on the desk in their room.

"It's so beautiful," sighed the woman. "I'd like to show it to a friend." In the interest of developing a relationship with the few people she saw in her daily life, Bluet reluctantly agreed. Besides, she was too frightened to say no.

It was a bad mistake. Aside from Marc's personal clothing, this framed portrait was one of his only remaining possessions, except for the simple blue-and-white Italian bone china cup and saucer he used for tea each morning.

When he discovered that the picture was missing, he exploded in rage. "Why the hell did you let her have it?" he barked. "You should have refused! You surely could have thought of an excuse."

"I was afraid," Bluet replied. "But she'll bring it back tomorrow. She promised."

He slammed down his briefcase. "By that time, the damage will be done. There'll be copies everywhere. A stupid move. You must be more careful. Far more careful," he repeated under his breath.

"They've begun following me, too," she told him quietly. "Were you aware of that?"

"Since when?"

"About a month."

He looked troubled. "It was not my doing. I'll try to put a stop to it. Don't worry . . ."

But Marc could not halt the surveillance. He discovered that the security agents were filing reports on every place she went, everyone she met, where she shopped, what she purchased, what she read, and even her conversations, if they could be overheard. Were they compiling a case so they could blame Bluet for Marc's waning zeal? It would not be the first time that they had condemned a foreign woman for undermining the loyalty of one of their own.

Only a few years later, an incident occurred that proved this point. When the chief of Soviet Intelligence in France was recalled to Moscow in the early 1930s, he brought along his mistress, Louise Clarac. Two years later he was asked to go to Shanghai alone, on a "vital mission." Shortly thereafter, he was reported missing. In fact, Soviet agents had shadowed and killed him in the back alleys of Macao because Louise had since developed a loathing for Soviet-style life and had returned to Paris. He had wanted to go back with her. So she was suspected of having subverted him. Whenever any man deep inside their network showed signs of political unreliability, that person could never safely be left alive.

Hotel Select,
February 1931

My darling, my darling,

I have been crying all day long. I cannot believe the news. Your letter arrived this morning in the same mail as the one from Mademoiselle. So I knew it had to be so. Believe me, my sweet, it is the most cruel blow in the world. I never expected Daddy to do this to us, but I'm afraid he has the right. I cannot fight him all the way from here. If he will not let you make the trip to see us this summer, then there is nothing I can do. Please do not do anything rash. I shall try to come to you. But it is not easy. There are formalities that have to be taken care of here before I can leave. But *believe me* I shall try my best to be with you as soon as I can.

Why didn't you tell me before how you were really feeling? Sonia did write a few times to say that you had been there for dinner almost every Sunday. But never once did she say that you had asked each time to see that silly old movie, the silent movie we made at Stony Point, running it over and over again just so you could watch me walking up and down. Maybe she didn't want to upset me.

I have not "abandoned you." I do still care. I do want to see you again. Do not listen to anybody who would make you believe otherwise. I did not leave you in New York because I thought you would be "in the way." How I would like to be there to tell you all these things personally so that you would know they are true. Please, my darling, try not to cry. I cannot bear the thought that you are so unhappy, so lonely. I am lonely without you, too. It takes so long for these letters to go back and forth that I keep thinking of all the weeks you will be fretting, still believing I do not care. I worry so much about your health and happiness.

How could I have suddenly changed so much? How could it possibly be true? We consulted you on everything. I would have never left if I had known what was going to happen. But you wanted me to go ahead and you seemed to understand, to appreciate that it was important for you to stay and finish your time at the Lincoln School so that you could go on to study all the things you wanted to study and be all the things you wanted to be. This is the only reason I left you behind.

What about your friends? In the other letters you sounded so busy and occupied. I can believe you when you say that the house feels empty and uninviting these days, especially with Daddy away or out of the house most of the time. But that is no reason not to want to go home after school. It is still your home. You know you can invite your friends at any time. Believe me, I miss our chats in the afternoon equally as much as you do. I miss our shopping expeditions. We had so much fun. We were so happy then.

Please, my darling, try to cheer up for my sake. Your birthday is in a few weeks, and seventeen is the most wonderful age for any girl. It is an age when you should be happiest, a time when you should be having the most fun of your life. And if you can't come here, then I will come there.

Do not listen to those rumors about me. They are all nonsense. As soon as I have definite news as to when I can come to see you and where that will be, I shall be writing again. It may not be immediately, as it is a very long trip and these arrangements take some time. Meanwhile, keep up your schoolwork so that I may be proud of my daughter. And be sure to arrange to spend a lot of time with all our friends. See them as much as you possibly can. I would be delighted to hear from any of them and I will always write back. Do not be discouraged or sad. I will see you soon. I will.

Kisses to you, my darling. Keep smiling for my sake.
Maman

WITH HER HAND STILL SHAKING from the emotional outpouring of the letter she had just written, Bluet put down her pen. She studied her words. The writing did not even resemble her own. It was double its usual size and scrawled untidily and unevenly across both sides of the notepaper. Tear stains blotted out passages here and there, but she had neither the energy nor the will to write it over.

Tonight she would tell Marc of her decision and ask him to bring home her passport immediately. She would leave Moscow as soon as possible. The decision had been taken out of her hands. She could no longer leave her only child in the kind of atmosphere that obviously existed with Max in New York. She felt wracked by guilt and annoyed at her immature quest for passion. She should have anticipated something like this. But then again, she had expected to lead a normal life in Moscow, one where they could have made a happy home for Anna, as well as for themselves. Now everything had gone awry on both sides of the ocean. There was not even time to wait and see if she could find a way for Marc to leave with her. She would have to go ahead and pray that somehow he could follow.

She walked down the hallway to fill a tall jug with water from the rusty faucet at the far end of the corridor and returned with the heavy steaming jug carefully balanced in both hands. She needed to wash her face. She did not want Marc to see her like this. They had arranged to eat dinner with friends and had tickets for a concert. She would tell him later.

At the end of the evening, as they trudged slowly back through the snow to the privacy of their room, she explained what she was about to do. At first, Marc seemed alarmed and bewildered, hardly believing what he heard.

"Let me see the letter from Anna," he said impatiently, as they climbed the stairs to their tiny room.

As soon as they were inside, she handed him the letter. He sat down on the edge of the bed to read it, not a glimmer of emotion showing on his face.

"I have to leave. I must go as soon as I possibly can," she begged as she watched him. "You can see that now, can't you?"

Reaching the end of the page, he looked up in silence before folding the letter to hand it back to her. He stood up and began to pace back and forth. After a time, he walked over to the window. He stared silently at the grisly black wagons as they entered the prison compound.

"You must bring my passport back tomorrow," Bluet pleaded. "I plan to leave as soon as I can."

She watched as he continued to gaze at the prison walls. "You will get it back for me," she repeated yet again. "I know you will."

But he shook his head vigorously, registering an emphatic refusal.

"No," he said hoarsely, without even turning around. "I don't have it."

Her eyes opened wide in disbelief. "Tell me, Marc. Where is it?"

"I handed it to the authorities when you arrived," he said in a whisper. "That's the way it works here."

"Then ask for it back."

He shook his head again. "No. No, I can't do that."

"What do you mean you can't? You mean you won't?" Her voice was rising. "You've been putting me off for weeks now. Why, Marc, why?"

He did not answer. Instead, he sat down again on the edge of the bed and swung his feet up to stretch out horizontally. He cupped his hands behind his head, then stared at the ceiling.

"Answer me, Marc!" she shouted. "I want my passport back. I want to leave. Get it for me!"

He continued staring upward, a glacial expression on his face, as if he no longer heard her words, as if she were not even in the room.

"Marc, *listen* to me!" The pitch of her voice rose in alarm. "What's the matter with you? Can't you see what's happened?"

But still he did not move. By this time, she was so distraught that she sank to the floor and began to cry. "Listen to me," she begged again. But it was no use. He completely ignored her. It was impossible to have an argument or even make a point with someone who didn't respond.

Watching him lie there, oblivious to her suffering and anguish, she sensed his growing mood of ruthlessness. He did not even move to pick her up from the cold floor. Apparently, he could not care less. How do you explain your anguish to someone who has never had a child of his own? she wondered.

"Tell them you are fed up with me," she sobbed. "Tell them I was just a foolish piece of fun, a cheap little tart you picked up and are glad to send away. Tell them I bore you. That I'm in your way. That you can't stand me any longer. It's true. I can't do you any good here. When they see I'm not out to hurt anyone, it will blow over. And you'll be glad it's over. You can even go back to Katya, where you should be now, anyway. Tell them, Marc. Tell them that."

He shook his head, indicating his disapproval.

"Then I'll say these things," she continued. "I'm not too proud. I'll say you are sending me away because you're fed up with me."

"It's not true," he whispered.

"Since when did the truth ever bother you?" she cut in cruelly. "All right. What if I promise to come back? I could do that, too. I could stay with Anna for a while and then come back here." She paused, coaxing him more quietly with, "Help me, Mitia, my darling, I want so much to go to Anna. I worry about leaving an emotional teenager in such a state. You can do it if you want to. You're the only person who can arrange these things."

But Marc was still gazing transfixed at the ceiling. His thoughts seemed to be somewhere else. It prompted her to murmur bitterly, "You only ever cared about yourself. If you really loved me, you would try to understand and let me go. I'm no better off than those poor souls across the street. I'm no freer than they are. I just have a different jailer, that's all."

But he had totally withdrawn. His stillness caught her by surprise, and suddenly a thought struck her in the silence. Had she not been so enveloped in her own distress, she would have remembered not to talk so candidly and loudly in the room. It was now too late. But it would take years and a far deeper understanding of the prevailing mood of ingrained Russian suspicion to appreciate that allowing her to go back to America—when they both knew she would never return—was tantamount to condemning her lover to death with her own hand.

Someone, she thought, must have overheard. She might have even compounded their plight. And she was certainly no closer to retrieving her passport.

Eighteen

It was worse than a crime, it was a blunder.

Joseph Fouché

BLUET WOKE UP WITH A START to discover that she was still lying on the cold floor. She had no idea what time it was or how long she had been lying there. Everything was now absolutely silent. There were no sounds in the corridor. The nightly shuffling in the adjacent rooms had ceased. It was pitch black and quiet down in the street, except for an occasional screech of brakes and the sweeping headlights from a never-ending flow of black vans with their pitiful nightly cargo, poking their way through the heavy gates of Lubianka. The devil's charnel house, she thought with a shudder. Perhaps Marc was right. Perhaps God had thrown up His hands in despair at what they had wrought.

She looked over at the bed. Marc was lying in the exact position that she remembered before falling asleep. He must have dozed off, too. He was still fully dressed, as she was. Obviously, she thought bitterly, he had no intention of picking her up and was content to let her spend all night on the floor, despite the savage cold.

Slowly, she tried to stand, but a sharp pain cut into her side. Her back and shoulders ached, and she could hardly lift her arms. She was shivering. The floor felt like a slab of ice beneath her body. She tried to raise her neck and found that it was stiff with pain. Looking down, she saw that she had been sleeping over rough-hewn floorboards that were dotted with raised metal nails. The pain was most severe on the left side—exactly where she had been lying.

Swallowing hard as she rose to her feet, she felt a further discomfort. Her throat was sore, and her chest was congested. She could hardly stand upright. The room dipped and danced in front of her eyes in a mad ballet that seemed like a fitting end to a horror-filled night.

With Marc sprawled over most of their narrow bed, there was hardly any space remaining. Nevertheless, she climbed up onto the small area still available, curling up as best she could. She did not even have the strength to undress.

Again she shivered. She tried pulling some covers over herself for warmth, hoping that by morning she would feel stronger again. But she could not sleep. She tossed and turned, convinced that she was condemned to die in this dreadful place as a punishment for abandoning her daughter.

In other circumstances, she might have accepted this sickness more in stride. But, upset by the evening's events, on top of what now appeared to be the onset of a fever, she found her thoughts rambling and increasingly maudlin. Her Catholic conscience was now working overtime. She convinced herself that there would be divine retribution for her selfishness. She would succumb to an illness from which she would weaken and never recover, or she would be arrested by GPU thugs. The final shot she would ever hear would be the one aimed at the back of her own neck. Thereafter, the authorities—in their usual manner—would disclaim any knowledge of her. She would become a nonperson. She would never see Anna again. What would become of her only daughter? Would Anna slip into a deep depression and even commit suicide? Highly strung adolescents did this sort of thing all the time. Max could not be trusted to notice her moods or care for her. Who would?

Bluet had reached a low point where she was fast losing any ability to care for anyone but herself and her child. Living in a cramped room without proper washing facilities; gnawed at by the cold, both indoors and out; being constantly spied upon; denied the freedom to leave, to make friends, to have a life; condemned to semi-hunger and the enforced boredom of not being allowed to participate in anything at all were depressing enough. But seeing Marc turn on her in such a vicious fashion, plus the overall fear that at any time she could disappear without a trace, left her feeling less than human. If this was supposed to be paradise, then hell had more to offer.

Once again, she tried clearing her throat. But the tossing and the turning, plus the noise of her choking, wakened Marc. He grunted, complained about the din, turned over on one side, and fell back into an exhausted sleep. She could not rely upon him any longer, she told herself. Bluet would have to look out for Bluet. The primeval urge to ensure her own survival and the desperate passion of a mother to be reunited with her only child had taken over.

By morning, her fever had heightened. Marc appeared concerned as he felt her pulse and checked her over. "You need a good doctor," he advised, as he flipped his Liberty scarf around his neck before leaving.

"It's no joking matter," she croaked from beneath the covers.

"I'm not joking. Stay in bed. I'll be back to look in on you in a few hours. Try not to get up. It would be better if you went back to sleep."

"You are going to get my passport today, aren't you?" Despite her illness, she had not forgotten.

"I'll do what I can," he replied. In almost any other country she could have applied on her own, despite him. But here in Moscow, the GPU and the party were all-powerful in these matters, and the request would only be referred back to Marc. Without U.S. recognition, she could not even go to the American authorities. There was no embassy, no consulate, no official representation. She would have to find a way to bypass Marc. But what if that caused him more trouble? She did not want to hurt him. Not really.

She dozed off again right after he left but was soon reawakened by the shuffling of heavy footsteps in the hallway. She could hear Marc talking to an older man.

There was a soft tapping at the door. It opened slowly. Marc walked in, smiling. He was followed by a bespectacled elderly gentleman who looked like the archetypal country doctor. The man was even carrying a worn black medical bag.

"Dr. Levin to see you," Marc announced smartly, as they both approached the bed.

"*The* Dr. Levin, the Kremlin doctor?" she inquired weakly in amazement. Everybody in Moscow knew Dr. Lev Grigorevich Levin. He was called the Kremlin doctor, because he had treated most of the top government leaders ever since the time of the revolution.

"Remember, I said you needed a good doctor," Marc was saying. "I brought you the best."

"You flatter me," said the old man, as he opened his bag and took out his stethoscope. Bluet glanced at Marc, about to comment upon this sudden new display of concern, but changed her mind and said nothing.

After completing his examination, Dr. Levin sent Marc to fill a prescription. In this respect, they were lucky. Marc worked in the Health Department. They could still obtain what they needed. As soon as the door closed behind Marc, Dr. Levin pulled a chair closer to the bed to sit beside Bluet.

"This is no place for you two to be living," he whispered, as he glanced around the room and sniffed the stale, rancid odor that permeated the entire hotel. "I can just imagine how Marc feels about it. He's such an elegant man. And what about you? I heard you had not one but two magnificent homes in America. That you gave dazzling parties. You must have loved Marc very deeply to give it all up for . . . it's no place . . . no place for you both."

She gave Dr. Levin a melancholy look in an attempt to convey all that she personally felt about their circumstances. "We're still waiting for somewhere of our own. It's taking much longer than expected," she explained. "We know that many people are living six or more to a room," she added hastily. She was now fully familiar with what she was supposed to say, no matter who asked the questions.

"Can't Marc do anything about it?"

Bluet shook her head.

The old man sighed, shrugged his shoulders, and continued sadly, "If Marc, of all people, can't get a place . . . " He stood up, smiled, patted her on the shoulder, and said, "I want you both to come to my house in the country as soon as you're better. You could use some fresh air. You'll meet my wife. I think you'll get along well together. She's an actress in the Moscow Art Theater," he added proudly.

"I'd like that," Bluet told him. "And thank you for coming over to see me."

Dr. Levin smiled. "Take it easy for the next few days," he suggested, as he slowly closed his bag. "I'll come back once more just to make sure. Marc was very worried about you this morning. You have no idea. He was most insistent that I come right over. He cares for you a great deal. Maybe more than you think."

Dr. Levin did not seem in a hurry to rush away. And she felt so warmly toward this kindly old man, who was so thoughtful and so interested, that she was tempted to blurt out her troubles to him. But she was too afraid to say anything.

Dr. Levin was as good as his word. As soon as Bluet was strong enough, he made arrangements for her and Marc to spend a full day in the country. It was the first of several visits to the comfortable frame home, which reminded Bluet of her own country house at Stony Point: easy chairs, rustic furniture, and hand-woven rugs chosen to reflect a combination of modesty and charm. It was simple, yet cozy. But food remained as difficult a problem in the country as it was in the capital. The meals were bleak, with each dish lacking sugar and fat. Outside the city, their hosts had managed to produce a few fresh vegetables. And away from the center city, Marc and Bluet felt so much more relaxed. The absence of tension was more apparent at the Levin house than anywhere else they had visited so far.

Even the conversation was less guarded, mostly tending toward the arts and the theater. For both of them, it was exhilarating to spend time in a real home again and to walk in the woods. Yet, by the same token, it only highlighted the hopelessness of their own condition, which the party stubbornly refused to alleviate. For as far as the party was concerned, nothing was to be gained. Marc's former enthusiasm was clearly waning. And Bluet was exhibiting overt signs of disaffection. Special privileges were not granted to renegades.

Bluet herself no longer cared because she was only concerned now with reaching Anna as soon as she could. "I have to go. I can't leave her any longer like that. You can't believe how it hurts me," she kept reminding Marc, insisting that the only reason she needed her passport was for a chance to spend a little time with Anna. It could not be construed as anything more, she said, pointing out that a short journey abroad of this nature could not have the unfortunate implications of someone opting out for good. What might happen to him if she never returned was something she blocked from her thoughts. Anna needed a mother who was both alive and available. That had to be her prime responsibility, even if it meant lying to Marc, even if it meant betraying Marc, even if it meant . . . Better not to go there.

WEEKS SLIPPED BY. Though the coming of March lessened the worst of the winter chill, there was no visible thaw in the stalemate over the passport. No matter. Bluet was prepared to keep up the pressure as long as it took to break Marc's resistance. Repeatedly, she tried to make him understand that she was perfectly prepared to take independent action if he did not change his mind soon. But the truth was that she had no contingency plan of her own. All she could do for the moment was to write regularly to Anna and beg her to understand that it was only a matter of time. Her passport, she still hoped, would come through shortly. But Marc refused to yield. He had a knack for twisting the problem around so that she felt disloyal for continually pestering him. He told her she should understand that they needed to pull together under these trying circumstances. They had taken on a certain obligation to each other. Did it mean so little? After all, Anna was almost seventeen and could surely survive adequately for a while longer without the constant presence of her mother. It might even do her good. She might develop a measure of independence.

Marc was playing for time.

But Bluet had neither his patience nor any faith that a viable solution could any longer be worked out to benefit them both.

She was therefore delighted when Marc mentioned casually, "Rhona's coming through in a few weeks. You'll be pleased to see a face from home." The woman in question was an earnest American woman in her early twenties who was currently acting as a courier for the Bolsheviks.

Bluet now had an idea. She would have to take a risk in order to carry it out, but it was worthwhile. What she had in mind was to take Rhona aside, outdoors naturally, and ask for a special favor. Rhona knew Anna well. She also knew how attached Bluet was to her only child. Bluet would therefore explain how desperate she was to go to New York because her daughter was having difficulties at home alone with Max. But Bluet had been unable to do so because the Russians were stubbornly refusing to let her leave. She would add that Anna could not possibly come to Moscow because Max had absolutely forbidden it. She would then ask Rhona to contact two newspaper friends whom Bluet felt might help.

The few American journalists permitted in Moscow in those pre-recognition days had found themselves becoming the unofficial liaisons between stranded Americans and the Bolshevik (increasingly called Soviet) authorities. Certain Americans who had capriciously been denied exit permits would slip word to one of them. The correspondents would then file a story, whereupon the Soviets (still anxious to seek friends abroad) would reluctantly but promptly release the individuals. The story would never get further than the censor's desk in Moscow. But it would create enough of a threat to do the job.

However, the only journalists she knew sufficiently well were both temporarily in the United States. She needed Rhona to reach them there, if necessary. "And even if they don't want to write about me," she explained to Rhona, "you could suggest that they find out what Max can do."

Max still retained a certain influence within the party—one that might be able to override Marc and the mighty GPU. Bluet felt sure that Max would want to see his daughter once again happily under the care of a mother.

While Bluet fretted and paced the streets of Moscow in despair, Rhona kept her word. Back in New York, she explained the problem to Bluet's newspaper friends. As anticipated, neither was eager to get caught in the midst of what seemed to them more of a family squabble than a public issue. Therefore, they simply forwarded the message directly to Max.

And that's when the trouble began.

Max's eyes widened with surprise and a delight he had difficulty concealing. It was the opportunity he had been seeking for months. Max still believed himself severely wronged, and he wanted to repay Bluet and her lover measure for measure. He had not forgotten that Marc had grossly humiliated him by capitalizing on his good name for Marc's own ends, while seducing and carrying off his wife. He could never forgive. With this request in hand, Max could not only part the lovers for good but, he hoped, exact his final revenge on Marc. He began an even more virulent assault, letting the party know all the details about Marc's unforgivable behavior in America, including his irresponsible and unethical behavior concerning Bluet. The Soviets were still working frantically for the cooperation of the American business community and trying feverishly to display a responsible and respected image, in the hope of achieving diplomatic recognition at last.

What Marc had done was not only a personal slight, Max insisted. It also undermined the credibility of the recognition effort. Max hit first upon the missing $6,000 donated in 1928 by his personal friend and an influential philanthropist, Francis Drury of Cleveland—the cash supposedly given for the passage and the expenses of two Russian physicians to come and study American hygiene, but who mysteriously never arrived. He let the Russians know that he had personally arranged for the money to be paid directly to Marc. And he only recently discovered from the bank that the money had been slowly withdrawn to pay "for his silk shirts, no doubt." Max demanded that the Soviets reimburse Drury for the entire amount. It took a great deal of negotiating, but the dollars—precious hard currency—were ultimately, though reluctantly, returned.

Max contacted the State Department and continued his attack. Don't let Bluet back in this country, he urged. She is a spy—an undesirable alien. Her recent actions prove it. Recalling his introduction to the chief of the GPU at a luncheon in Moscow some years ago, Max also seized upon this direct line to the top. He wrote a personal letter to the GPU chief, telling him the truth as well.

Indeed, during all that dark and dreary March, while the winds howled through the cobblestone passages and whistled down the broad avenues of Moscow, Max was busy in New York and Washington. He made telephone calls. He showered his friends with letters. He made the rounds of social events, the end result of which he sincerely hoped would exact maximum revenge on Marc.

But neither Marc nor Bluet were aware of this. Marc had become involved in a new escape plan of his own, unbeknownst to anyone, and Bluet had grown so despondent that she was already revealing her dilemma to her closest Moscow friends. She particularly singled out the Yulins. She knew they were very powerful and would do a great deal in the name of personal friendship. After not hearing a word from New York for weeks, she presumed that Rhona had simply failed to follow through.

Nineteen

THE GENTLE RAINDROPS OF SPRINGTIME fell in dizzying patterns. They danced down the windowpanes, washing away the last of the winter snows from curb and crevice and exposing, all too abruptly, the scars of buildings left untended in the passage of time. Along the banks of the Moscow River, huge ice slabs were breaking up into smaller, jagged chunks, crackling and squeaking until suddenly the waters burst free to flow again, beckoned onward to the call of the faraway sea. Spring had returned.

Spring meant renewal. And a people dulled and haggard from another winter of hardship still found time to tend a window box, to nurture a tiny green shoot of a bulb until the blaze of multicolored blossoms promised that life itself would be renewed. Days grew longer and nights were less frigid. Young girls sported gaily colored kerchiefs on their heads. Lovers, walking hand in hand, still found time for the intimacy and the wonder of romance, while the whole city hummed with activity in expectation of upcoming May Day celebrations.

That year the papers announced that the festivities would include five immense wall banners proclaiming "The U.S.S.R. is the shock brigade of the world proletariat," as a backdrop to a stupendous parade. Sixty thousand troops were to march in a daylong procession. The highlight would be a spectacular display of field guns, each drawn by four white horses galloping alongside one another. As they thundered past the reviewing stand, forty of the nation's newest airplanes were scheduled to fly overhead, displaying their pilots' finest aerobatic skills. Whoever sat in that reviewing stand would be keenly watched, as it signaled who was rising and who had fallen from grace.

It was also Bluet's birthday. In recognition of the occasion, Marc had purchased tickets for the Bolshoi Ballet, "two of the best seats in the house." Knowing that the Bolshoi was one place where people still took extra care to look their best, Bluet had spent a good deal of time rummaging through her large black steamer trunk to find just the right dress for the occasion. She sorely missed having the opportunities to dress more formally. Clothes had always been a personal passion and one that Max had encouraged. He had liked to think of his wife as a well-dressed woman. Now she could no longer dress well, and it made her feel less desirable and even less feminine. Earlier, she had treated herself to a leisurely, steaming bath at Yulina's house, taking along what was left of her favorite lotions, creams, and fragrances.

Yulina hovered about uneasily that morning. She finally blurted out something that seemed to be nagging at her thoughts. "Could someone like me, with my secretarial skills and languages, find a job easily in America?" Bluet was astonished. Had the Yulins had enough, too? Were they as anxious to leave as she and Marc were? Did the Yulins see their friendship with her as a way to nurture a valuable American contact, should this become necessary? Bluet assured Yulina that she would have no trouble, especially since the couple already knew so many well-placed Americans.

Bluet had devoted extra care and attention to her bath that morning. Something about nearing age forty made these rituals all the more compelling. Everyone said she still had the youthful appearance of a woman ten years younger and the thick flaxen hair of a girl in her twenties. But the number forty was personally devastating. Added to this was the fear that after so many months of Moscow life, lines were beginning to disfigure her face, her hair was starting to thin and streak with gray, and she had begun to develop the careworn appearance of so many Russian women.

She chose to wear a simple black couture dress that evening, one of her favorites. It had been expertly cut and tailored to her exact measurements by her beloved dressmaker in Paris (who by this time, Bluet mused, must surely be wondering what had happened to such a faithful customer). How she would love a visit! A gossip. A fitting. An open checkbook, like in the old days. What luxury! She took out the dress and laid it on the bed, then sighed. Even the dress seemed to recoil from such inappropriate surroundings. But Bluet was determined to enjoy her birthday. So she hunted for a brand-new pair of silk stockings, her last. Finally, digging to the bottom of the trunk, she turned up a pair of black calf pumps. She rarely wore them anymore. Felt boots and thick walking shoes were more practical for negotiating the icy cobblestones and fractured pavement of Moscow. That was the trouble with a proletarian paradise. There was nothing stylish about it. No excuse to dress, few colorful occasions to celebrate, and not even a home to decorate. Faces were drab. Interiors were drab. Lives were drab.

She slipped the dress over her head and peered at herself in the long mirror attached to the inside door of the wardrobe, aghast at how much weight she had lost. But the dress was so beautifully cut and the fabric so soft and supple that it still clung to her in gently flowing lines. She tried on the new silver peasant-style belt with a miniature dagger clasp that she had discovered in an antique shop a few weeks earlier. But she discarded it in the end. Somehow, it was just not quite right. Was she becoming as unadventurous as her surroundings? Surely not.

To turn this basic outfit into something more glamorous for the evening, she picked out her favorite diamond earrings, a gold and ruby brooch, and a solid-gold evening purse, which she carefully placed on the bed. Then she gave her hair dozens of hand strokes with her natural-bristle hairbrush. Curiously, this brush was the possession most envied among her women friends of Moscow.

Instead of arranging her hair in its usual chignon, she decided to leave it loose. She lifted and tucked it away from her face by folding slender strands to meet at the back in a tiny metal clasp. Then she settled down in a chair in front of the long mirror and carefully applied her makeup, remembering to use it sparingly, as she was not sure when she might be able to find these particular colors and brands again. Even the idea of cosmetics was still abhorrent to most Russians. She was just about to put away the irreplaceable jars when Marc walked in.

Coming through the door, briefcase in hand, he halted abruptly. His eyes opened wide in amazement. "You look magnificent," he said. "You look absolutely magnificent."

"I was just trying to dress up like my old self," she replied. "It feels good once in a while, even though I know I shouldn't."

He lay his briefcase on the desk and glanced down at his own suit, tailored in Rome but now worn, stained, and faded. Walking over to the mirror, he grimaced at his own image. "You make me feel shabby," he murmured. Unexpectedly, he added, "We've both changed, haven't we, my darling?" Suddenly, a smile crossed his face, as he said more cheerfully, "But by the time I leave this room in one hour, I'll be worthy of such a beautiful escort, I promise you that."

He stooped to lift her from the chair and take her in his arms to kiss her. "Happy birthday," he whispered. "We can still say happy birthday, comrade Bluet," he added with a chuckle. "Even comrades have birthdays.'"

245

He stood back, staring at her again in admiration, and grew nostalgic. "I remember, way back when I was still a student," he began. "There used to be a flower seller sitting in front of the Foreign Office, near where Vorovsky's statue is now. The young men would stop to buy their ladies a long-stemmed rose before taking them to the opera or the ballet." Marc paused for a moment, as if he wished he could recapture some of that charm. "But now there are no roses in Vorovsky Square. If there were any left, I would run right down and buy you the most beautiful one of all."

She fell silent. It was such a long time since he had spoken this way. "That would have been nice, Marc. I would have liked that," she replied softly. "But I'm not surprised. Nothing as delicate as a single rose could possibly survive here. Only a weed," she observed wryly, "only a weed, sneaking up between a tractor and a Five-Year Plan."

He was not listening. He was deep in his previous thought. Brandishing a wooden hanger in the air before changing his clothes, he continued, "In Rome I could have found you a rose . . . a dozen beautiful red roses . . . in Paris . . . in New York."

She smiled. "You'd better start getting ready, or we'll be late. You Russians are never on time for anything except the theater. I've noticed that nobody dares to walk in once the curtain has gone up."

He took out his cherished suit from Saks, murmuring guiltily, "I didn't even bring you a gift."

Marc must have been deeply affected by the moment because he took longer than expected to shave, to wash in the putrid bathroom at the end of the corridor, and to dress to his impeccable standards. Seeing him in his former debonair attire brought a lump to Bluet's throat.

All the sartorial fuss made them late, so they had to run the short distance from the hotel to the Bolshoi, with Marc dragging her along by the hand as if they were children hurrying off to enjoy the sights and the delights of a fairground. Crowds were already scurrying into the theater by the time they arrived, only moments before curtain time.

There was an air of excitement and anticipation before the start of these performances that could not be matched anywhere else in the city. The Bolshoi was one of the few gatherings that had retained the flavor of imperial elegance—tarnished elegance though it was. Formerly distinguished men, now humbled and old, dusted off frock coats and striped trousers, shiny with use, and paraded forth dressed up in this faded badge of lost grandeur, accompanied by pompous wives in old-fashioned fur wraps that had also seen better days—ghosts of a bygone era eager to redeem their stolen station of grace, if only for an evening.

The ballet itself and the attendant rituals were so intrinsically old Russian that even the Bolsheviks had not dared to change it. Ballerinas were an elite; they were allocated choice apartments, special food privileges, medical care, and the finest training and were the most sought-after companions and lovers of the mighty. Politics and sex aside, to have a daughter chosen for the Bolshoi remained one of the proudest honors that could be bestowed upon any Russian family.

For Bluet, the ballet had added significance. The glittering performance reminded her of the halcyon days when evenings such as these had been commonplace events in her own life, followed by the most stylish of parties, sometimes at her home and sometimes in a room set aside at one of the better restaurants. The full corps de ballet would congregate and gossip, fawning over Max in the hope that the closer they were to him the closer they would be to stardom. In those faraway days the extravagant life had been exciting, but the man intolerable. Now her life was sordid, but the man in her life—Marc—remained magnificent.

Soon she submerged herself in the delicate perfection of the ballerinas and the precision and the grace of the male dancers. Warmed by the special tenderness Marc had displayed earlier in the evening, she soaked up the harmonious tones of the music and the gaiety and the glamour of the moment. When it was time for the intermission and an offering plate was passed round, as was the custom, for donations to "charity" (a coin, a small piece of jewelry; the government never missed an opportunity for *valuta*), Bluet struggled to pull off Max's plain gold wedding ring, which she still wore on the fourth finger of her left hand, in a rush to drop it into the passing plate. It was a gesture to Marc, not a commitment to the questionable charity. As she fumbled with the ring, their eyes met in an intimacy that had almost disappeared from their life together. Nothing was said. Marc gently reached out to place his hand for a moment over the pale spot where the ring had been. It wasn't a time for words. The look that passed between them was more meaningful than any spoken words could have been. It was as if, fearing what lay ahead, they were begging for just a little more time, just a few more weeks, just a few more opportunities like this to let one another know how they felt.

Ma grande chérie,

Somehow I feel that all the things I should write to you must keep
until I see you. Letter writing is becoming more and more painful for
me. I am only afraid that if I do not write to you that you will worry.
So it forcibly gives me the necessary push.

Your own letters are my life these days, but I can say so little. I am
alone, quite alone here at the moment. Kayho has been sent away on an
inspection tour and is not due back until the end of the month, maybe
longer. He could not take me with him. So I am here, all by myself.
How I miss you and wait anxiously each morning to see if there will be
a letter from you. One day you will know what I am trying to say and
understand.

Thank you so much again for the magazines, the wonderful books
by Romain Rolland, everything. Please continue to send as much as you
can. I read everything from cover to cover.

Thank you, my sweet, for remembering my birthday. It meant a lot
to me. Did you get the cable I sent you for yours? Seventeen! I cannot
believe it. I was so unhappy all the day long, thinking that we could not
be together on this special day of yours and wondering what you had
planned. I told all my friends that it was my darling Anna's birthday,
and I think they knew how I felt. I wanted so much to be with you. I
am still hoping to make arrangements to come and see you very soon,
but these matters take so long to arrange from here. You cannot believe
how hard I am trying to work it all out. I am sure something will be settled by the time the summer vacation is with us. At least, you sounded
brighter in your last letter.

I am happy to see your German is getting better. Do not worry about
the A- in English. I suppose the minus is on account of your spelling.
Your report on O'Neill interested me. It was very well done. Always
send me these school papers, my sweet. I do love to read them, and I
will tell you exactly what I think. As for your knowledge of O'Neill, I
am sure that by now with so much study and analysis you must know
more on the subject than I do. The report was beautifully and originally
handled.

Your photograph on horseback came last week. Thank you, my darling. You look so grown-up and attractive. I am so proud of you. You
seem to have grown. Have you? Five feet what? I am so glad, as I did not
want you to be a little shrimp like me.

It is wonderful to know that you are planning to go sailing at the end of May. I am thrilled and excited because I know you will have a wonderful time. I was also excited to hear about your visit to the country with David, to the estate. It must have been quite a day for you. I know just how I would have felt in your place. Just a little fear, much happiness, and great excitement. Is that so? Of course, his people were anxious to meet you because I seem to remember that Miss Daringer told me you were one of the only girls in which he showed an interest. So I expect they wanted to know what you were like. I am sure you looked charming, well groomed, and soignée. To be soignée is the most attractive attribute of any woman. How I am longing to hear about everything. You have no idea. Have you invited David after that visit? And your other friends? Tell me all the news. How is Nina? I am always thinking about you and what you are doing.

It is true, my darling, that we discussed smoking and that I agreed that you could smoke after graduation. I did not forget and thank you so much for keeping your promise to me. But I only hope that you will not learn to like it too much. I still hope that you will not like it at all because in the end it becomes a very harmful habit and a necessity.

The snow is completely gone, but by evening it is still snappy and quite cold. Nevertheless, we are going toward warmer weather and I am glad of that.

Did I tell you that Kayho took me to the Bolshoi for my birthday? It was a magnificent evening. Walter Duranty, the correspondent from the *New York Times* was there that night, and while we were talking I happened to mention I had been able to follow so many of his dispatches, thanks to you, my love.

Keep well, my darling, and stay happy and busy. I am with you all the time in my heart, and the day I see you again will be one of the dearest of all my life.

Always yours,
Maman

BLUET HAD BEEN COMPELLED, as usual, to conceal the truth. Marc had come home the week before, distraught and strangely weary, to inform her that he was being sent on a lengthy tour of the Volga region. The relentless purge of the kulaks had left some of the most devastating chaos in that area. Famine and disease were rampant. There were also reports of stubborn rebellion. Questions were being asked from abroad and the Red Cross needed a firsthand report on the extent of the upheavals and the requirements of the local people, regarding medical and food supplies.

Bluet greeted all this with cynicism. It sounded too genuine, too much like real Red Cross work. Just what kind of a job had they carved out for Marc this time? It was so far removed from his accustomed role of training agents and coordinating the operations of overseas teams. She could only surmise that it was yet another unholy scheme to further torment her man—and her.

Probably, she concluded, she was again to blame. Whose loyalty was being tested now? Knowing Marc's personal antipathy to the kulak policy and his value to the Bolsheviks in the field of foreign affairs, it seemed idiotic to waste a month on something like this. There had to be a method to their madness, even if there was madness in their methods, she thought.

Marc opened his briefcase that night, with further news. He removed a document, an official paper written entirely in Russian characters, and asked her to sign at the bottom of the page, "but in the Russian way. Here," he beckoned, pulling a pen from his jacket pocket. "Let me show you." He picked up a scrap of paper lying on the desk and wrote it out for her. "Just copy this."

"What am I signing?" she inquired cautiously.

"An extension of your stay. You've been here for over six months. You must renew your permit. I don't want any trouble while I'm gone. I should have attended to it sooner," he added, sounding decidedly uneasy.

"And if I don't sign?" she asked, thinking she would be only too delighted to be required to leave.

"Don't be foolish," he urged. "It can only make more trouble. And I'll worry." He placed his hand on her shoulder and added softly, "Don't create extra problems for us right now. Please. I'm concerned enough at having to leave you alone for so long. You must promise to be exceedingly careful about everything—everything while I'm gone."

She signed.

It was only later, a few days after he had left, that she discovered what she had really signed.

It was Yulina who told her, the one friend who always seemed to know exactly what was going on and who occasionally even dared to speak her mind. Yulina explained that it was not an extension of Bluet's stay. It was an official application for Russian citizenship.

"Russian citizenship!" echoed Bluet. She sank into a chair in Yulina's apartment and exploded with a rage directed mostly at her own gullibility. "I don't believe it. I don't believe Marc would do such a thing. It's a cruel, underhanded trick."

"Hush," warned Yulina. "Remember where you are."

"How could I fail to remember where I am after something like this? I might as well forget I even have a daughter. What kind of people have we become when we scheme like this against our own?" But she knew she was not without guilt herself. She had schemed against him for the return of her passport.

Still, with the stroke of a pen, she had committed another devastating blunder. Not being a native-born American and possessing American nationality only by virtue of her marriage to Max (a privilege derived from the American immigration laws of the day and one she could lose because of her divorce), she had signed away the rights to her cherished passport, her only way out. She was ashamed to admit that in a masterly move, professionally and swiftly executed, Marc had checkmated all her efforts.

She shook her head, mumbling oaths at Marc beneath her breath.

Yulina took a totally different view.

"I don't think Marc intended to trick you," she suggested. "He loves you too much for that."

A look of disbelief crossed Bluet's face. "No, I mean it," Yulina insisted, then added softly, "It's a perfect day for a walk, don't you agree?" Yulina had given her the usual signal that something confidential was to be discussed. Bluet nodded and grabbed her coat.

As they slowly wandered along, Yulina continued, "I think you're looking at the matter from the wrong viewpoint. You're always complaining that none of us trusts you. Well, maybe Marc was trying to prove a point. It's no secret that the party insisted right from the beginning that he had committed a serious error in judgment by bringing you here. He has always argued to the contrary.

"Don't you understand?" Yulina continued. "This is a sort of written declaration of your loyalty. If you have this paper in hand, nobody can accuse you of wanting to go abroad for anything but a temporary family matter— merely a mother wanting to spend time with her daughter, which we all know is the real truth. Isn't it, Bluet?"

Bluet stared at the pavement in guilty silence.

"Perhaps they won't even process the paper," Yulina went on. "The fact that you were willing to sign might be enough. Have you ever considered that Marc might be more sympathetic to your dilemma than you think? You're too critical of the man. You even refuse to acknowledge the Herculean efforts he's making to get the two of you a real apartment of your own—and a modern one right in the center of town, like you want. How many people in all of Moscow live like that? What did you expect?"

"Then why didn't he speak to me openly?" Bluet asked. "Why did he use such devious tactics?"

Yulina laughed. "You actually believe you would have signed such a paper knowing what it really was? Let's be honest, at least between ourselves. Have a little faith in the man. Have some compassion. He's in a very difficult position right now. He's fighting more than one battle. And do be careful while he's away. You never know what can happen in Moscow these days. Be careful."

EARLY ONE MORNING, a few days later, there came a tapping at the door of her hotel room. Bluet wondered who it could possibly be. Nobody ever came to see her in the room. With Marc already gone for more than two weeks, visitors were not expected. Perhaps it was a mistake.

But the gentle tapping continued. She walked to the door and opened it just a crack. She was surprised to see Marieka, the Dutch wife of another GPU foreign department official, standing in the hallway. They had met at various social gatherings. They knew each other well. And Bluet had always sensed a genuine friendliness about the woman, probably because they shared a common bond as outsiders.

"Can I come in for a moment?" Marieka asked.

Bluet nodded. She was somewhat apprehensive, although she did not quite know why. Maybe it was all those warnings about taking extra care while she was on her own. But here was a good friend. An old friend.

"I just thought I'd stop in to say hello while I was in the neighborhood. I hear Marc's away," Marieka continued casually, "and I thought I'd look in on you."

"Everything's fine," Bluet insisted, still somewhat curious. "Would you care to sit down?"

"No, I only have a minute. I stopped in to invite you to have lunch with me tomorrow, if you're free. I thought it might be a break for you. I've been

252

given an opportunity to have a meal at the sports club and wondered if you'd join me?"

The sports club was a unique restaurant, noted throughout the grapevine as the only eating place remaining in the capital where the food and the service could match anything offered in the West. Who was allowed the privilege of dining there—and why—was never discussed. Marc had never taken her, though she knew it was just the kind of place he would probably go if he could. Sensing that a good meal lay ahead and warmed by the charm of Marieka's friendly approach, Bluet decided to forget her apprehensions and accept the invitation.

The next day Marieka picked her up at the hotel, as promised. Marieka had arrived in one of the rare taxis still operating in Moscow, and they rode together to the restaurant. Marieka would not hear of Bluet paying even a portion of the cost, though Marc had left her ample money, insisting before he left that Bluet indulge herself in visits to the theater, shopping, and anything else she could find to brighten her drab existence.

"It's my treat," Marieka said.

Stepping inside the restaurant, Bluet had difficulty restraining a gasp. It was the most elegant setting she had seen since she arrived. The small round tables were well spaced on the thickly carpeted floor and dressed in clean white linen, with full settings of embossed silverware, fine stem glasses, and bone china. A small vase of fresh flowers decorated the center of each table. Waiters were neatly attired in crisp white uniforms. The low hum of conversation in a variety of languages was as sophisticated and cosmopolitan as in any of the capitals of Europe.

The food was nothing short of remarkable, considering that the entire country was struggling through such chronic shortages that most people were grateful merely to fill their daily ration of bread. As they were escorted to their table, they passed a dazzling array of Russian zakuski and sturgeon on a long buffet table. Mounds of caviar stood in huge glass bowls of cracked ice. There were platters of smoked salmon and a mouth-watering display of cocktail sausages and cold meats. At individual tables people were enjoying portions of grilled kebabs, beef stroganoff, roast beef, fresh vegetables, and a selection of pastries, cakes, and creamy desserts such as Bluet had not seen since she entered the country. Mounds of sweet butter and crusty French bread adorned each table. And as she passed by, there arose the kind of aromas she had not enjoyed for nearly a year—glorious, glorious food.

"I remember you telling me once that good food was a special love of yours," Marieka said as they sat down. "I had a hunch this would be a treat."

"I never could resist a good meal. It's a French weakness perhaps," Bluet admitted.

"I understand the chef here is French," the woman told her. "Apparently, he was with one of the great families in the old days."

It had become a regular practice in the early years after the revolution to comb the jails and pluck people from the old nobility, or those sympathetic to the old nobility, to use for a particular job the revolutionaries could not fill from their own ranks. Many a minor aristocrat or his faithful valet had bought their freedom this way. Marc himself had rehabilitated one young woman, a fine linguist, to handle all the regular foreign correspondence of the Russian Red Cross. Dozens of similarly jailed aristocrats had been freed earlier in the decade to act as interpreters for the international relief workers pouring into the famine areas and even at some of the embassies. But there were strict GPU conditions attached to these jobs. They had to serve as informers, too.

"Would you like an aperitif?"

Bluet was surprised to see a wine waiter smiling down at her. "We have just about everything here," he explained, noting her look of amazement.

"Indulge yourself. Let's enjoy it while we can," Marieka urged. Soon Bluet was consuming not only an aperitif but several glasses of a delicate French wine as well. And the lunch was truly sumptuous, tasting so much more special because of the months of privation: a plate of superbly prepared paté, followed by a delicious portion of chicken Kiev, served with crispy matchstick potatoes, tiny green beans, and a salad. Completing the meal was a plate of flaky Viennese pastries overflowing with fresh whipped cream.

Cradled into a glorious sense of well-being by the unaccustomed effects of the wine, the flavor and the quality of the food, and the atmosphere of the restaurant, Bluet soon found herself unusually relaxed and talkative. She refused to acknowledge that maybe this had been the whole point of the lunch and that perhaps she should be using discretion, as she had been warned. But here was a foreign woman like herself. They shared a bond.

It was not long before the matter of visiting Anna came up. Bluet decided to ask her new friend how to handle it, how this woman managed to travel back and forth to Holland with no difficulty whatsoever. "I help them quite a bit," she replied, searching Bluet's face for a reaction. "It's a question of give and take."

Although the discussion was being handled with the utmost delicacy, her companion was definitely trying to convey a subtle message and was also searching for information. At first, Marieka seemed interested only in Bluet's attitude toward her life in Moscow and her relationship with Marc, all personal questions. The wine had loosened Bluet's tongue. Her replies slipped out spontaneously—so quickly, in fact, she could never quite recall from one moment to the next what she had been saying. At one point she became exceptionally candid about her hotel room.

"Nobody could possibly be content living like that," Bluet confided, grimacing. "It's a disgrace." Then she added even more critically, "I know everyone's going through hard times, but I do think Marc deserves better treatment, considering his years of service."

Marieka took it all in—carefully. "The matter of your apartment has been under review for a long time, as Marc must have told you," she said. "There are so many *deserving* cases and so few available." The innuendo was inescapable.

But not until the coffee was served did Bluet appreciate just what becoming a deserving case might entail. And, in fact, what was probably behind the lunch in the first place.

As the waiter brought the cups and set the steaming coffeepot down in the center of the table, Marieka leaned over and whispered, "You've enjoyed your lunch here today, I can see that."

Bluet nodded vigorously.

"I imagine we'd all like a chance to come here more frequently," Marieka continued, pouring the coffee slowly into each cup and watching the steam rise upward, carrying the delicious aroma.

Again Bluet nodded, slowly sipping the freshly brewed coffee with unconcealed delight.

"How would you feel about working with us . . . entertaining . . . acting as a hostess to foreigners who come here on business? It would mean lunching at places like this fairly frequently . . . possibly having somewhere better to live . . . letting us know what they're up to. . . . "

"Entertaining?" Bluet questioned. "Acting as a hostess? You mean with Marc?"

"Well, sometimes, but mostly by yourself. He's so busy. You would show them around . . . you know . . . find out . . . give them the right impression . . . make them happy . . . give them what they need. . . . "

Lulled by the delectable sensation of her stomach being satisfied by a real meal and the possibility of spending time away from that miserable room, which she now seemed condemned to inhabit forever, Bluet found herself desperately trying to interpret the offer as a relatively benign assignment.

Yet she felt a hint of foreboding, despite her pampered senses. "I'd better talk it over with Marc before I make any commitment," she responded. "He should be back in a few days. You do understand."

Though she fully realized that her duties would be sexual as well, she could still think only of having more of that wonderful food if she agreed. Deprivation had done its work.

Twenty

THE WEEKS DRAGGED ON, with still no word from Marc. Bluet was worried. She knew it was conceivable for someone in his precarious position to conveniently fall victim to an accident, especially in an outlying district where the real facts could never be ascertained.

She tried telephoning his office at the Department of Health. After endless transfers from one desk to another, she was told that he might be back any day, although, on the other hand, he might not. So she tried the unofficial route, starting with Yulina, thus far her most reliable source. But even Yulina could not find out anything more definitive. Marc had been delayed somewhere—that was all she could learn. So Bluet asked Dr. Gurevitch, still nominally the man in charge at the Department of Health, although he was now mostly involved with foreign trade. It made more sense for Gurevitch, as a physician, to remain officially listed as a representative of the Department of Health, especially when he needed a foreign visa for travel abroad. Visas were still most easily obtained for a physician. They were granted faster and with less delay than were requests from other sources. And host countries were less likely to keep tabs on medical personnel—the secret, of course, behind Marc's successes. But even Dr. Gurevitch was unable to help, merely explaining that Marc had been due back some time ago and might turn up any day now.

Along with being worried, Bluet was also impatient. It was already early June. Anna would be finishing school soon and would expect some definite news from her mother regarding summer plans. So Bluet intensified her efforts to get out of Moscow by telling anybody and everybody—mentioning only, of course, that she desired to spend part of the summer vacation with her daughter. The Yonoffs were especially sympathetic. She visited them often and made it clear that she would welcome any direct assistance they could offer. In her weeks of solitude, it had occurred to Bluet that it really did not matter what passport or paper she was given, provided the authorities just let her go.

Later she could sort everything out at the American embassy in Paris. She doubted that the Americans would really withdraw her U.S. citizenship. They were very sensitive about being accused of separating parent and child. She was even prepared to give Marc the benefit of the doubt and acknowledge that he may have recognized this all along and was just trying to protect his own position, as Yulina had suggested. Or perhaps he had employed the Russian citizenship idea as a means to extricate them both. Once she had shown her willingness in this direction, they could apply for a trip abroad together.

Bluet mulled over all these thoughts as she drank her morning tea and downed her daily breakfast of black bread covered with a few final drops of precious olive oil. Suddenly, she became aware of a scratching under the bed and looked up with a welcoming smile. She knew who was there.

A few moments later a whisker appeared. Then a twitching nose. Finally, her furry friend came scampering out with an expectant, hungry look in its eyes. "Well, hello," she said out loud. "I haven't seen you in weeks. Where have you been? You won't tell me? It's a secret? Everything is a secret around here, so I'm not at all surprised. You look thinner. Do you want some breakfast? Same menu as ever. Never changes. You'd prefer *white* bread, you say? Not so loud. That's counterrevolutionary talk," she chuckled.

"Why are you so thin? Is it difficult to find food? Aren't you getting your usual rations? Maybe you haven't been a good Bolshevik mouse. Is that true? They still suspect you are a Romanov mouse." She looked him over closely. "Well, you're not red, that's clear. But neither are you white. You're gray. *Mon dieu!*" she gasped. "That can only mean one thing." She leaned toward the mouse mischievously, "A counterrevolutionary mouse."

The mouse twitched violently. "I'm so sorry," Bluet apologized. "I didn't mean it. I'm not going to tell anyone. Your secret is safe with me. But a counterrevolutionary mouse in GPU headquarters. *Mon dieu!*" she cried again, throwing up her hands in mock horror. "The government will fall.

"Where have you been all these weeks? To a wedding, you say. To a cousin who lives just across the Polish border? That was a long trip. But I'll bet you didn't need a passport or even a visa. What are passports, you ask? Silly papers humans must carry so they can go in or out of a country. You just go where you like, I suppose, spending the night in a friendly hole along the way.

"Those Polish cousins really know how to cook, you say. Better pickings that side of the border. If the Bolsheviks aren't careful, you'll tell all your friends and soon there won't be any mice left. The world's first socialist society will be mouse-free!

"Your cousin married a German mouse with some very strange ideas? But you're still speaking to each other anyway. You're right. But it's not that way around here. Unless you are born in the right place and have the right ideas—I mean, the left ideas—you are not accepted. Sounds silly? Obviously, everyone doesn't think alike. Then you're not a good Bolshevik mouse, are you? Ants make far better ones. They are disciplined, conformist, industrious. But it's not a good philosophy for a mouse, you insist. Mice like their own private holes. They don't want to belong to a large colony under rigid rule. They like to do and say as they please.

"You're enjoying our little talk, I can see that. You're not hurrying away. I'm enjoying it, too. Will you come back every morning? I'll keep some crumbs and even see if I can get a lump of cheese. That would be a treat. Nothing is too good for such an understanding friend. You can come visit any time of the day or night. Marc's not here. I don't know when he's coming back. You'd like Marc. I think he'd like you, though he'd give me a medical reason why it's not good to have mice around. I worry about him. I love him. But everything I do seems to hurt him. He doesn't even talk to me much anymore. I have a daughter. But I can't speak to her either. You have two daughters, you say. And you can speak to them any time you like."

There was a rattling at the door. The mouse's eyes widened in alarm.

"Don't run away," Bluet urged. "It's probably a mistake. I'm not expecting anyone." But the rattling continued. The mouse, panicked, darted under the bed.

"Come back!" she called.

But it was gone.

The noise continued. Buttoning her long robe, she crossed the room and opened the door just a chink.

It was Marc.

He looked so disheveled that she had difficulty choking back a scream. His ashen face was sunken at the cheekbones. His eyes were swollen and glazed. Several days' growth of stubble was visible around his chin. And his suit, caked with mud, was also covered with a fine dust that he tried to brush away as he stood in the doorway. By his side stood a small brown suitcase. He was trying to reach for the door handle, yet for some reason he had trouble steadying his hand to turn the knob.

He smiled weakly. For a moment they just stared at each other. Then he said impatiently, "Don't look so shocked. It's not as bad as all that. I'm just exhausted, that's all." He continued to brush himself off as he muttered, "The villages were nothing but mud ... we stood all night on the train ... it was delayed as usual ... for hours ... breaking down all the time. ... "

Guiding him by the arm, she picked up his suitcase and helped him inside, then closed the door quickly. Whatever had happened could wait. He needed comfort, not questions. Slowly, she directed him toward the bed. He just sat down and stared, clearly too worn out to speak anymore.

Bluet pulled off his shoes and helped him take off his jacket. She raced down the hall to fill a jug with water, to make a hot drink on the small electric ring next to the tap. Knowing his fondness for his special Italian cup and saucer, she took it down from the top of the bureau and filled it with steaming tea, then handed it to him as he sat motionless on the bed.

He took it from her eagerly. But he had trouble holding it steady. When she tried to reach out and hold it for him, he shook his head violently, as if to tell her to leave him alone.

"Be careful," she cautioned. "It's all you have left."

"Isn't that the truth?" he said. "And you," he added, looking up with a weak smile. "I still have you."

She brought a chair over to sit next to him and asked gently, "Now can you tell me what happened?"

Only later would she learn how Marc had been devastated that month, not by any act of violence directed against him personally, but from seeing with his own eyes the extent of human suffering that the party's current policies had caused. In the postwar catastrophe of 1921, Lenin had appealed to the outside world for relief from a famine caused by internal strife. But this particular famine was the result of deliberate policy run amok, and it was purposely being covered up. Marc himself would have to openly deny its extent whenever the International Red Cross made discreet inquiries, following widespread rumors that had circulated abroad.

The horrors themselves were appalling: thousands left to die of starvation, while food was exported; half-naked children with wraithlike limbs and gargoyle eyes staring vacantly into space, their bellies swollen from lack of nourishment and their feet bleeding and torn from lack of shoes; emaciated adults with matchstick legs and skeletal frames, eating weeds for sustenance and chewing bark off the trees; endless truckloads of kulaks transported at gunpoint to prison camps for refusing to plant their crops, even under the shadow of the whip.

After working a lifetime for what he believed was a new and better society, Marc was now unable to rid himself of a personal sense of responsibility for having played such an active role in fostering a regime that had engineered such barbarism. Even worse, by having to publicly disclaim it, he was plagued by the awful realization that he was both powerless to change it and unable to escape it. He had become impotent. No earthly gain, no future wonderland, could possibly justify anything as hideous as what he had witnessed.

For days afterward, he remained shaken and withdrawn. Bluet again cursed this misbegotten land, where an individual could not even air his distress in the privacy of his own home, for fear it would be used against him. She was afraid that he was on the verge of a breakdown. Time and again, she tried to reassure him by reminding him that he was shouldering the burden and the guilt of others. It was not his personal policy; it was not his personal doing. Perhaps if his reports could convey the extent of the suffering. . . . It was a naive idea, but she suggested it anyway.

Then she told him about the sports club.

"Damn it!" he wailed. "They gave me their word they would leave you alone. You said no, of course?"

She was embarrassed to tell him that she had wavered. What she might have done if he had not returned, she did not want to dwell upon.

IT WAS GROWING uncomfortably warm in Moscow. An oppressive summer heat had descended upon the city. Nothing moved. Even the terror abated somewhat. Yet Bluet could no longer conceal her tears, even in front of Marc. She cried openly whenever she read her daughter's letters. Anna, despairing of ever seeing her mother again, tinged her letters with sadness and a growing bitterness. She no longer believed that Bluet was interested in arranging a trip out. Anna considered it all a charade. And, as she had originally suspected, she was being discarded entirely in favor of the lover. To have Anna feel this way was a particularly cruel blow for a mother who had been rejected by her own mother years earlier. The depth of Bluet's melancholy spilled over in conversation, no matter where she went.

Even Yulina asked her over more frequently. Fearing to leave Bluet alone, Yulina invited neighbors and friends up for a chat, a walk by the river, or simply an outing somewhere. Anything to make sure Bluet did not remain in that bleak room by herself.

Then one hot afternoon in August, as Bluet trudged up the hill to Yulina's apartment, she heard her friend shouting from the balcony above, waving her arms back and forth with a great deal of excitement.

"Come quickly," Yulina called. "Hurry! I have wonderful news!"

Bluet ran the rest of the way, then darted upstairs to find Yulina standing by the open front door, a broad smile spread across her chubby face.

"I can't wait," Yulina blurted out. "I can't wait to tell you. Come inside."

Pulling Bluet by the arm, Yulina made her sit down first, before exclaiming, "You're getting your passport back. You're getting it back. You're going to see Anna any day now."

Bluet's mouth dropped wide open. She could not hold back the tears welling up at the corners of her eyes. "Are you certain?"

"Quite certain."

"Then why didn't Marc say anything about it?"

"He will. I'm sure of it. Ask him tonight. He may even have it with him," Yulina continued excitedly. "I was so delighted when I heard the news that I was going to run over to the hotel and tell you right away. I couldn't wait to see your reaction."

But Bluet's mind was already going in so many different directions, she was hardly listening. She could not escape the fear that it was only a rumor. She had yet to see the passport. She dared not plan ahead. Yet she felt compelled to say something appropriate.

"May I leave some of my winter things with you?" she asked Yulina. "I'll probably be back before the worst of the cold weather, so I won't be needing heavy clothes. Do you have enough room?"

"Of course," Yulina agreed. "Leave as much as you like. Everything will be safe with me. I've plenty of space. Is there anything else I can do for you?"

"No, nothing I can think of right now," Bluet assured her. She stood up and walked around nervously. She could not relax.

The early evening hours found her pacing up and down in their small hotel room, waiting impatiently for Marc to return. She had never watched the clock before to see exactly when he came in. But this evening the minutes seemed to crawl. He appeared to be so much later than usual. At long last, she heard his footsteps in the hallway outside.

As soon as he came through the door, she blurted out, "Yulina told me I'm getting my passport back."

The exit visa that ultimately cost Marc his life.

Closing the door slowly behind him, he nodded. "That's right," he said in a monotone. "I'd have told you sooner, only I was waiting until I actually got it. I only picked it up a few minutes ago. That's why I'm so late." He walked over to the desk and put down his briefcase before opening it with a sharp click. Shuffling through a pile of papers, he took out the little red American passport that had somehow never seemed quite so precious.

"Here," he said and quickly turned away.

She grabbed it from him and flipped it over several times in her hands to make sure it was really her own. Leafing hurriedly through the pages, she wanted to be certain that the exit permit was also stamped inside. She found it at the back, looking absolutely official and entirely in order. It gave her just a few weeks in which to make her arrangements and leave. She was so overjoyed, it barely registered how dirty and worn the passport had become and how many new stamps were inside.

"There's some other news," Marc began, while she frantically turned the pages of her little red book. "Our apartment, a real apartment of our own, has finally come through. We can move in any day. It's just up the street. Right in the middle of town, like you wanted. It's only tiny by your standards. But I tried. Just for you. . . . We have our own bathroom and kitchen and hot water . . . we can get the big bed out of storage that you brought from Berlin. There is a small alcove for your clothes. You can fix it up any way you like."

"What is it, Marc?" she asked, looking up from her passport. "I didn't hear. I was wondering when the next sailing was out of New York so maybe Anna could meet me in Paris. . . ."

"I said our apartment has finally come through," repeated Marc. "Our apartment . . . we can leave this room tomorrow if you like."

At that emotional moment Bluet never stopped to consider that the timing of the apartment might be the crucial test of her loyalty. Her thoughts were already miles away, far across the Atlantic. She ran over to a pile of old issues of the *New York Times* stacked in a corner and searched the pages. She hoped to find out which boat to cable her daughter to take so that Anna would be in Paris by the time Bluet arrived. Hurriedly, she flipped through until she found the page where forthcoming departures were listed.

"Come on, Marc," she said as she got up from the floor. "We'd better go downstairs right now and send a cable to Anna. I can't seem to find out when the next boat leaves. But I'll ask her to check and let me know the arrangements as fast as possible."

"Didn't you hear me?" he repeated yet again. "Our apartment. . . . "

"Apartment?" she questioned. "Oh, Marc. Oh, no! Not now. . . . " The bitter months of struggle, fear, hunger, and compulsory inactivity had taken their toll. She hated herself for totally losing sight of his struggle and his needs. The guilt that would torment her for a lifetime had begun its caustic work.

THEY MOVED THE NEXT DAY, but Bluet could not generate any interest in turning the apartment into a home. It was too late. The apartment would suffice as it was for the next two weeks until she was ready to leave. Instead, she spent her time shopping for going-away gifts for her Moscow friends.

No longer concerned about appearances, Bluet cashed several travelers' checks at the store reserved for foreigners, purchasing precious commodities that were unavailable elsewhere: lemons, coffee, butter, cheese, noodles, and olive oil, to distribute to those who had been the most kind to her during her stay. The remaining dollars she spent on gifts for her American friends: embroidered tablecloths, lacquered boxes, decorated blouses, nests of hand-painted Matryoshka dolls, miniature balalaikas, and other assorted sou-venirs. She arrived back at her new apartment late in the day, piled high with boxes and bags, just like the old days in New York. She was getting out. Soon she would be strolling arm in arm with her daughter along the boule-vards of Paris, with the nightmare of Moscow erased as they happily dodged traffic and enjoyed the bustle of a city teeming with life.

The memory of Marc and what he might be suffering would be far more difficult to remove from her consciousness.

Bluet received a return cable from Mademoiselle, assuring her that there was no problem about the voyage. The governess would accompany Anna personally. They hoped to be in Paris by the middle of the month.

Bluet hurried to the railway station to purchase an advance reservation for a first-class overnight sleeping compartment to Berlin. Such a luxury involved standing in line for several hours. But she did not care. She was getting out.

IT WAS RAINING LIGHTLY the day she left, the city gray and brooding under a wet mist. Marc had stayed home to see her off, puttering around aimlessly most of the morning while she packed her few remaining belong-ings into her cabin trunk and valise. He alternately stared out the window, blurred and speckled with raindrops, and back at her as she sat on the floor, stuffing her suitcase. When she was finished and it was almost time to leave, she sat back on her heels, snapped her luggage shut, locked it, and looked up at him.

Watching him standing there, his once-impeccable tweed suit hanging limp and shabby on his skinny frame, his tie slightly loose at the collar, she could not help but compare his present appearance to the very first evening they met. He had been so debonair, so magically endowed with life and hope and self-assurance—in full command of himself and his future. In the relatively short time that elapsed since then, he had aged significantly. His shoulders sagged, and he stooped over slightly as he walked. The lines on his face had deepened, and he had the look of a tired man. He had lost weight.

He was no longer slender but painfully thin. He appeared thoroughly down-cast, as if life itself had played a cruel joke upon him.

She felt torn, leaving her lover in the claws of a despot who understood neither compassion nor pity nor love.

Impulsively, she gathered together all the jewelry she had brought with her. It was the only personal wealth she had retained when she left Max: her favorite ruby brooch, her gold bangle bracelets, her beloved set of dia-mond earrings. She had been wearing them all, but she took them off and piled them neatly on the floor beside her. She even reopened her trunk to grope around for the solid-gold evening purse she had tucked away in a corner.

She scooped them up and ran to his side as he stood by the window. One by one, she stuffed them into the jacket pockets of his suit until they sagged from the weight, making the outfit look more ill fitting than ever.

"For you . . . for anything . . . so you can . . . ," she stammered, tears streaming down her cheeks. She never finished what she was going to say. They both understood. Whether to purchase some small comfort or—if fate or luck permitted—buy his way out of the country.

He put his arms around her for the last time. They stood there silently together. Moments later, an urgent tapping at the door forced them apart. A taxi had arrived. It was time to go. The train was scheduled to depart in an hour.

They did not talk on the way to the station, but stared silently out at the drab streets of Moscow. There was nothing more to say.

The taxi pulled up sharply in front of the station. They climbed out. A porter carried the luggage over to where the international express stood waiting, its engines hissing and huffing. The Yulins had come to see her off. They stood whispering to each other on the platform. Bluet and Marc walked up to them, and Yulina handed Bluet a little package. "A 'going away just for a while' gift," she said. But Yulina knew. And her husband knew. And Marc knew. Bluet had made her choice. She would not return.

"Look after my things 'til I get back," Bluet reminded her. "You know how much I need those woolens for the winter," she added, giving them both a warm hug.

Then she turned to face Marc, who stood sulking in the background, shuffling uncomfortably from foot to foot. The magical sparkle had disap-peared from the eyes of this proud man. He shook his head sadly and smiled weakly, as if to ask whether she really knew what she was doing. For a long moment Bluet and Marc just stared at one another. She tried to kiss him good-bye, but he turned his face away. Finally, he came forward, gently guiding her as she climbed up into the coach, his hand hesitating for just a fleeting moment as he slammed the door that would separate them for all time. She leaned out of the lowered window.

Up and down the long platform, they could all hear the clapping sound of other doors slamming shut with the same finality. The whistle of the train shrieked its mocking cry. A huge cloud of heavy smoke billowed from the engine up ahead, draping them in a thick gray shroud. The enormous black wheels began to churn along the track. As the train inched slowly out of the station, the Yulins glanced at Marc and then at each other. Sasha Yulin fumbled for the comfort of his wife's hand, then grasped it tightly. Bluet waved. The Yulins waved. The train picked up speed.

Marc, seemingly transfixed, stood alone, staring after her. Suddenly, catching them all by surprise, he broke into a run and began chasing after the train in a mad sprint. Bluet could see the tears streaming down his face. He was shouting to her, calling out over and over again, but his words were drowned by the clatter of the wheels and the roar of the engine. He ran until he reached the farthest end of the platform and could run no further, then pounded his fists in desperation on the wooden end posts.

"Go back!" she cried through her own tears. "Go back!"

Such an emotional outburst in public was suicidal. A man like Marc was not supposed to be pining in public for a foreign woman who was anything but a loyal communist. She had never seen him so distraught. Even when seething with anger, he had always maintained his composure. Onlookers were already turning to gaze at him quizzically. Someone would surely report the incident to the authorities.

But Marc would not stop. The Yulins cringed. Sasha Yulin wisely restrained his wife from rushing to Marc's side.

Crestfallen and drained, Marc waited until the train was no larger than a speck of dust suspended on the distant horizon. He turned and wandered wearily back down the platform.

WHO WOULD REMEMBER? Who would even care? He had sold his soul for a slogan. He had sacrificed his wisdom and medical skills for an ideology gone sour. He had abandoned his sense of caution and judgment for a passion he could not control.

The new world he had hoped to build was no better than the old. Perhaps they had all been responsible for creating this petty, deranged, loathsome despot who was no different from any other czar. It had come full circle, though in time this new czar would go on to haunt and torment more than his own land.

Marc knew full well that Bluet would never return and that, ultimately, the authorities would come for him. It was only a matter of time. Certainly, they would never let him out. He posed too great a risk. He knew too much.

With the back of his hands, he wiped away his tears and stalked out of the station, passing the Yulins as if they were not even there. He thrust his hands into his pockets, where he could feel the trinkets she had left him, and strode across town toward the coveted apartment he knew he would have to face alone. There was no point in going back to Katya, something that Bluet repeatedly urged him to do. Her words echoed in his ears, "So, my darling, you can climb to where you want to climb. So at least you can *survive.*" He would do that only if he wanted to regain some standing with the party. But he had long since lost interest.

Caution be damned. Tomorrow he would write Bluet a letter.

MARC CHEFTEL NEVER DID return to Katya. Instead, he continued to write letters to Bluet for more than a year. They arrived regularly at two-week intervals and were always sent by registered mail to the home of her closest friend on the Upper West Side of Manhattan. Bluet had suggested that Marc write to this address, in case she could not find anywhere permanent to live.

They were passionate and painful letters, full of longing that he and Bluet would one day be reunited. He continued to send them, despite knowing how dangerous it was to correspond regularly in a foreign language with a Western woman with whom he had been intimately involved. Frantic over the financial difficulties Bluet encountered on her arrival back in New York, Marc also took the incredible risk of sending her some dollars through a friend. Any private transaction involving scarce foreign currency was considered one of the most serious crimes against the state.

He had written his own death sentence, but he no longer seemed to care. Marc had become politically "unreliable." His actions could not be tolerated for long.

In 1932, Aldous Huxley completed his novel *Brave New World.* Starvation raged inside Russia. F.D.R. was elected president. The Lindbergh baby was kidnapped. Thirty million people in the capitalist nations were unemployed. Ziegfeld died. They sang, "Brother, Can You Spare a Dime?" "As Time Goes By," and "April in Paris." *Show Boat* was revived. Cole Porter produced *The Gay Divorcée.* Auguste Piccard reached the dizzy height of 17.5 miles in his stratosphere balloon. A second Five-Year Plan was launched.

And as the summer faded and the leaves turned the color of chestnuts to die upon the trees, the authorities came and took Marc away.

In September he was arrested and sent to the disease-ridden, mosquito-infested slave labor camp at the Volga Canal, the most infamous of the entire gulag network. Fittingly, the actual details of his exile and death remain as private as the manner in which he chose to conduct his life.

Only one thing is certain. In the summer of that year, realizing his arrest was imminent, he called upon a close friend and told him, "If they come for me, be sure to send Bluet a note and let her know. I can't bear the idea that she might think I'd stopped writing because I'd stopped caring."

So at the close of October, expecting to receive her usual letter, Bluet arrived at the home of her Upper West Side friend to be told that, instead, a postcard was waiting for her. Not knowing quite what to expect and what had happened, but feeling an unusual sense of panic, she hurriedly picked it up. It bore a Russian stamp and a Moscow postmark. In English, in a hand that was entirely strange to her, was written, "Mi has been sent away from Moscow. He will not be able to communicate with you any longer."

Sadly, she took the postcard and went to see Dubrowsky. He promised to try to find out what had happened to Marc. Some weeks later, Dubrowsky confirmed what she already feared. Marc had been arrested. And from what Dubrowsky heard, she would be better off forgetting about him.

She now had only his letters, a small black jewelry box, and a miniature cameo picture of him.

It was over.

Epilogue

BLUET ENCOUNTERED severe financial problems and a total rebuff from Max upon her return to the United States at the height of the Depression. Eventually, she settled down again, becoming part of a select group of former communists who embraced the extreme right in a sort of purging of the political soul. She also rejoined her former friends from the theater and concert world. In a duplex apartment only paces away from where Lincoln Center now stands, she provided them all with a political and cultural salon in the truest European tradition. It was a nostalgic and gracious haven, attracting influential and gifted people, blending many old friends from the Rabinoff days with new ones. An evening at Bluet's apartment was an evening of wit, politics, and intellect.

She did all her entertaining in a vast two-story living room furnished with faded French antiques. A tiny drawer in a small antique chest at one corner of the room was reserved for a cameo photo of Marc Cheftel, carefully mounted in an embossed metal frame, as though she always wanted him close by her side. Folded into the back of the frame was a tattered article she had cut out of a 1960 edition of the Paris newspaper *Le Monde.* In bitter terms, the news story described a resurgence of anti-Semitism inside Russia. It was as if she was trying to tell him that, sadly, he had been right. In the end, it had all been for naught.

Bluet died in a small apartment on the Upper East Side of Manhattan on January 31, 1976. She was eighty-five.

After revealing his secrets to the Dies Committee in 1939, Dr. Dubrowsky became part of Bluet's circle. But he never relaxed. He was too fearful of being murdered by Soviet assassins for what he had revealed. He drowned his terror in endless shots of vodka. His main concern in those declining years was that he should outlive Stalin. He did not get his wish. Stalin outlived Dubrowsky by almost three years. Dubrowsky died on June 23, 1950. He was sixty-two.

Max Rabinoff spent much of the early 1930s organizing the Cosmo-politan Opera Association. It later evolved into the City Center in Midtown Manhattan, often called the "people's theater" and retaining, to this day, Max's philosophy of making great dance, opera, and theater more affordable and available. In 1935, his colleagues gave him a gala celebration in honor of the twenty-fifth anniversary of his career as an impresario. But that was where it ended. Afterward, he faded into obscurity. Others rose to take his place. Also, having constantly ignored the need for a solid financial base of his own—one that was not used to finance another stab at success—he ended life with very little money. His final years were spent living alone in a small Upper West Side hotel and working intermittently on his autobiogra-phy at Columbia University, where a selection of his papers and personal photos is still held. A testament to his continued anger over Bluet's actions can be seen from the way some family photos have giant holes in the center or at one side. He literally excised Bluet from these group shots, apparently using a large pair of scissors and cutting away her image with deft strokes, which must have provided its own sort of therapy. Max never reconciled with his former wife or their daughter, shutting them both out of his life. He died after collapsing alone and penniless on the streets of Manhattan on April 18, 1966. He was eighty-nine.

Anna, known informally among friends and family as Johnny, graduated from Bennington College and Yale University, devoting her life to teaching drama in Catholic parochial schools and colleges in the United States. She never married. A heavy smoker, Anna died of lung cancer at fifty-seven.

Anna's friend Nina Fonaroff became a distinguished dancer and a cho-reographer, joining Martha Graham's troupe and later expanding upon the Graham style in performances at venues that echoed Max's philosophy, such as the 92nd Street Y. Like Anna, she also devoted much of her time to teach-ing. She died in London in August 2003 at age eighty-nine.

Katya lost her apartment soon after Marc moved out and was given a shabby room in a filthy, overcrowded house, into which she crammed, some-what incongruously, her cherished pieces of Italian furniture. Appointed the director of a Moscow hospital, she retained the post until being swallowed up by the Great Purge of 1937, when she disappeared forever.

Louis Fischer left Moscow for the United States in the late 1930s, thor-oughly disillusioned. Father Walsh remained an outspoken critic of com-munism and a controversial figure on all matters pertaining to U.S. foreign policy. The Jesuit order named a college after him—the Edmund A. Walsh

School of Foreign Service at Georgetown University in Washington, D.C. Its mission remains, as always, to prepare students for leadership roles in international affairs. It continues to flourish. Walsh is listed as its founder and first dean.

The revolution tore apart the Cheftel family. Ill equipped to weather the physical and mental strain, the gentle Solomon died soon after the initial revolution of 1917. After struggling to keep her family alive and fed by bartering cloth during the civil war, an inconsolable Maria sought refuge in the relative quiet and stability of Prague. Following a brief and unsuccessful marriage, Marc's sister fled to Italy, remaining there for the rest of her life. The second son emigrated to America, spending the rest of his days in New York City. After a brief period in Prague and Italy, the youngest son returned to Moscow to pursue a career as a chemical engineer.

Disappeared or executed in the purges of the 1930s: Sasha Yulin and his wife; Dr. Mikhail Gurevitch and his wife; Dr. Lev Grigorevich Levin (the Kremlin doctor); Schuster (the official from Amtorg mentioned in the Fish hearings); Piatakov, Zinoviev, and Kamenev, three of the leading Old Bosheviks, and even Krylenko, the prosecutor at the Ramzin trials. And, of course, dozens of others like Marc and Katya, whose names were not sufficiently noteworthy to be included in most of the accounts of those times. When Bluet visited Trotsky's widow in Mexico in the early 1940s, she recalled that they had what amounted to a graveyard conversation. All the Russian friends they had in common were dead.

Author's Note

This historical tale was re-created with the cooperation of the following individuals: Bluet Rabinoff, the wife of impresario Max Rabinoff; Sabrina Sheftel (the wife of Marc's brother in New York); Congressman Hamilton Fish Jr.; the ballerina Nina Fonaroff; surviving members of the White Russian nobility; and famine relief workers who served in Russia in the 1920s, plus a number of former Soviet sympathizers who begged to remain anonymous for understandable reasons.

In addition, the following unpublished documents were consulted: the incomplete memoirs of Bluet Rabinoff and passages from the personal letters she wrote to her daughter from Moscow during the winter of 1930 (now in safekeeping with the author); the Special Collections section of the Lauinger Library at Georgetown University (the papers of Father Edmund A. Walsh); the Rare Book and Manuscript Library at Columbia University (the papers and transcripts of interviews with Max Rabinoff); the archives of the American Friends Service Committee (Quakers) in Philadelphia and London; the Rockefeller Archives Center in Sleepy Hollow, N.Y.; the Hoover Institution at Stanford University (unpublished memoirs of Max Rabinoff); the Italian State Archives in Rome; the London Records Office, London, England; the Police Cantonale in Lausanne, Switzerland; and the International Red Cross in Geneva.

U.S. government sources included files compiled by the CIA/FBI, obtained under the Freedom of Information Act, and verbatim excerpts from the 1930 congressional hearings into communist activities. Published works are listed in the following biographical note.

I wish to thank my agent, Carolyn French, of the Fifi Oscard Agency in New York, for her continued faith in my work, as well as my editor at Wiley, Hana Lane. I would also like to thank my good friends Clifford Forster and his wife, Joan, for their help in obtaining many of Bluet's personal papers and photos. I would also like to thank the many librarians and curators at the archives and the libraries that I used for the care and attention they gave to my research needs.

Bibliographical Note

The following books, listed in alphabetical order by the author's name, can provide further insights into this period in Soviet history and the world inhabited by Marc and Bluet. Many were written at the time or shortly thereafter. It gives them an immediacy that can help the reader understand the strong emotions that surrounded a political experiment whose attraction at a pivotal economic moment may have accelerated the development by the capitalist world—the very one these revolutionaries deplored—of social programs that might otherwise have been ignored or delayed. Thus, in a roundabout way, it did achieve some of its espoused goals. However, as a vehicle for eradicating anti-Semitism, communism proved to be only a passing salve. The titles of these works, together with the dates of publication, make their content self-evident.

Agabekov, Georges S. *OGPU, The Russian Secret Terror.* New York: Brentano's, 1931. Reprint, Westport, Conn.: Hyperion Press, 1975.

Barmine, Alexander. *One Who Survived.* New York: Putnam & Sons, 1945.

Bessedovsky, Grigory (a.k.a. Grigori Besedovskii). *Revelations of a Soviet Diplomat.* London: Williams & Norgate, 1932.

Bukharin, N. I. *The Great Purge Trials.* New York: Grosset & Dunlap, 1965.

Dallin, David. *Soviet Espionage.* New Haven, Conn.: Yale University Press, 1955.

Deacon, Richard. *A History of the Russian Secret Service.* London: Muller, 1972.

Deriabin, Peter. *Watchdogs of Terror.* New Rochelle, N.Y.: Arlington House, 1972.

Duranty, Walter. *I Write As I Please.* New York: Simon & Schuster, 1935.

Eaton, Quaintance. *The Boston Opera Company.* New York: Appelton Century, 1965.

——— . *The Miracle of the Met.* New York: Meredith Press, 1968.

Fainsod, M. *Smolensk under Soviet Rule.* Cambridge, Mass.: Harvard University Press, 1958.

Fischer, Louis. *Machines and Men in Russia.* New York: H. Smith, 1933.

——— . *Men and Politics.* New York: Duell, Sloan & Pearce, 1941.

Fischer, Louis. *The Soviets in World Affairs*, vols. 1 and 2. New York: Jonathan Cape, 1930.

——— . *Why Recognize Russia?* New York: Jonathan Cape, 1931.

Florinsky, M. *World Revolution and the U.S.S.R.* New York: Macmillan, 1933.

Gallagher, L. J. *Edmund A. Walsh, S. J.: A Biography.* New York: Benziger Bros., 1962.

Gorchakov, Nikolai A. *The Theater in Soviet Russia.* New York: Columbia University Press, 1957.

Haines, Anna J. *Health Work in Soviet Russia.* New York: Vanguard Press, 1928.

Hammer, Armand. *The Quest of the Romanoff Treasure.* New York: W. F. Payson, 1932.

Heifetz, Elias. *The Slaughter of the Jews in the Ukraine in 1919.* New York: T. Seltzer, 1921.

Lockhart, R. H., and R. H. Bruce. *British Agent.* New York: Putnam & Sons, 1932.

Lyons, Eugene. *Assignment in Utopia.* New York: Harcourt, Brace & Co., 1938.

Moorehead, Alan. *The Russian Revolution.* New York: Harper & Bros., 1958.

Palmer, Francis. *Russian Life in Town and Country.* New York: G. P. Putnam & Sons, 1901.

Reswick, William. *I Dreamt Revolution.* Chicago: Henry Regnery Co., 1952.

Scott, Richenda C. *Quakers in Russia.* London: Michael Joseph, 1964.

Walsh, Edmund A. *The Last Stand.* Boston: Little Brown & Co., 1931.

Webb, Sydney, and Beatrice Webb. *The Decay of Capitalist Civilization.* New York: Harcourt, Brace & Co., 1921.

——— . *Soviet Communism: A New Civilization?* New York: C. Scribner's Sons, 1936.

——— . *Truth about Soviet Russia.* New York: Longmans, Green and Co., 1942.

Weizmann, Chaim. *Trial and Error: The Autobiography of Chaim Weizmann.* Philadelphia: Jewish Publication Society, 1949.

Williams, William A. *American-Russian Relations.* New York: Rinehart, 1952.

Zweig, Stefan. *Joseph Fouché: The Portrait of a Politician.* New York: Viking Press, 1930.

Index

Page numbers in *italics* refer to illustrations.

Abarbanels, 222–223

Alexander I, 92

Allies, White army and, 110, 113

All Russian Textile Syndicate, 131

Amazar, 64–65

American Institute of Opera and
Allied Arts, 20, 21, 22, 46

American Red Cross in Russia, 111,
127

American Relief Administration
(ARA), 127

Amtorg Trading Corporation
congressional investigation of,
159, 160, 166–167
Delgass exposes, 166–167
Rabinoff and, 8, 48
subterfuge by, 131–134

Anisfeld, Boris, 21, 34

antireligion movement, 74, 105, 119,
217–218, 221

anti-Semitism
Nicholas II and, 96, 98
resurgence of, 151
in Russian revolution, 112–114
Stalin and, 75–76, 151, 219–220
Whites and, 110
Zionism as response to, 97

Babb, Nancy, 128–129

Bakst, Leon, 35

Ballet Russe, 15, 34–36

Berlin, Bluet in, 67–70

Bessedovsky, Grigory, 152–154,
155, 156, 157, 160

Bezymensky, Alexander, 203

Big Red Scare, 47–48

Binger, Dr., 67, 68–69

Bolshevik revolution, 79, 109. *See also*
Russian revolution

Bolsheviks, Old, 30, 61–62, 196

Bolshevism
appeal of, 58–60
Catholic Church's opposition to,
118
criticisms of, 61
fear of, 16, 17, 33
godlessness in, 119
Golden Age of, 16–18
Jews and, 109–110
Quakers and, 127–128
recognition of, 114–115
rise of, 79
spread of, 115–116
women under, 60, 148
See also communists; Soviet
government

Bolshoi Ballet, 246–247

Borah, William E., 148

bourgeois element, 17

Britain, 113–114, 129

British-American Quaker mission,
128–129, 130, 138

capitalism, 30
Catholic Church
  Bolshevism and, 118
  funds diverted to Bolsheviks, 118,
    119–120
  plan to regain influence in Russia,
    119
Chaliapin, Feodor Ivanovitch, 35,
    37, 133
Cheftel, Katarina Timofeyeevna
    (Katya)
  as agitator, 109
  bond with Marc, 108
  as GPU operative, 115–116,
    124–125
  housing problems and, 84
  in Italy, 110–111
  later years of, 272
  leaves Italy, 124–125
  Marc's affairs and, 108
  marriage to Marc, 107
  as physician, 108, 109, 111
  political beliefs of, 18, 107, 109
  refuses to divorce Marc, 164–165
  returns to Russia, 162–163, 272
  Russian Red Cross and, 136
  in United States, 19, 139,
    140–141
Cheftel, Marc Solomonovitch
  advances toward Bluet and, 39
  affair with Bluet and, 42–45
  as agitator, 109
  Anna and, 25, 40–41, 52, 161,
    227
  background of, 29, 30
  Bessedovsky exposes, 154–159
  Bluet's move to Russia for,
    160–162
  Bluet's return to United States
    and, 265–267
  Bolsheviks and, 114

Catholic funds confiscated by,
    118, 119–120
  childhood of, 92, 93, 94–98
  communist agitators and, 148
  death of, 265–267
  death obsession of, 216–217
  defection considered by, 152
  Delgass exposes, 166–167
  eloquence of, 14, 15–18, 28–29
  escape from prison of, 103–104
  exiled, 268
  GPU activities and, 87, 115–120,
    124–125, 126, 128, 135,
    141–142, 171–175
  imprisonment of (1905), 99–103
  introduction to Bluet, 9, 10, 150
  in Italy, 105–106, 107, 110–111,
    116–120, 123
  as Jew, 94–95, 104–105, 217,
    221
  Katya refuses to divorce,
    164–165
  in Lausanne, Switzerland,
    122–123
  leaves Italy, 124–125
  Levin and, 238–239
  loses hope, 267–268
  loss of prestige, 182–183
  love for Bluet, 83, 160, 185
  marriage to Katya, 107
  Max and, 19, 21, 25–26, 135,
    142, 144, 145
  medical studies of, 105
  meets Bluet in Russia, 72–73
  personality, 5, 14, 29, 95, 185
  photograph of, 6
  physical appearance, 14
  as physician, 106, 108, 109, 111
  plans to marry Bluet, 164
  plots entry into United States,
    120–130, 134–139

political beliefs of, 30–31, 96, 98, 102, 104–105, 109, 151
power and, 15, 32
private meetings with Bluet and, 27–33, 38–40, 150
Quakers and, 126–130, 134, 137, 146, 151
returns to Russia, 47, 53, 124–125, 160–162, 163
Russian Red Cross and, 9, 111, 114, 116, 118–120, 142–144, 172
sexual passions of, 107–108
in Social Revolutionary Party, 99
Sokolniki apartment and, 81–82
Stalin and, 227–228
in Ukraine, 112–114
in United States, 9, 19, 139, 140–141, 145–146
in Vatican, 116, 117–120
in Volga region, 249–250, 260–261
White Russians and, 114, 115–118
at Yulins' party, 202–208
Cheftel, Maria
background of, 92
later years of, 273
Marc's imprisonment and, 100–101, 102–104
as mother, 94
physical appearance of, 93
political views of, 98
as spokeswoman, 94, 100
Cheftel, Solomon, 92, 93, 95, 98, 100, 103, 273
Cheftel villa and sanatorium, 116
Cheka, 115
Chicherin, Georgi, 104, 117
civil war between Reds and Whites, 109, 110
Clarac, Louise, 230

collectivization, 62, 74–77, 81, 152
Comintern (Communist International), 17, 112, 115
Communist Party, 48, 148
communists
agitators, 148
congressional investigation of, 159–160, 161, 165–167, 174, 183
Depression and, 48
fascists and, 117, 124
sympathizers, 48
congressional hearings, 159–160, 161, 165–167, 174, 183
Conradi, Maurice, 121
Cossacks, 113
counterrevolutionaries, 181
czars, new, 61–62

Delgass, Basil, 161, 165–167, 183
Depression, 31, 48
Diaghilev, Sergei, 34
Drury, Francis, 26
Dubrowsky, David, 136–137, 142, 144, 269, 271
Duncan, Isadora, 37–38

economic blockade, 147

famine, 76, 260–261
famine relief, diversion of, 118, 119–120
fascists, 117, 124
fear as means of control, 76, 77, 182, 195
fellowship program for doctors, 146–147
Fischer, Louis, 149, 177–178, 184, 198, 200–201, 272
Fish, Hamilton, Jr., 48, 148, 159, 161, 165–167, 183

Five-Year Plan
 collectivization and
  industrialization under, 75
 miseries caused by, 181–182
 need for American technology,
  130
 Stalin initiates, 62
Fonaroff, Nina, 272
food shortages, 68, 75, 85–86
Fouché, Joseph, 101–102
French Revolution, 101

Garbo, Greta, 38
Gatti-Casazza, Giulio, 34
Genoa Conference of 1922, 33
Germany, violence in, 69
gold, 133
Golden Age of Bolshevism, 16–18
Gomberg, Alex, 131
GPU (secret political police)
 faction against collectivization in,
  75
 Katya's involvement in, 115–116,
  124–125
 Marc's involvement in, 87,
  115–120, 124–125, 128, 135,
  141–142, 171–175
 recalls Marc, 160
 Stalin takes over, 56
Graham, R., 124
Great December Show Trial, 195–200
Great Illusion, 60
Great Purge of 1937, 272, 273
Gregg, Alan, 138–139, 146
gun running, 145
Gurevitch, Mikhail, 134–135, 182,
  226, 257, 273
gypsies, 218

Haines, Anna, 126–130, 137, 138,
  140, 146, 151
Hammer, Armand, 17, 131

Hitler, Adolf, 69
Hoover, Herbert, 147
Hoover Mission, 127
Hopkins, Harry, 46
Hotel Select, 186–187, 190–191
housing
 collectivization of, 76–77, 81–82
 problems obtaining, 84
hunger, in 1930s Soviet Russia, 77.
  See also famine; food shortages

industrialization, 62, 74, 75, 80–81
Industrial Party Plot of 1930, 183
intellectuals, 75, 76
intelligentsia, 76
international socialist groups, 104
Italian Communist Party, 106, 116
Italian Riviera, 116
Italy
 appeal of communism in, 115
 Bolshevik recognition in,
  114–115
 communists in, 106, 115
 Marc in, 105–106, 107,
  110–111, 116–120, 123
 Mussolini's takeover of, 120
 recognition of Soviet government
  by, 114–115, 124
 socialists in, 114–115
 unrest in, 115
Ivan the Terrible, 78

Japanese expansionist activities,
  130–131
jewels, 117, 133
Jews
 bias and actions against, 92,
  96–98. See also anti-Semitism
 Bolsheviks and, 109–110
 communist, 105
 exodus of from Russia, 97
 massacres of, 112–114

282

of the Pale, 92, 94
in Palestine, 97
privileged, 92–93
Stalin's purging of, 75–76
Zionist, 97

Kaganovitch, 220
Kamenev, 151, 219–220, 273
Kharkov, Ukraine, 93, 113
King, William H., 148
Kollontai, Alexandra, 60, 61, 107
Kollontay. *See* Kollontai
Kremlin, history of, 78
Krylenko, Nikolai Vasilyevich, 198,
    199, 200, 273
kulaks, 74, 75, 249, 250, 260–261

Lazareff, Dr., 73, 165, 184
Lenin, 16, 62
Levin, Lev Grigorevich, 237–239,
    273
liquidation of kulaks, 75
Little Father of all Russians, 98,
    99
living conditions in Russia, 76–77,
    81–82, 163, 181–182
London, Bluet in, 66–67
Lubianka prison, 79–80, 196
Luxemburg, Rosa, 107

Majestic, 4, 6–7
Marieka, 252–256
Matteoti, 124
May Day, 243
medicine, socialized, 60, 127
Mordkin, Michael, 34, 35
Moscow
    culture in, 79
    in Golden Age of Bolshevism,
        16–18
    history of, 77–80
    industrialization in, 80–81

Museum of Anti-God, 217–218
Mussolini, Benito, 120, 123, 124

Napoleon, 79
Nervi, 116
New Economic Policy (NEP)
    arrest of traders, 75
    benefits of, 125
    Lenin allows, 16
    Stalin ends, 62, 152
New York Sun, 155–159, *158*
Nicholas II, 96

OGPU. *See* GPU
Old Bolsheviks, 30, 61–62, 196
overcrowding, in 1930s Soviet
    Russia, 77

Palestine, Jews in, 97
Palmer, Jean, 24
Pavlov, Ivan, 118
Pavlova, Anna, 15, 34, *36, 37*
peasants, 74. *See also* kulaks
"people's theater," 272
performers, Russian, 133, 143
Peter the Great, 78
Piatakov, Yuri, 206–208, 273
pogroms, 92, 96–97
Poland, Bluet in, 70–71
political prisoners, 101
poverty, in 1930s Soviet Russia, 77
proletarianism, 16–17
propaganda, financing of, 132
Protocols of the Elders of Zion, The, 110
purges of 1930s, 272, 273

Quakers, 126–130, 134, 137, *138*,
    146, 151

Rabinoff, Anna Pavlova
    birth of, 32
    Bluet's attachment to, 10–11

Rabinoff, Anna Pavlova *(continued)*
  Bluet's move to Russia and, 50,
    51–52, 55–57, 227
  as Catholic, 52
  death of, 272
  feels abandoned by Bluet, 261
  later years of, 272
  Marc and, 25, 40–41, 52, 161,
    227
  Max and, 25, 52, 231
  Max prevents Russia trip, 231
  naming of, 35
  photograph of, *23*
Rabinoff, Helene (Bluet)
  accused of spying by Max, 241
  affair with Marc, 42–45
  Anna and, 10–11, 50, 51–52,
    55–57, 227, 261
  asks Max to help, 240–241
  in Berlin, 67–70
  as Catholic, 32
  childhood of, 8–9, 11, 14
  Communist Party and, 183
  as confidante, 24–25
  considers returning to United
    States, 193–194, 208–210,
    232–234
  death of, 271
  despondency strikes, 242, 261
  divorce from Max, 4, 7, 53–54
  efforts to leave Russia and,
    240–242, 257–258
  in Hotel Select, 186–187,
    190–191
  illness strikes, 236–238
  introduction to Marc and, 9, 10,
    150
  later years of, 272
  leaves Russia, 265–267
  leaves United States, 4–7, 50–57,
    58, 62–70

Levin and, 237–239
  in London, 66–67
  love for Marc and, 4, 7, 83, 185
  Marc's GPU involvement revealed
    to, 87, 171–175, 184
  Marc's plans to marry and, 164
  marriage to Max and, 32–33
  Max's treatment of, 4, 5, 7, 8,
    11–12, 32–33, 45
  Moscow arrival of, 80
  moves to Russia for Marc, 72–73,
    161–164
  passport and, *71*, 72, 161–164,
    201, 209, 233, 239,
    262–263,*263*
  photographs of, *5, 23, 37*
  physical appearance of, 7, 27
  in Poland, 70–71
  political views of, 31
  private meetings with Marc and,
    27–33, 38–40, 150
  Russia arrival of, 71–73
  signs Russian citizenship
    application, 250–252
  social life, 7–13, 24
  Sokolniki apartment and, 81–82
  sports club and, 253–256, 261
  surveillance of, 228–229, 230
  at Yulins' party, 202–208
Rabinoff, Max
  accuses Bluet of being spy, 241
  American operatic school and, 20,
    21, 22, 46
  Anna and, 25, 52, 231
  background of, 29–30
  Bluet asks for help, 240–241
  Bluet's affair and, 45, 47, 150,
    161, 174, 178, 182
  Bolsheviks' wooing of, 144–145
  as Bolshevism promoter, 20, 33,
    114

death of, 272
diplomatic role of, 8, 33, 145
divorces Bluet, 4, 7, 53–54
financial difficulties of, 46–47,
    150
gun running and, 145
as impresario, 4, 11, 15–16, 20,
    30, 34–36, *35*
influence of, 8, 35, 144
later years of, 272
Marc and, 19, 21, 25, 135, 142,
    144, 145
marries Bluet, 32–33
personality of, 8, 11, 32–33, 45
philanthropy of, 25–26
photographs of, *12, 23*
revenge against Bluet and Marc,
    214, 231, 241–242
Russian dealings and, 8, 15–16,
    20, 25–26, 34, 131, 144–145
sexual encounters of, 7, 11, 15,
    33, 38
social life of, 8, 9, 12–13
treatment of Bluet and, 4, 5, 7, 8,
    11–12, 45
"rackets," 132
radical left, era of, 31
Ramzin, Professor, 198–199
Red-baiting, 32
Red Russians, 80, 109, 110, 111,
    112
Red Scare, 47–48
Red Square, 78
religion, discouragement of, 74, 105,
    119, 217–218, 221
Revelations of a Soviet Diplomat
    (Bessedovsky), 154
Rhona, 240, 241
Rockefeller Foundation, 138, 139,
    146
Rubenstein, Helena, 63–65

Russia. *See also* Soviet Russia
    Bluet arrives in, 71–73
    food shortages in, 68
    in Golden Age of Bolshevism,
        16–18
    living conditions in, 76–77, 161,
        181–182
    privileged Jews in, 92–93
    terror machine in, 59
    women in, 60–61, 148
Russian Orthodox Church, 119
Russian Red Cross
    as Bolshevik operational center,
        111, 118, 119–120, 136
    diversion of medical supplies and,
        118, 119–120
    Katya and, 136
    Marc and, 9, 111, 114, 116,
        118–120, 142–144, 172
    New York mission and, 9, 136,
        142–143, 144
Russian revolution, 79, 109,
    111–114

Sasha, 86–87, 173
Scheftel. *See* Cheftel
Sheftel. *See* Cheftel
Shot, The, 203
socialism, 16–17, 96, 109
socialized medicine, 60, 127
social revolutionary movement, 96,
    99
Social Revolutionary Party, 99
Sokolniki, 80, 83, 85
Soudeikine, Serge, 10, 21, 24, 34
Soviet government, diplomatic
    recognition of
    by Italy, 114–115, 124
    need for by United States,
        130–131, 134, 135, 147–149
    in Western Europe, 130

Soviet Russia. *See also* Russia
  Britain and, 129
  economic blockade of, 147
  new politics of, 58
  trade with United States,
    131–134, 147
Spinoza, 104, 105
sports club, 253–256, 261
Stalin, Joseph
  brutality of, 59, 75–76, 152,
    196
  collectivization under, 75, 152
  intelligentsia feared by, 76
  Jews persecuted by, 75–76, 151,
    219–220
  kulaks liquidated by, 75
  Lenin and, 62
  Marc meets with, 227–228
  movement against, 181
  as new czar, 61–62
  rise of, 56, 61–62, 137–138
  treatment of "unreliables," 62
  Trotsky and, 61, 62, 151,
    219–220
St. Basil's Cathedral, 78
St. Petersburg, 78–79
St. Petersburg massacre, 98–99
Stony Point, 20, 21–24, *23*, 46

Taganrog, 91–92, 93
terror, 59, 152
"theater of illusion," 35
Thomas, Wilbur, 146, 151
Thompson, William Boyce, 111
Togliatti, Palmiro, 215–216
trade, American-Russian, 131–134,
  147
trade envoys, 133–134
Trotsky, Leon
  aims of, 17
  death of, 76

expulsion of, 17, 62, 151
as Jew, 219–220
Stalin and, 61, 62, 151,
  219–220

Ukraine, 93, 112–113
United States
  economic blockade of Russia by,
    147
  fear of Bolshevism in, 16, 17
  Soviet operatives in, 132–134
  Soviet's need for recognition by,
    130–131, 134, 135, 147–148
  trade with Soviet Russia,
    131–134, 147
U.S. House of Representatives,
  159–160, 161, 165–167, 174
U.S. State Department, 133, 134
valuta, 133, 247

Vatican, 116, 117–120
Volga region, 249–250, 260–261
Vorovsky, Vatslav, 117, 120–123

Walsh, Edmund A., 118–120,
  147–148, 149, 161, 174, 175,
  183, 272–273
War of 1812, 79
Whalen documents, 48, *49*, 159,
  160
White, Dorice, 128–129, 137, *138*,
  151
White Russians
  Allies and, 110, 113
  anti-Semitism of, 110
  Marc spies on, 114, 115–118,
    143
  war against Reds, 80, 110, 111,
    112, 113
Why Recognize Russia? (Fischer), 149
women in Russia, 60, 148

workers' revolution, 104, 106
World War I, 30, 80, 108, 110

Yonoffs, 65, 257
Yulin, Sasha, 201, 242, 266, 267, 273

Yulin, Yulina, 201–203, 207, 242, 244, 250, 261–262, 266, 267, 273

Zinoviev, 64, 151, 219–220, 273
Zionism, 97